THE

ROAD

HOME

THE
ROAD
HOME

A Contemporary Exploration
of the Buddhist Path

ETHAN NICHTERN

FOREWORD BY SHARON SALZBERG

North Point Press
A division of Farrar, Straus and Giroux
New York

North Point Press
A division of Farrar, Straus and Giroux
18 West 18th Street, New York 10011

Grateful acknowledgment is made to Seth Freedman
for permission to print the image on page 55.

Library of Congress Cataloging-in-Publication Data
Nichtern, Ethan, author.
The road home : a contemporary exploration of the Buddhist path /
Ethan Nichtern ; foreword by Sharon Salzberg.—First edition.
    pages   cm
    ISBN 978-0-374-25193-2 (hardback)—ISBN 978-0-374-71196-2
(e-book)
    1. Meditation—Buddhism.   2. Buddhism.   I. Title.

BQ5612.N53 2015
294.3'444—dc23
                                                          2014030912

Designed by Abby Kagan

North Point Press books may be purchased for educational, business,
or promotional use. For information on bulk purchases, please contact the
Macmillan Corporate and Premium Sales Department at 1-800-221-7945,
extension 5442, or write to specialmarkets@macmillan.com.

www.fsgbooks.com
www.twitter.com/fsgbooks · www.facebook.com/fsgbooks

1 3 5 7 9 10 8 6 4 2

For my parents, who set me on this path.
For my teachers, who keep me on this path.
For my colleagues and students,
who keep me honest on this path.

CONTENTS

FOREWORD

BY SHARON SALZBERG

I started reading my advance copy of *The Road Home* while in a hotel room, far from where I live. Internet access was in fits and starts, the busy highway outside left me stranded in this little enclave, and there were no restaurants open anywhere. I was at the tail end of a book tour (seven cities in ten days!) and had woken up that morning directly into the cliché "Where am I? I don't know at all where I am." I was so tired I felt lucky I wasn't waking up to "I don't know at all who I am."

My experience of fragmentation and unease was perfectly captured by Ethan in the early part of this book, in his description of a "commuter," someone always on the go, someone anchorless.

Sitting in that hotel room, I saw right away that I wanted a stronger sense of community than the one my iPhone could offer in those fits and starts of Internet access. I very much wanted to find renewal and openheartedness, so I could be in the next place with the next people in a good way. I also wanted some greater quiet—not isolation, but a sense of repose, stopping, being at ease. I wanted the relief and support of being at home.

Thanks to my many years of meditation study and practice, I knew how to directly find and actually follow a road home, even though I wasn't going to be seeing Massachusetts anytime soon. This is the best kind of home—independent of conditions, accessible even if my plane was once more delayed, unencumbered by the need for successful and timely baggage delivery.

The Road Home is a guide to taking this special kind of journey into our own hearts and minds, a true refuge for us wherever we are. And we're home not just for a tiny, fleeting visit, only to recall it distantly and nostalgically when we are once again far afield, feeling lost, wondering where we are. "Remember that great time, when I felt connected and aware? That was a really good time! Ah, to be back there." It's not a journey to a finer address, or an exotic voyage to foreign lands, or an effort to go back to the past and build a monument to what once was and then irrevocably slipped away. It's a journey that we can have confidence in right here and now when we remember to embark.

The road home Ethan describes includes looking deeply at what meditation is and isn't, to carefully hone self-awareness. It includes examining often misunderstood concepts in Buddhist teaching, like karma, ethics, and emptiness, to transform our sense of what is possible for us. This road explores the awakened heart, empowered by the basic truths of interdependence and relationship, and the strength and vitality of wise compassion. And it encompasses looking at our shared communities and societies, to discover cultural, social, and political meaning to our journeying.

While writing in a completely contemporary idiom, Ethan draws here from different perspectives and schools within the Buddhist traditions, including the Shambhala tradition, of which he is a second-generation member. This journey home has been a part of Ethan's world his whole life.

When Ethan asked me to write this foreword, he also asked me not to say anything that would embarrass him, reminding me of the time when I did just that by introducing him to one of my teaching colleagues, Sylvia Boorstein, saying, "Ethan is the future of Buddhism." But it fits very well in the flow here, it's quite a good closing statement, it's kind of fun to embarrass him, and I mean it sincerely. So, I'll just close by expressing my great respect for this work and by strongly encouraging you to use it as a practical guide, not a mere abstract reflection. And I'd like to specifically add, "Ethan is the future of Buddhism."

THE

ROAD

HOME

INTRODUCTION
Where Do You Live?

Where is home? Is your address your home? Is your body your home? Do you feel at home in your own mind? Where, oh, where is home?

In many ways, these have been the central questions of my life. The quest to answer these questions—or at least to feel more capable of understanding them—is the primary reason I have chosen the path of Buddhism* and the primary reason I practice and teach the path to others.

For me, the question of home is emotional. It's a poignant metaphor. It's rarely been a literal dilemma. I've always found a place to crash, at least, and have never faced a serious threat of losing the roof over my head. In that way I'm luckier than many people. This relative safety and comfort allow me a privilege I try to never forget: adequate space and time to contemplate existence.

*Literally, Awake-ism.

Still, the main question this book asks about "home" is an existential one; we aren't talking about a physical address. We are asking: Where, when, and how do we *feel* at home? How do we handle the fears and insecurities of not feeling at home?

It's possible, maybe even likely, that you don't feel completely at home right now. That might be the whole reason you picked up this book. If you're currently in commute, watching the world stream by through the isolating window of some train, plane, or bus, then you know the feeling. Or if things recently fell apart for you, in one of those limitless ways that Things Fall Apart for us mere mortals, then you're probably in a time of transition. If that's true, you may know what I mean about home in a very immediate way, and you might be hoping for something to come along to end this disorienting commute, to get you back to a place where you belong, where you are safe and sound, loved and understood.

But what if you're actually reading this at home, at the place where you lay your head most often, the place your mobile phone bill gets delivered, the place where you most often caffeinate? You might be lounging in the most comfortable chair you've ever owned, with the most creatively named pet snuggled in your lap. And yet, there still might be a hovering aura of stress or anxiety, an underlying insecurity that makes you feel shiftless, just a little bit uncomfortable about everything. Maybe feeling not-at-home makes you check your newsfeed way too often or scratch an itch that isn't quite there. Or, maybe you're just dreading the next time you're going to have to leave the comfort of home and head back out into the big strange world in which the pretense of knowing what you're doing is a constant prerequisite, that world in which there is still no manual on how to be you.

The sad fact—the fact that binds us together in our shared struggle as human beings—is that even when we actually are at home, it is so damn difficult to feel at home.

The tradition that I study, practice, and teach—Shambhala Buddhism—traces the journey that we each make to find where we belong, and describes what happens when we get lost in transit. First and foremost, practitioners of this tradition look at how we have lost touch with a feeling of belonging and trust in our own mind. Then, we can examine how the feeling of not-at-home makes us avoid the trickier aspects of our human relationships. Finally, we can look more broadly at how our inability to settle with our own being leads to communities and societies of mutual distrust, cyclical dissatisfaction, and violence.

LOST IN COMMUTE

The Sanskrit word *samsara*—which traditionally represents the summation of all our confusion and destructive patterns of behavior—literally means "wandering around." The Tibetan word for a sentient being caught up in confusion—*drowa*—could be translated as "always on the go." I like to think of this word as meaning "commuter." From the standpoint of our struggle, we are wanderers, commuters addicted to a state of transit, always thinking that we will be most satisfied somewhere other than here. We may struggle our whole life, on a relentless and unsettling journey from cradle to urn. Lacking the tools to get comfortable in our own skin and safe in our own mind, we get lost again and again in the existential transitions of life, blindly hoping that a true and permanent home lies around the corner, after just a bit more struggle to prove ourselves, a bit more time figuring out how to belong in our life. So often our idea of home is whatever we hope will magically be waiting for us after the current disruption. For the commuter, "home" becomes a shifting mirage in an increasingly repetitive desert.

In this desert, we experience our past as a collection of lost opportunities: Maybe I already missed my chance at a true home? Memories blend into a potpourri of nostalgia: Maybe I really was at home, once upon a time, back in the day, but then I lost it, or it was taken away from me. The future becomes a carnival of hope and fear. We clutch at the belief that "home" will be waiting for us at the end of our current transition: "Life gets better, it's gotta get better, I just need to find the right _____." Filling in this blank is fraught with stress and anxiety.

From this point of view, human life is a nonstop quest for anything that makes us feel temporarily safe within the rudderless journey of aging. Ultimately, what we are seeking is a feeling of belonging in our life. It's the feeling of relaxation that comes with knowing there's a place for us right here in this present moment. But if we never feel like we belong in the present, we quickly become cynical and apathetic, human zombies on a commute from moment to moment, day to day, year to year. Below is a version of such a dark story from the point of view of samsara, the cycle of restless wandering.

THE COMMUTER'S STORY

When the commuter is born, he cries from the depths of his being, not knowing where or who he is. Breath is both a gift and a burden. As a baby, the commuter clamors for safety in a world in which he is utterly defenseless. His parents try to protect him as best they can, but they, too, struggle to deal with the anxiety, regrets, and uncertainty created by their own commutes through life. They don't dare tell him the whole truth about their own struggles, afraid that they might poison his chances at happiness. Childhood brings many lighthearted moments, but few answers to the many questions that define his personal cosmos. As he moves through his world, "why"—a word full of wonder and terror—becomes a constant on the young commuter's lips. Why the sun? Why these grass stains? Why does strawberry ice cream have to melt so quickly? And, most important, why all the sadness that the grown-ups never really talk about? Sometimes he gets a real answer to these questions, but even those answers almost always strike him as incomplete or beside the point, simply opening the door to new "why"s.

In his free time, the child commuter begins to invent his own fantasies, private creation myths to explain this universe and his place in it. He feels disempowered by an inability to reconcile his vast imagination with the confining rules of this place he is slowly learning to inhabit. Taller, fatter people called "adults" make all these rules, which they pass off as objectively true. They tell him that when he grows a little more, he will begin to belong to this place, this society, this earth. If only he commutes through life a little longer, they say, everything will start to make sense to him. He will get it. He will arrive at home. He awaits high school as if it were some holy Mecca.

Adolescence brings longer limbs with which to roam, but little that helps him understand how people treat themselves and each other. Nobody explains to the commuter how to just BE, much less how to BE with others. So he travels onward, imprisoned in a rapidly changing body, adopting a persona of shifting interests and preferences. He discovers only one apparent constant among the flickers of his perceptions, a feeling of tender awkwardness underlying all his steps, a vulnerability he may spend the rest of his life trying to pretend does not exist.

He becomes disillusioned by existing systems and hierarchies, coming to the cynical teenage view that most of the adults in his midst have as much of a clue about what's really going on as did the toddler he used to be. To make matters worse, some of these clueless adults have a ridiculous amount of power over other people, tremendous control over the systems that govern the world. But don't worry, he lets himself be convinced: after graduation, after he leaves his native home, the story goes, is when the real experience begins, when he gets to find his own place on this earth.

He dives into postadolescence, privileged enough to enter the invisible bubble of a university, and watches fellow travelers move on to some of life's other institutional pit stops. In college, the other commuters he befriends nervously tell each other that when "we" get out into the real world, that's when life starts to get good, even though "the real world" is just the name of an old reality TV show.

The commuter stumbles his way into intimate relationships. But without knowing his heart, without knowing himself, it's a maddening dance to share another person's affections. He struggles to learn the unique language of someone else's mind, the floor plan of chambers inside another heart. He feels the accumulation of deep wounds. His capacity to let himself stay open seems to weaken with each disappointment. Wandering through the emotional ups and downs, he gets insatiably lonely when single and relentlessly restless in relationships. He tells himself that eventually, if he just wanders onward a little further, he will find the right person, or at least someone to keep the bed warm. Then he will feel at home—safe and, above all, understood. But romantic disappointment turns saviors into tyrants in the blink of an eye. He decides to take a break from the tyranny of intimacy, and he journeys on alone.

For a while, the commuter builds his home out of a righteous independence from the bondages of human connections. Maybe liberation lies in the freedom from having to depend on anyone or anything, he decides. For a while, this spiritual libertarianism becomes his favorite place to hang his proverbial hat. He could practically write a manifesto on self-reliance. But, in the end, building an off-the-grid existence with an isolationist heart doesn't help if his relationship with his own mind is unsustainable.

He journeys onward, pursuing a career, making his life purposeful, angling to leave a mark through his labor, his achievements. He commutes through graduate school and work life: socially networking, linking in profiles, exaggerating skills on résumés, passing out business cards, dissing bosses and coworkers behind their backs, searching for status, success, and, above all, security. But what, from the point of view of this narrative of dissatisfaction, is a career, anyway? It's just the many hours spent between literal commutes, a blur of moments staring at the movements of a clock, waiting to head back to a home that doesn't quite feel like one.

The commuter finds time to travel abroad, wandering like some Xerox of a Xerox of Kerouac across this lonely planet. He decides that maybe a little spiritual odyssey will open his eyes, and lend him the perfect Kodak moments to post on Instagram. On his pilgrimages to places that are sacred to someone else, he takes brilliant pictures of filtered sunsets. As the light flees each day, each day one closer to death, he accumulates passing "likes" from all the other commuters out in cyberspace. Who doesn't want to be the most popular wanderer?

Eventually, he settles down and finds a partner, a partner with whom the miscommunication is bearable and the snuggles are sheltering, and they give birth to children, welcoming a new generation of commuters. He convinces himself that this nesting process will bring the home he and his partner were always seeking. He lets himself feel cautiously optimistic that they will erase the neurotic mistakes of their own generation, which are version 2.0 of the mistakes of the previous ones. He will provide these new, improved little beings with a home and a clear path to belonging. But parenting brings a new kind of commute through upheaval and groundlessness.

It turns out, of course, that everything brings groundlessness, because everything comes from groundlessness. But he just can't settle with this liberating and terrifying truth: everything that starts, ends.

So he commutes onward, idealizing the oncoming Valhalla of the middle-aged—the empty nest. That's when he'll really be able to get some time back to himself, to finally deepen his relationship to his own being, to achieve spiritual insight or else complete long-forgotten creative masterpieces. Or maybe he'll just take a good long nap on the couch.

Finally, he decides, it's when he retires, if he is lucky enough to afford retirement, that he'll really be able to relax, to explore spiritual pursuits easefully. Then he will have the time and space he needs to transform an entire lifetime of neurotic motion into some kind of experiential wisdom, like the carefree sages of ancient times. He will leave behind a road map for future wanderers, complete with step-by-step instructions, stating exactly what they should do to find their way home. Or maybe he'll give up on the idea that life offers any lessons at all, and just write a tongue-in-cheek memoir, sarcastic and witty enough to undermine anyone's need to believe deeply in anything. But, after retirement, the fossil fuels of hope and fear that drove his constant commute through life continue to pollute his mind. He finds little rest. Finally, there is only one commute left, a choiceless journey into old age and death, a kind of mass transit that even the most seasoned traveler might be unprepared for.

Even with all the assumptions and generalizations of this story, how unsatisfying and isolating would such a life lost in commute be? To make this story even more of a downer, all of the above is just the best-case, most privileged scenario for a life spent in anchorless commute. The above is a life defined by what friends of mine like to call "first-world problems." Many of us don't even have the option of wandering all the way into an unsatisfying old age. Sickness, accidents, and violence can cut this story short before its climax. And the great majority of humans on this planet not only face these existential dilemmas, but are also oppressed by the external forces of systemic poverty and bias produced by the greed, intolerance, and delusion that have gone viral across the globe.

The commuter's narrative is a tale of resentment, grasping, and isolating fear, a story with which most people I've met are familiar.

THE GOOD NEWS

Our lives and societies certainly generate a lot of bad news for anyone brave enough to pay attention. It's a mark of great maturity to realize that we can't become properly optimistic about life, and can't take responsibility for the state of the world, until we're willing to very honestly face the confused side of our situation. This honesty is where the road home has to begin. The historical Buddha first taught about the truth of dissatisfaction that comes from not knowing how to deal with our own mind to a group of intensely depressed spiritual seekers who were literally torturing themselves in the pursuit of happiness.* Given this context, I've

---

*This teaching, where the Buddha set in motion the body of his work, was called the four noble truths, which simply outlines the root causes of human dissatisfaction (*duhkha*) and the basic road map of a path to contentment: (1) the truth of dissatisfaction, (2) dissatisfaction's cause, (3) the possibility of contentment, and (4) the path to contentment.

always thought that the Buddha's description of our dissatisfaction with the commute through life was simply meant to create a moment of honesty and relief in which his students could admit that they were having a hard time. This is my favorite phrasing of the first noble truth: *It's always okay to admit you are struggling.* Why are we struggling so much? To reinterpret the second noble truth in the language of home: people struggle because we don't know where we belong, and we always assume that home lies somewhere other than here and now, a mistake that sets us on an exhausting commute.

The first noble truth—the simple acknowledgment of our struggle—is actually good news. If we start any journey with rose-colored glasses or false promises, we end up disillusioned. If we start with an acknowledgment of reality, free from shame or embarrassment, connecting our own struggle with the struggles of others, then we can move toward a genuine optimism.

The good news about being human is this: the commuter's story is based on a mistake, a fully workable mistake, which is the third noble truth. Our life is never told in just one story or one story line. If the commuter should ever find a way to feel at home, the whole vantage point of life changes. If we change the lens through which we view our experience, then the narrative always shifts as well. Cynicism can quickly become optimism. If he finds a road home—a path outlined in the fourth noble truth—then the commuting zombie eventually turns back into an empowered human being.

All of us have at least glimpsed another way of moving through life, an alternative narrative that arises in parallel to this story of alienation. Sometimes, even for just a moment, something in us shifts, and we don't fixate on whatever will happen at the end of this particular transition. For a moment, we actually arrive in the present, feeling safe, belonging right here. A whole new realm of possibility emerges when it feels like we actually belong in our present experience; we start to appreciate life in a way that is impossible to express verbally. It's nothing magical, unless you consider experience itself to be magic. It's just the feeling of reality shining through the gauzy filters of hopeful daydream and fearful nightmare. If we can learn to consciously reproduce the feeling of returning home to the present, we start developing confidence that we belong here. Maybe we belong here even as much as the great saints and sages of human history, the enlightened people who actually figured something out about life.

If we feel like we belong here enough, we experience the great relaxation that comes with not competing against idealized images of a different, better "me," ideals that by definition we could never live up to. Shame and guilt about who we are slowly subside. Momentarily liberated from deeply engrained forces of self-punishment, we start to take responsibility for what happens to us. We smile and recognize our own mental agency. Then we open our eyes and start looking other people in the eye, listening to their stories more deeply. True friendship and intimacy take shape only when we are present enough to experience more than just one narrative, as well as to participate in our shared human experiences. Suddenly inspired and naturally energized, we can even begin to take responsibility for belonging to planet Earth, for feeling at home in relation to all of this planet's commuting inhabitants.

In this alternate story, our experience of time itself ceases to be one of cyclical entrapment, the déjà vu pain of just going through the motions. Life is no longer about just trudging onward toward oblivion. In this alternative, empowered narrative, the passage of time starts to represent spontaneous opportunity. Every day is new, every moment fresh, every relationship sacred. In this story, no one is ever doomed. "Now" is always the moment of creative potential. In this alternate story, we are awake.

WHERE DO *YOU* LIVE?

My father, David, has been a meditator for forty-five years and a Buddhist teacher for almost forty years, all while maintaining his day job as a composer and musician. Dad tells a funny story of a conversation he had with a Tibetan teacher, or Rinpoche, when the teacher was staying at our old loft in New York's NoHo neighborhood. This lama, named Khenpo Tsultrim Gyamtso Rinpoche, is widely renowned for his meditative prowess. He is also renowned for being impossible to engage in small talk. If you asked Khenpo Rinpoche a question about, say, gluten-free pancakes, he would give you an answer about the nature of mind. Ask him about his favorite painter, and the response would be about emptiness-luminosity. It's a pretty interesting experience to talk to someone who has no interest in chitchat. Imagine trying to send him an instant message. How do you even start a conversation? My father (who loves small talk) decided not to ask a question about the Buddhist teachings. Instead, he asked Rinpoche a small-talk question: "Where do you live?" It was a simple enough question, a little dose of chitchat to blend with all that profundity. "Where do you live?" Dad asked. "When you aren't on the road— traveling, moving around, teaching—where do you live, Rinpoche?"

When he heard the question translated, Khenpo Rinpoche raised the brows above his wide eyes and said something in Tibetan to his translator. My father didn't break his gaze with the powerful little man. I imagine this was quite an eye-locked moment, brow to brow, mind to mind. My father heard the translator's voice ethereally in his ear as he stared into Rinpoche's eyes. Cue climactic theme music.

"Rinpoche says to tell you that he lives in the center of his awareness!"

"You know you've met a true yogi when you get that kind of

answer," my father finishes the story. "As for me, I live on Great Jones Street!"

That's quite an answer to a simple question. When Rinpoche said, "I live in the center of my awareness," I believe he was saying, with full confidence, that he had developed the tools to experience complete acceptance and relaxation within the space of his own thoughts, perceptions, and emotions. He was claiming a kind of fearless intimacy with his very being, a comfort with oneself that is rarely seen. He was saying, "It doesn't matter where I live, because I always feel at home. I belong HERE. No matter where HERE is. If you were HERE, you'd be home by now."

In psychological terms, this space of basic awareness, the home for all our subjective experience, is called the mind. In more romantic terms, it's often called the heart. The totality of our personal experience—what the Tibetan teacher called his awareness—involves our cognitive, emotional, and intellectual processes, all at once. For that reason, the path of awakening views our intellectual intelligence and our emotional wisdom as completely entwined, existing in a unified space of consciousness that needs to be experienced and developed in an integrated way. "Mind" alone doesn't seem like a sufficient word for this space, and neither does "heart." Let's instead talk about the "heartmind," and how to learn to live there.

Our heartmind is where we will always live, where we will always come home. Whether we live well in our awareness, or whether we trash the place, is quite another story, but the fact is that our heartmind is where we must lay out the welcome mat. What could possibly be more important than taking care of our true home?

The decision to prioritize your relationship with your heartmind is deeply connected with what it means to practice Buddhism. People often ask, "What's the definition of a Buddhist?"

I've always done my best to answer, but there are a lot of possible responses—it's very personal and definitions are always debatable. Of course, there are formal vows that you can take to become a Buddhist, and many people do, but not everyone chooses this path. The vast majority of folks I've worked with on the Awake-ist teachings are interested in some definition that is accessible and relevant to life in the fast-paced, global society of the twenty-first century. Most of us are not looking to take on anything that sounds like a new religion, preferring a socially relevant and ethically responsible psychology and philosophy.* As Eastern ideas converse with Western science, culture, art, and politics, and especially Western psychology, the definition of a Buddhist is open to an increasingly lively debate, and the range of definitions seems to evolve almost daily. Some people are adamant about what does or doesn't make someone a true Buddhist, or a "good" Buddhist, a real-deal practitioner. Of course, every tradition has its purists, obsessed with policing authenticity. However, the purists end up simply authenticating—within a huge array of traditional perspectives available to them—the aspects of the tradition that support their narrow claims.

Here's my personal definition of a Buddhist: someone who prioritizes cultivating her relationship to her own heartmind—and her relationship to other sentient beings—above whatever else she might achieve in life.

An Awake-ist is anyone who has come to the decision that her heartmind is her true home, and develops the tools to train to live in her awareness with skill and compassion. An Awake-ist uses contemplative and ethical tools to travel the road home, and to help others feel at home in whatever way she can. For me, in this

---

*Some people still think Buddhism is a religious designation. I'm not one of them. I will discuss this more in chapter 10.

vast and diverse world, the only meaningful definition of a Buddhist is this broad and inclusive one.

It turns out that my father's small-talk question to the Tibetan lama was actually immensely profound.

In thinking of home, we have to move beyond considering home as a physical address. We have to start asking what home feels like. My main teacher and guru, Sakyong Mipham Rinpoche, emphasizes that it is never enough to have good ideas—we need to familiarize ourselves with how experiences make us feel, on a deep and personal level. It is beneath the frameworks of ideas, in the very taste and texture of experience, that true insight is born. We use language to describe and communicate feelings, but the feelings described by language are actually the most important thing to befriend. To be a sentient being literally means that we feel first, and that we think and act later, on the basis of these feelings. So, how does it *feel* to feel at home? How do we act when we feel like we belong?

When I feel at home (or when someone else truly makes me feel at home), I feel comfortable, supported, safe, and relaxed, like I don't need anything. At those times, my past ceases to be a neon marquee of regrets, and my future is no longer an unending to-do list, bullet-pointed by unrealistic expectations. Feeling at home is the feeling that I can just be myself. It would be wonderful if there was a more psychologically complex description of this feeling with which to impress some academic journal. I'd love to concoct some seven-syllable yogic word that sounds mystical, ancient, brilliant: JUSTBEYOURSELFASANA. But, in fact, the simplicity of being ourselves is actually the ideal outcome of traveling the path of awakening. When I feel at home, I can also begin to feel truly available to others, because their presence no longer compromises my identity or threatens my safety. When other people no longer seem like threats, I open my eyes and take greater interest in the society we share, this earth on which we are all natives and locals.

Is it ever really possible to feel completely at home all the time, to be free of anxiety and struggle? What's the actual difference, anyway, between someone who lives fully in the center of her awareness, and a confused person? Are awakened beings born that way, neurologically or spiritually different from the rest of us? Is that Tibetan lama made of a different substance, a more enlightened bloodline? In this era of self-aggression and idealistic celebrity, there is always a tendency to "other-ize" positive qualities, a tendency that is unfortunately amplified by the fact that the Buddhist teachings originate in a foreign cultural context.

You could say, from the perspective of the tradition of meditation, that there is actually very little that separates an enlightened being from a zombie commuter. Both have to deal with the pains and pleasures of life; there's no way to bypass them. The only difference is that the confused person is constantly lost in commute, grasping for home among the slippery and unstable objects along the road. The enlightened person is already at home, living in the center of her awareness. The enlightened person has made the space of her own being into a sustainable home, with immeasurable square footage. The awakened person has plenty of mental space to accommodate and deal skillfully with the entire range of life's emotional experiences—making room for fear, lust, anger, uncertainty, jealousy, and all the other emotions that come with being human.

We could ask this very same question about confusion and wisdom on a larger scale: What's the difference between a confused society and an enlightened society? A confused society, a deeply endangered society, is a group of people all lost in nightmarish commute. The systems, institutions, and culture of such a society discourage people from feeling the trust and belonging that come with being at home in your world. A confused society is a society of isolation and exclusion, one in which fear becomes profitable and self-reflection becomes a threat to established bureaucracies.

An enlightened society is one where the culture encourages time for self-awareness, belonging, and connection. An enlightened society would actually foster cultural and social relationships to help commuters find their way home. It's that simple—in theory. But "simple" should never ever be confused with "easy." Our personal journey is rarely easy, and our global journey is even less so. Because everything is interdependent, we have to work on both of these levels at once. Trying to change society without deeply understanding our heartmind won't work. Your own road home can never be separated from society's journey. We need a unifying theory and language that allow us to link the lessons of our personal journey with the situation facing our world. The important question then, a question laced with a gorgeous irony, is, "How do we get home from here?" Or, maybe more appropriate, "How do we get here from here?"

NOT AT HOME: THE CRISIS OF MATERIALISM

What word best describes the epidemic arising from a life of constant commute? What happens when we have to clutch fearfully at the objects of experience in an attempt to find security? What happens to a whole society of people who systemically feel ashamed about being with themselves and are taught that their best option is to become comfortably numb to their experience? What psychological damage do we enact on ourselves, how do we torment each other, and what environmental havoc do we unleash on the world when we repeatedly avoid working with our minds? From the Shambhala standpoint, the word to describe this illness is "materialism."

When we call somebody materialistic, we usually mean that he has superficial or petty values, that he has mistaken beliefs about what really matters in life. For me, a Madonna song comes to mind. But what the tradition means by "materialism" is something subtler, more metaphysical, and more universal. Materialism is the belief that "consciousness" is unimportant, that the mind is reducible to the brain, and therefore that the path to happiness involves precise chemical manipulation. Materialists don't believe in the importance of the mind itself and instead reduce life to the pursuit of pleasure. As such, they have grown deeply insecure about their relationship to their own awareness. Every bad choice we make in life, and every destructive and greedy system at work on this planet, comes from this insecurity, from the actions of human beings who don't feel at home.

To understand the theory of materialism, we must have a basic understanding of the subject-object nature of human experience, and how the Awake-ist tradition leads us to bravely encounter our own heartmind. We are each a subject, one who exists and perceives objects of experience within the space of our lived awareness. When a subject can't feel at home within his own subjectivity, he has no choice but to attempt to solidify home by grasping for safety "out there." This process of objectification is the basic fuel of our nightmarish commute through samsara—a road trip spent oscillating between chasing after, and then rejecting, a range of experiences, trying to arrange all the right moments in all the perfect ways, and doing anything we can to avoid discomfort.

A basic fact of reality, however, is that all experiences we encounter are fundamentally unstable (in other words, impermanent).

The attempt to create a real and lasting home out of any collection of impermanent objects is going to eventually produce recurrent stress and deep anxiety, instead of lasting comfort and safety. Whether it's a physical object like a remodeled kitchen, or a mental object like a feeling of inner bliss, both are bound to change. Even though they might make us feel safe for a while, neither object is reliable as a true home. Rather than taking the impermanence of all experiences as a message to focus more attention on his own heartmind, the materialist takes impermanence as a kind of "beat-the-clock" challenge to collect as many meaningful experiences as he can before time inevitably runs out. On the coarsest level, this leads to a culture of consumerism as the materialist in each of us constantly seeks new objects to replenish our collection of worthwhile experiences. For example, the materialist remodels a kitchen and only focuses on the cabinets and the fixtures, without any awareness of how his mind is responding to the experience of inhabiting the kitchen, how he lives in his awareness as he moves through the space. Eventually, the shine wears off the refrigerator and he decides he needs a brand-new kitchen all over again, just to feel temporarily at ease once more. With all of his mental energy tied up in pursuing the next object, he usually avoids any meaningful awareness of himself as a subject, the very "me" he was trying to make happy in the first place. In a scary, impermanent world, the materialist lives as far away from his awareness as he can. Such a life is spent in "object management" mode, suppressing pain and chasing pleasure, prostrated before the flight-or-fight part of the nervous system, obsessed with short-term fixes, defending constantly against short-term threats. When you don't want to look at your own subjective experience, the best thing to do is to live by what you can touch most viscerally, which is the reliable chemistry of pleasure and pain.

Materialism—the human illness that arises from the objectification of home—is not something to be judged. Materialism is simply an immature response to reality, one that has existed throughout human history and that has been repeatedly fortified by culture and philosophy, a response that we all fall victim to in one way or another until we complete the path of learning how our heartmind really works. Let's not judge Wall Street or anyone else too harshly for making the same mistake of objectification that beings have been making since the dawn of . . . well, beings. At the same time, nonjudgment certainly doesn't mean passivity; if we understood materialism's mistaken cause, we wouldn't continue empowering greed as a social norm.

Our materialistic impulse is totally understandable, the way a child's temper tantrum is totally understandable. We can't do anything about our materialism unless we develop some real empathy toward it, along with a sense of humor. When a child is throwing a tantrum, we try our best to be skillful and compassionate and appreciate where the child is and how his fears are valid. But that doesn't mean we don't hope that the child eventually matures and learns to regulate his emotions more effectively. The same goes for an adult's immature attempts to control objects, to solidify the fluid phenomena of his life into some kind of lasting home. We each start where we are, of course, but we try to head to a more mature place.

The Awake-ist path is all about slowly learning to regulate our materialistic tantrums in the face of reality's rules. To recognize, with a playful attitude, that we have a childish relationship to reality is where this path begins. The path is never about discarding emotions; it's about cultivating more emotional maturity, which means having more awareness of how our emotions operate, learning that they contain deep intelligence, but that they also present us with destructive obstacles. To call materialism immature is not a value judgment, but simply a recognition that it makes us want to convert objects into what objects cannot become—solid and permanent.

At the same time, we can't pretend that the outer world has no effect on our consciousness. Objects matter. We will feel differently on a day when it is warm and sunny than we feel on a cold, rainy day. Living in poverty, versus living in privilege, has a huge effect on how people experience their lives and their minds. A person recovering from intense trauma is in a different situation from someone who hasn't experienced difficulties to the same degree. To become a student of Buddhism does not mean forsaking the outer environment and how it affects us. Awake-ism means becoming curious students of the *relationship* between inner and outer circumstances, and between subject and object.

THE ANCIENT PHILOSOPHY OF MATERIALISM

Materialism was an actual philosophical system in India that paralleled the spread of the Buddhist meditation tradition.* What the early materialists believed was sophisticated and at least somewhat scientific: they thought all reality was material (i.e., matter) and that the universe was just a huge sequence of random chemical and physical arrangements, arising from four basic elements or chemical building blocks. For them, what meditators call "consciousness," what the Tibetan lama called "awareness," what I'm calling the "heartmind," was all just a perceptual myth, a romantic idea of philosophers and contemplatives. In today's terms, a pure

---

*This school of thought was called Carvaka or Lokayata: I sometimes joke with friends that we can take comfort that our dominant worldview is traceable to an ancient Indian system.

scientific materialist would say, "I don't see any mind. I only see a brain and a nervous system that can be chemically and biologically regulated and manipulated." (It's actually hard to argue with such a person on his own terms, because the only way that the heartmind can be experienced is personally and subjectively. That's why meditation is such a crucial tool.)

For ancient materialists, human existence was little more than an accident, a throw of cosmic dice at an intergalactic craps table, a fleeting, random occurrence. There could be no path to awakening, the materialists thought, because a path to awakening requires the belief that the most important asset in human life is our consciousness itself. The materialists, by definition, didn't believe that consciousness actually existed, so they didn't believe there was any need to work with our habitual tendencies or conditioning. Nor did they believe in any ethical basis for choosing what to do and what to avoid. Why would you even bother to argue about ethics? Why does it matter how you treat people, when only matter matters?

The materialists made living pleasurably the highest spiritual pursuit of life, and the spiritual paths they advocated were the ones that evoked a veritable feast of blissful feelings. This philosophy has repeated itself in many forms throughout human history. At their height, the materialists were sort of like emotional foodies, suckling on sensation, drizzling their days with moments of ecstasy, garnishing life with comforts. At their most profound, the materialists were scientific naturalists, producing great poetry borne from an epicurean interest in the richness of the present moment. At their most superficial, they were addicts and hedonists, sipping on the champagne of the day like ancient Jay Gatsbys or Don Drapers, laughing ironically, undermining the logic of anyone who dared to lecture them about ethics, morality, or the powerful momentum of habit known as karma. The hedonists obsessed over the haute couture of their era, investing their entire lives in the pursuit of pleasure, shrugging off the idea that we have a responsibility to help others, unless it was to help others share pleasure.

Let's face it—the materialist embedded in each of us knows two important things, two truths you can't really argue with: (1) life is short, and (2) pleasure feels a hell of a lot better than pain.

THREE TYPES OF MATERIALISM: PHYSICAL, INTELLECTUAL, AND EMOTIONAL

The founder of the Shambhala tradition, Chogyam Trungpa Rinpoche, didn't just discuss this materialistic tendency to objectify reality in relation to physical possessions. He saw the physical objectification of our world, its reduction to an input of dead matter for consumption, as an enormous problem and the root of environmental devastation. Still, he taught that materialism can cause us to fixate on even subtler objects. He realized that we make the mistake of chasing after home not just on the level of physical comfort, but on deeper psychological levels as well. On the level of intellect, we fixate on ideologies and shut out opposing views, vilifying those who disagree with our perspective. In an even deeper way, we fixate on our emotions. And, at the deepest level of materialism, we objectify what it means to be a spiritually mature person.

Physical (Sensory) Materialism

Of course, the most obvious, external way that we chase after safety is by looking for instant gratification through our senses. The sense perceptions can create pleasure and comfort and temporarily ease the anxiety of not feeling relaxed in our own being, but sense pleasures can't ever solve the fundamental issues created by avoiding your own mind.

Intellectual (Ideological) Materialism

Ideas and ideology serve an important purpose—they communicate experience and create new ways to understand our journey. Being able to think clearly and consider ideas is very important. Sometimes people falsely believe that a good spiritual path should be anti-intellectual. Nothing could be further from the truth. If we aren't able to think clearly, then how are we ever going to find our way through the vast and complex world that we inhabit? Thoughtful ideologies can help us to describe the world; ideas are the source code of great technology, art, and discourse.

But ideas are unable to do one thing: become a true home for our experience. The map of Barcelona is never the experience of Barcelona. A menu is never a replacement for a meal. Ideologies, by their nature, are fixed descriptions of a world that is constantly in motion. If we try to create a lasting home from our ideologies, we will always fail, ignoring the moments when reality shifts its terrain and where our ideas need to shift as well.

Emotional (Spiritual or Psychological) Materialism

In a seminal spiritual work, Chogyam Trungpa Rinpoche discussed the idea of turning the highest pursuit of spirituality, or awakening, into another means to objectify reality. From the standpoint of materialism, the purpose of spirituality (or psychology, or any practice related to the mind, for that matter) is to use spiritual practices to reliably produce a certain emotion, like joy or ecstasy. In their subtlest forms, emotions are actually objects, too, objects that arise within the space of our awareness. Emotions are not where we live—like any other object, they are just regular visitors in the home of our heartmind. When we try to decorate our experience with certain "spiritual" emotions, like happiness, peace, or bliss, and throw out other emotions, like sadness and anger, we invalidate a huge amount of what actually happens to us. A spiritual materialist fixates on feeling like a spiritual person, and tries to make a permanent home out of the heightened emotional states that he attributes to his spiritual practice. In that state of innermost hedonism, we only pursue human relationships that make us feel peaceful or ecstatic. We might fall in love, but only so long as the intoxication lasts. We might work with a mentor, therapist, or guru, but only if they tell us what we want to hear. We might practice meditation or yoga, but not if it means confronting difficult feelings like anger or jealousy. If we leave a practice session feeling less than perfect, we think the practice is not working for us. We might buy incense and statues, but only until the odor bores us, and the statue's sheen wears off. We turn human examples of wisdom into robotic representations of peace and happiness, rendering them safe to reinforce the boundaries of our narrow comfort zone.

The problem with spiritual materialism is that if our heartmind were truly an inviting home, we wouldn't be rejecting the emotions that are often deemed "less" spiritual, less "peak," like sadness, anger, disappointment, loneliness, and remorse. We wouldn't turn other humans into superheroes or villains based on our latest spiritual elation or disappointment. If we were at home in our own mind, we wouldn't have to spend life chasing after only a small range of prized feelings to arrange like trophies on a shrine, rejecting all other emotions as lesser, unworthy of our experience. This is a subtle and difficult point, but the path of awakening is not about objectifying certain emotions as worthy and others as unworthy of visiting our home. We cannot find comfort by chasing after mind states that feel "divine." If we do this, we will spend most of our life rejecting what we are actually experiencing, pretending that we are on some holy path while we're really on an evasive journey away from our own humanity. Our blissful smile will be knit together by a deep, underlying sense of self-loathing. If we don't work compassionately with whatever comes, we will be forced to constantly defend against the invasion of unwanted emotions. Without the experience of all emotions, our journey will cease to be a human one. The road home is a human journey *through* feelings, not around them. Meditation is a practice of accommodating feelings, not a way to sanitize them. This understanding should be the starting point for anyone who attempts to meditate.

In his very first teaching on the four noble truths, when he discussed the causes of our dissatisfaction, the Buddha implicitly linked emotional materialism to the source of all our confusion. One major cause of dissatisfaction, as he described it, was an attempt to annihilate the feelings we experience in the present moment. Attempting to limit and quarantine the range of emotions only serves to compound our pain. Likewise, when we react to feelings blindly, we also avoid facing them. Suppressing and acting out against feelings are the markers of our innermost materialism. In both cases, we are trying to defend against the intensity of actually living. Trying to defend against feeling what we are feeling is the subtlest form of mental violence, and leads to a lifelong path of internal warfare, a boxing match where reality and fantasy bludgeon each other with no clear winner. In this tradition, this kind of inner emotional violence is considered to be the root of all the systemic greed, hatred, and avoidance we experience as a society.

Because there is no way to defend against feeling our feelings, there is also no way to make our peak (blissful, sacred, divine) emotions into a permanent home. Nor will we find any salvation in idealizing the relationships—romantic partners, creative muses, spiritual gurus, etc.—that we think will deliver only bliss-ful emotions, ecstatic insights, and heightened experiences. If we are going to conquer materialism, we have to make the heartmind into a place in which the full range of human emotions can feel at home.

BEGINNING THE JOURNEY

This book follows a fairly traditional structure with four parts representing four main bodies of teachings. While most of the teachings (especially in the first three sections) are derived from an ancient Indo-Tibetan tradition, my interpretation of each of these bodies of insights comes from the perspective of looking at the heartmind as our true home, examining how that insight af-fects our relationships and our understanding of our collective identity as a human society.

In the book's first section, we look at the journey of self-awareness. This is traditionally called Hinayana in the early texts of the Indo-Tibetan tradition, or literally the "small vehicle," be-cause the scope of practice is limited to one's own subjective expe-rience. Here, we look at the mechanisms of our mind as the basis for coming home to ourselves. First, we'll investigate some simple insights and lingering myths regarding the increasingly popular practice of meditation (chapter 1). Then we will look into the teachings on karma, where we'll explore the habitual conditioning and stuck patterns of behavior that keep us caught up in the com-muter's mentality (chapter 2). Then we will discuss how the practice of self-awareness permeates every aspect of daily life through the practice of ethics (chapter 3). Finally, we will explore how the journey of self-awareness can shift our idea of the self and trans-form our view of human nature altogether (chapter 4).

In the book's second section, we look at the journey of relationships, traditionally called Mahayana, or literally the "expansive vehicle," as the scope of practice becomes broader and more interpersonal. We broaden the focus to include relationships not only because living in awareness reveals that we are accountable to others, but also because we come to recognize that our very sense of who we are as individuals is cocreated in relationship to others. This cocreation of our sense of self begins very early with our parents and continues with everyone else we meet. First, we explore the basic interdependence of self and others to see how compassion meditation practices can help us to understand other people better (chapter 5). Then we discuss Buddhist teachings on human communication, extending the insights of mindfulness into the realm of effective listening and speaking (chapter 6). Then we look into the often misunderstood concept of emptiness, seeing that if we misapply this potentially liberating idea, we might end up using our spiritual practice to bypass the difficult relationships of life, rather than to deal with them (chapter 7). We go on to the practical implications of trying to live a compassionate life by considering a Buddhist approach to boundaries in relationships (chapter 8). This section ends with an exploration of various types of student–teacher relationships that may help guide us along the path (chapter 9).

In the book's third section, we look at the idea of sacredness, traditionally the third body of teachings in the Indo-Tibetan tradition, called Vajrayana, or literally the "indestructible vehicle." In this body of teachings, also known as Buddhist Tantra, every aspect of life and practice, as well as every emotion, is said to have the potential to reveal that our mind is a profound and sacred home. First, we examine the ways that we unnecessarily divide our secular experience from our spiritual path, and explore the view that these secular and spiritual truths can be completely integrated into one enterprise in which spiritual practice and worldly life support, rather than fight against, each other (chapter 10). Then we look at the practice of visualization to see how we can transform our imagination into a space where we view ourselves and the world as sacred (chapter 11). Finally, we look at the Shambhala principles of windhorse and *drala* to see how the subject-object relationship can be seen as the basis for a sacred relationship to emotions as well as ecology, and can prepare us for full engagement with the larger world (chapter 12).

In the book's final section, we look at our shared path as a community and society. We look at various ideas for evolving the teachings of Buddhism beyond the individual and the interpersonal into a cultural, social, and political space. First, we look at how seeing the reality of interdependence causes us to develop our understanding of the journey beyond the traditional three-part framework above into an exploration of how the personal, interpersonal, and collective aspects of practice can all be worked with simultaneously (chapter 13). Then we discuss how the institutions of a confused society mirror the confused habitual patterns that arise in an individual, and how those institutions might transform into supportive systems for enlightened society (chapter 14). Then we look at the role of culture, art, and creativity as practices of transformation that affect the environment of our collective experience (chapter 15). Finally, the book concludes with some advice for making the Buddhist teachings your own, in order to truly come home in your own way (chapter 16).

See you on the road.

PART I

The Journey of Self-Awareness

The longest journey a man must take is the eighteen inches from his head to his heart.

—UNKNOWN

I

MEDITATION

Accepting Your Own Friend Request

M editation has become incredibly popular. Well, at least popular in theory. Aspects of Buddhist meditation have already had a profound influence on a wide swath of our culture, as mindfulness and other techniques have been widely integrated into Western psychology, medicine, arts, social justice work, and even early childhood education. This has all happened very quickly, in some ways far more rapidly than Buddhist thought was integrated into the new cultures it migrated into throughout its Asian past. I am part of the second generation of the American Shambhala Buddhist community, and many of the obstacles that the first generation faced in establishing its practice are now greatly diminished, thanks to the hard work of dedicated pioneers in integrating Eastern practices into Western culture.

I imagine that when my parents each told friends and family in the early 1970s that they were practicing meditation, the response they got was quite different from what I get when I disclose my own practice now. I know my parents were met with many confused looks and worried questions behind their backs about swamis and cults. I especially like to imagine the look on my grandparents' faces circa 1973 in the small farming town of Stuttgart, Arkansas, when my mother, Janice, tried to explain to them that she was now following a brilliant and wild Tibetan man, receiving teachings on the nature of mind.

Things have changed drastically since the 1970s. Rarely a day goes by that my social network doesn't light up with a widely shared link to an article about the proven health benefits of meditation practice. Now, wherever I go, when I tell somebody I teach Buddhism, it's never greeted with frowns, and is almost always a big plus for my credibility as a human being. "That's so awesome!" people usually say. Often they will follow by telling me about their own practice or experience with Buddhism, or else they might start talking about their yoga practice, or maybe the dialectical behavioral therapist they work with. Every once in a while when I reveal what I do, the person I'm talking to will put his hands together at his heart center and say a quiet *namaste* in a semireverent tone—a gesture totally out of context— and I have to catch myself from cracking up in front of him.

The thing that happens most often when I tell people I meditate is actually pretty strange: after singing the theoretical praises of meditation, the person says something like, "I wish I could meditate. I just can't. I tried. I just couldn't empty my mind. It just wouldn't stop." Because of these seemingly countless encounters—where people highly praise meditation and proudly say things like, "If I'm anything, I'm a Buddhist," only to turn around in the next breath and say they aren't cut out for meditation— I often joke that meditation has become the thing we're all really happy that *other* people do.

DEFINING MEDITATION

Why is meditation so popular in theory, but less so in actuality? Why do people encounter so much difficulty with even a foundational practice like mindfulness of body, where we simply take a comfortable posture, connect with the present moment, and try to gather our attention to the feeling of our body breathing for a few brief minutes? Countless studies—and, much more important, the personal experience of millions of practitioners—have already verified the many positive and transformative effects, as well as the health benefits, of a sustained long-term meditation practice. There is even evidence to suggest that a small but consistent amount of meditation practice might amplify the expression of positive genetic traits!* Techniques that have been formally studied include mindfulness, compassion meditation, and now even more esoteric visualization techniques. Why, then, aren't people walking the streets of our major cities with meditation cushions strapped across their backs, the same way they do with yoga mats?

Part of the issue is that there are some lingering misconceptions about what meditation practice means and what it offers. Exploring two traditional Buddhist translations for the word "meditation" can help to demystify this confusion and make the practice more accessible, as well as to clarify common misunderstandings about its purpose and effects.

Definition One: Cultivation—No Fast Food in This Garden
Like almost everything worth doing in life, meditation is a longterm endeavor, meant to be practiced a little bit each day over a long

---

*From Richard Davidson at the University of Wisconsin: www.news.wisc.edu/22370.

period of time, along with occasional periods of retreat to deepen your experience. I know so many people who have tried meditation once or twice and then gave up on it because they didn't instantly get the results they were looking for. The results we are looking for, unfortunately, often include stopping our thoughts altogether, or destroying unwanted emotions. One simple reason meditation is difficult to sustain is that the principal benefits of meditation are not short-term, and it is generally hard to convince ourselves to engage in anything that has mostly long-term effects. Our global culture and the animal portion of our brains are geared toward activities that have short-term rewards, and our culture and our brains both fight hard to keep us away from activities that provoke short-term resistance. This is part of the commuter's mentality; when we wander through life, we tend to privilege short-term convenience.

The first traditional definition of meditation points to the need to view it as a long-term process. There is a word in the Pali and Sanskrit languages of early Buddhism, *bhavana*, which is generally translated as "meditation practice." *Bhavana* means something like cultivation, developing, or growing. It has the feel of gardening. This word points to the fact that meditation helps us cultivate qualities of mind that truly make a difference in life: mindfulness, compassion, love, intelligence, patience, and fearlessness. These are, after all, the qualities we hope people will remember us by. I, for one, hope that when I'm gone people have more to say about me than, "He could watch every single episode of his favorite show in one marathon session, without ever leaving the couch. Now that's stamina!"

From the standpoint of *bhavana*, meditation functions very similarly to physical exercise, like the slow training of a healthy body. Sakyong Mipham Rinpoche points to the fact that everyone at least theoretically agrees that physical exercise is a good thing. At least we agree around New Year's Day, when making our resolutions. Though we rarely think that our mind can be exercised, it is, in fact, arranged as a group of muscular systems that we need to develop slowly through training.

To take this analogy further, think about how you feel when you watch a world-class athlete. When we see this athlete, of course we might think much of their success comes from natural talents, but we also know that their abilities were developed through a lot of training. Nobody thinks Michael Jordan got where he did without a whole lifetime of practice. He was in the gym all the time (he got cut from his high school team, by the way).

However, when we see an incredibly compassionate person, our mind makes different assumptions. We tend to just assume that they (the Dalai Lama, Dr. King, Aung San Suu Kyi, etc.) were "born that way," that there was no training involved, no resistance confronted, no bravery required in becoming who they became. The best we can do as mere mortals, we figure, is to maybe get a distant blessing or a deep hug from such a saint. Maybe then some of their magic aura will rub off on us. Believing that great people are born without having to work with their heartminds reveals a lack of understanding that we ourselves can develop our minds. Through meditation, we come to see that mindfulness and compassion are like mental muscles that need to be worked daily. That's the remarkable fact: compassion is something you have to train in.

When we don't realize that we can cultivate our mind over time, we feel stuck, helpless, resigned to a schmuck's sorry fate, disbelieving that we could ever transform how we perceive ourselves and how we interact with the world. Without our realizing it, this misguided view leads us to a very harmful place, because it causes us to abdicate responsibility for the cultivation of compassion, always leaving the hard work to somebody else. But if humans are going to thrive (or even survive), we each need to manifest as a decent, mindful, and compassionate person in this world. We can't wait for the right person to get elected (we already tried that one) or, for that matter, the perfect teacher or guru to show up on our doorstep and bless us, removing all veils and obstacles.

A few years back, I joined a CSA, or community-supported agriculture program. Once a week, we city dwellers would pick up a load of fresh vegetables and produce delivered from an organic farm upstate. It was March when I signed up for the farm share. Feeling ecofriendly and hipster green, I proudly asked over the phone when we could pick up our first load of produce. The woman responded, "Oh, probably the first week of June." The first week of June was almost three months away. My knee-jerk thought was "What a rip-off!" Then I remembered the truth of how slowly good things come into being. "Oh, I forgot. They have to grow the food first. Right."

Our inclination to get caught up looking for immediate solutions mirrors our tendency as a society. So many of our global systems seek fast-food solutions for our shared problems. Our political and economic systems are overly bound to outcomes that can be quickly achieved, outcomes that almost always sacrifice the long-term health of our society and planet. These instant gratification approaches always seem the most profitable, but only when profit is defined as immediate comfort with minimal effort. As a society, we need to contemplate why we've come to prefer quick gains over long-term sustainability. Likewise, as individuals seeking happiness, we need to come face-to-face with our problematic addiction to immediate gratification and convenience.

Meditation gently forces us to confront just how much the habit of instant gratification has led us astray, into a commute of dissatisfaction. In fact, the more we practice, the more practice begins to short-circuit our animalistic wiring to seek pleasure right now.

Of course, it makes total sense that we look for a quick-fix version of mental well-being, something that might reduce stress and reliably make us feel good immediately. Let's be honest: if quick fixes actually worked, then the smartest thing to do would be to go for the quick fix, every single time. However, there is no fast-food version of meditation and, if there were, it would probably be about as healthy for the mind as fast food is for the body.

To be a committed meditation practitioner, you have to sit down for, say, ten minutes each day, thinking about the effects of your practice ten years in the future, rather than just hoping to feel awesome the moment the timer goes off. Some days you do feel great at the end of the session, whole and balanced, capable and even fearless. But some days when the gong rings, you just feel cranky and defensive, rubbed a little raw by your time on the cushion, like you lost a few layers of skin. To become a student of meditation is to become a student of life, a student of process itself. In my experience, becoming a student of meditation leads to studying everything else—art, culture, politics, relationships—more fully. You establish a basic rhythm of being more process-oriented, and you are willing to stick with all processes more appreciatively, more patiently. You generally become, in the words of Pema Chödrön, one of the Acharyas, or master teachers, of the Shambhala lineage, more "curious about existence."

This is not to say that meditation doesn't offer any short-term benefits such as stress reduction, settledness of mind within chaotic life situations, clarity of intention, and heartfelt empathy for others, to name a few. These effects have all been verified by multiple studies that have examined a wide range of the effects of practice on both brand-new and highly experienced practitioners.* But if you try to use your meditation practice to feel a certain way every time, to experience a reliable bliss, you eventually end up with the kind of spiritual objectification that is the very source of the commuter's confusion. Meditation just doesn't work that way, because reality just doesn't work that way.

The fact is, there are much better ways to feel short-term pleasure than to meditate. I'm sure you are familiar with some yourself, whether they are rated G or NC-17. But meditation is the best way I've found to feel at home in my experience, which leads to a kind of sustainable satisfaction that can begin to pervade every situation you encounter, whether pleasant or painful. It takes a lot of time to begin to trust that meditation works. The journey of practice provides so many bumps and curves, so many chances to lose and then to recover our trust in the whole process, so we have to remember our long-term view again and again and again.

Interestingly enough, in the Buddha's earliest teachings, when Siddhartha speaks of whether it is possible to truly cultivate your mind like a garden, he tells his students to just trust him. He says, "If it were not possible to cultivate healthy and wholesome qualities of mind, I would not ask you to do so." Usually, in his oral

---

*These range from findings of reduced instances of depressive symptoms among beginning meditators in mindfulness-based stress reduction eight-week courses to radical and unprecedented increases in activity in the left prefrontal region in master practitioners such as Matthieu Ricard and Mingyur Rinpoche during monitored sessions of compassion meditation, findings that earned them each, alternately, the title of "World's Happiest Man."

dialogues, Siddhartha demonstrated things that could be verified by lived experience and thoughtful contemplation, and he told anyone who was listening never to take his word for anything. After all, this is generally the best form of teaching: the best teachers provide a supportive framework and timely sparks of inspiration for the student to gain confidence in her own experience. But here, when it comes to our deepest insecurity—our tendency to disbelieve that we can actually change our mind— the Buddha just says, "If you don't trust yourself, then trust me. I wouldn't ask you to practice if you couldn't do this." I always thought this was a very interesting teaching, because it sounds like he is demanding blind faith. Even so, whenever I've felt hopeless and stuck in my practice, or my life, it always helps to think of the encouragement of mentors or genuine heroes who have already cultivated the qualities I'm working to cultivate. As we've said, those people weren't "born this way" (if they were, what use would they be as examples for us?). Rather, they were brave enough and patient enough to slowly develop themselves, to till the fertile soil of their own minds over time.

If we try meditation once and then return to our habitual mode of commuting through objects, looking for something shiny and disposable for our spiritual shopping cart, we'll only feel the same old dissatisfaction when the new method no longer glows. Meditation only works if we give it lots of time. My advice is to practice at least a year, ten minutes each day, and go on at least one retreat during that year before you wonder too much about results. A year is not too much time to invest in your true home. Honestly, a lifetime wouldn't be, either.

Definition Two: Making Friends with Yourself
There is a deeper reason yet, I think, that meditation is hard to engage in, which goes right to the heart of what it means to come

home to ourselves. When we meditate, we are engaging in something that for most of us is a completely new style of education. In our society, most fields of learning are about the world of objects, people, and relationships "out there." Most, maybe all, of our formal education is based on understanding objects. When we learn about engineering, or we learn to cook, or we learn painting, we are studying the rules of how the world "out there" operates, how the perceptual or intellectual objects of our experience work together with each other, how these objects can be understood and manipulated. This style of education even influences the way psychology has been traditionally studied in Western culture. Ironically, it is still possible that somebody could earn a Ph.D. in psychology and have mostly gained expertise in the study of other people's minds, or an abstracted mind.

But what about us, the subjects? For many of us, our education is a matter of pride, something that has cost us many years, many resources, and lots of toil. We may know countless facts, we may have fancy degrees or titles, but have we directly studied how our mind perceives, feels, experiences, grasps at, reacts to, and projects onto the world "out there"? It's quite possible that a person has multiple framed diplomas, and still he doesn't know much about his own true home, his heartmind. This can be quite a difficult and embarrassing fact to come to terms with. As a teacher and a student, I know that an educational process is always the hardest when a student feels that the subject at hand is something she is already supposed to know about. We may be adults, but in terms of our direct relationship to our own mind—what you might call our contemplative education—we may have only a kindergarten level of understanding. When we meditate, we have to leave all our diplomas behind for a moment and be willing to go back to an inner kindergarten, to the most basic level of contemplative education. We have to embrace a new kind of subjective learning process, with all its awkwardness and uncertainty, but also with its playfulness, in order to overcome whatever inadequacy we might feel when we realize that we may never have developed the simple skill of being able to spend ten minutes alone with our own mind. After all, kindergarten is supposed to be fun, with graham crackers and apple juice galore.

A second word defining meditation practice, *gom*, comes from the Tibetan tradition and means something along the lines of "familiarization" or "getting to know." When we meditate, we are becoming familiar with our mind's subjective experience in a direct and intimate way. This definition points again to the idea that when we meditate we are entering an educational realm that is new to us, that we have to take a lot of time and patience to become familiar with.

Chogyam Trungpa Rinpoche used to say the purpose of meditation is to make friends with yourself. This is not what many people think meditation is all about—many people I talk to seem to think that meditation is about hiring an inner ninja assassin to secretly kill off the thoughts and emotions you no longer want to have. Instead, meditation is actually about befriending our thoughts and emotions, befriending the space of our own awareness. In thinking about this definition, I have often thought about how we feel when we are in the early stages of a new relationship that we're genuinely excited about. It could be a new friend, a new love interest, or an artist, writer, or thinker whose work moves us. Consider the excitement you have waiting for your second encounter with a person, in a situation where the first date went really well. What would happen if the person made a little mistake, like she was fifteen minutes late? Chances are, you would forgive her, and think something like, "Oh, I guess she got caught in traffic,"

or "Because she is so cool, she probably has an eccentric relationship to the space-time continuum." But if somebody you've known
forever, say a spouse, is fifteen minutes late, you can't handle it.
And if you yourself—your very oldest and dearest frenemy—
should make a mistake, heads will roll.

When he said that meditation was about making friends with
yourself, I think Chogyam Trungpa Rinpoche was basically inviting us, each time we work with meditation, to take the same
attitude of curiosity and excitement we would have hanging out
with somebody we are really interested in. We need to look at our
minds with enough curiosity and friendship to not judge and condemn what we find. This is what it means to get to know ourselves
through meditation. It's about accepting your own friend request.

I've noticed again and again that the people who are most successful at sustaining a meditation practice are the ones who are
curious, maybe even fascinated, by the process of getting to know
their own minds. Of course, we might be worried that this self-
fascination could lead to other problems. Unfortunately, contemplative practice often gets dismissed as narcissism or self-indulgence.
It's important to be clear that taking time to work with our own
mind is not self-obsession. Self-awareness is actually the opposite
of self-obsession; it's helpful to everyone around us, and taking
time to familiarize ourselves with our own mind is a crucial form
of education. Ironically, it's when we don't take time to get to know
our own mind that we get obsessed with stuck narratives about
"me." In my experience, when we avoid ourselves, that's when
we start harming others as well. Self-avoidance is the true self-
obsession.

TYPES OF MEDITATION

There is a confused belief that meditation is just one thing, just one tool or technique. This leads to disagreements about which approach to meditation is the right one. The Shambhala tradition, as well as the larger Buddhist tradition, has many different techniques of meditation that we learn at various points along the journey. These meditations approach the mind from different directions, all with the two basic purposes stated above: getting to know ourselves and cultivating positive qualities of the mind.

Mindfulness-Awareness

Mindfulness is the foundation, the ground-level tool we cultivate in meditation. In the Shambhala tradition, the main form of mindfulness meditation is often called by its Sanskrit name, *shamatha*, which means something like "developing peace" or "calm abiding." Most, but not all, forms of this mindfulness-awareness meditation involve using the breath as an anchor for our attention in the present moment. These techniques allow the mind to settle into the present, to recognize thoughts and recurrent patterns of thought, without getting caught up in them. Again, none of these mindfulness-awareness techniques are about stopping the mind from thinking. The key skills developed through mindfulness-awareness techniques are (1) direct recognition of our thoughts and feelings, as well as direct recognition of when we get caught up in recurrent inner narratives or story lines, (2) an ability to deal nonreactively with space and boredom, and (3) a basic attitude of familiarity and deep friendliness with our true home.

The ancient words that translate as "mindfulness" have both a precise and a much broader meaning. In the precise sense, mindfulness refers to the development of a particular mental muscle group, muscles that operate to direct and deepen one's attention to a chosen object in the present moment. Practicing mindfulness is how we can decide what to focus on and what to be with, choosing among the many different sense perceptions, thoughts, memories, plans, and feelings that populate any given present moment. Mindfulness is what is allowing you to place your attention on reading this page right now. In Buddhist teachings on cognition, it is said that, in each moment, mindfulness can take only one object at a time. Our experience of simultaneity—of many things happening at once—is actually an approximation of many tiny moments of experience happening closely together. Exercising the muscle of mindfulness allows us to gain some control over where we place our attention at each moment.

Awareness is the corollary to mindfulness. It is like the involuntary muscle of our mind, like our heart or smooth muscle. As mindfulness helps us to place our attention more and more on our actual experience in the present moment, we begin to become more aware of the general context in which we are placing our attention. Mindfulness is what focuses your attention on the words in this book, while awareness is what keeps you cognizant of the environment you are reading in. And awareness is also what notices thoughts and emotions; it especially notices when we get lost in thought, disembodied within our physical environment.

Contemplative or Analytic Meditation

Some meditation techniques direct the thinking process to develop insight and clarity in a particular area. This could be as mundane as contemplating what you want to do for a living, or it could be a deeper contemplation, such as coming to terms with the truth of death and impermanence, or else contemplating the meaning of interdependence. Contemplative meditation teaches us to use the thinking and analytical mind skillfully.

Compassion Meditation

Compassion meditations, such as *metta* (lovingkindness) or *tong-len* (a Tibetan compassion practice) work to generate empathy, and to help us to develop caring and nurturing attitudes toward ourselves and others. These techniques prepare us for the difficult work of being present in human relationships, which will be discussed in the book's second section.

Visualization (Imagination) and Mantra Meditation

Visualization meditation works with archetypal forms that represent the most heroic and holistic qualities of the mind, such as a fully realized experience of compassion, wisdom, or skillful effectiveness. In visualization or imagination meditations we bring to life these archetypes in order to gain confidence that we also possess these qualities. These are primarily practiced in Vajrayana or Tantric Buddhist meditations, although they also form a crucial aspect of compassion meditations. Visualization will be discussed in chapter 11.

Meditations on the Nature of Mind

Within the Shambhala and Tibetan traditions, as well as within Zen, there are several bodies of teachings on looking directly at the nature of awakened mind, and learning to rest within our own unconditioned awareness, to fully come home to awareness in the present moment. These increasingly subtle meditations focus on accommodating any experience of thought or emotion that could possibly arise, without fixating on or rejecting the experience.

In the Shambhala teachings, one such style of meditation is called windhorse, which has the direct intention of fostering confidence in the pure energy of emotions, without fixation, so that the wisdom of our emotional states can be used skillfully to help ourselves and others.

No matter what meditation technique is employed, the purpose of all Buddhist meditations is to get to know our own mind more deeply and to cultivate the tools to actually be at home in our own experience. We do this so that we can begin to look directly at the habits and patterns that keep us caught up in commute.

2

KARMA

Taking Responsibility for Home

W hen we start to work with our mind in a consistent, rigorous, and disciplined way, we start to become more and more familiar with our own conditioning and habitual patterns of thought and behavior. We see the patterns of our mind more clearly when we slow down and look at them through meditation. The study of our habitual conditioning and how habit leads us to react is the study of karma. On the meditation cushion, these patterns often manifest as recurrent thoughts or fantasies or, more subtly, as a certain inner tone of voice that comments on our experience.

Karma has become quite a loaded term in the modern Western lexicon and is one of the most co-opted ideas from all of Eastern philosophy. Even among Buddhist philosophical schools, the idea is talked about in many different ways—there are pithy teachings and immensely complicated explanations of human cognition. One of the problematic approaches to karma evolves from a materialistic point of view in which karma is portrayed as some kind of commodified spiritual account, a kind of credit line extended by the Bank of the Cosmos for good deeds we've done. While this kind of "credit score" outlook can lead a person to actually engage in positive behavior, the reasons for doing so are often suspect.

Karma becomes most relevant if we simply examine it as a psychology of habit. Karma is about beginning to see the general script we act from, the strategies we employ when confronted with familiar obstacles along our commute. This approach to studying karma as our acquired habitual patterns is much more practical and useful, since, in adopting it, we avoid the danger of a spiritually materialistic belief system where we are constantly acting with ulterior motives to maximize "good" karma, trying to rig the roulette wheel of circumstance, betting on actions that lead to pleasure, and engaging in ethical behavior only because we think, "If I do the right thing, the universe owes me one." Simply put, karma is not your cosmic bank account, and it's not a Las Vegas casino, either.

Another difficulty with the subject, however, is that it can induce feelings of great guilt and shame. We often view karma as some indictment for all the awful things that have happened to us, and all the awful things that have happened in this world. For example, after hearing a bit about karma as a child I remember thinking that, as someone with asthma, I must have done something terrible in a past life to not be able to breathe very well sometimes. That kind of "blame the victim" approach offers us a convenient new narrative for the recurring story of our self-aggression, as well as a reason to continue to isolate ourselves from the plight of others. In this ultraseparatist approach, if bad things happen to other people, then they probably deserve them, and I can't help them anyway. I have even heard friends who were mugged being told, with some pseudospiritual logic, that they got mugged because it was their karma. In a world of oppression and conflict, what a horribly demeaning view that is. At this extreme, karma becomes a kind of spiritual libertarianism, a way to praise the privileged and blame the oppressed. This kind of isolated worldview cannot hold up when we look at the larger interdependent forces that shape our world and when we recognize that everything and everyone's actions are affecting each other all the time, that nobody lives in a vacuum of their own making.

There is a huge difference between saying that we are implicated in everything that happens to us and saying that what happens to us is our fault. The former is a statement of accountability, necessary for our awakening, while the second is a statement of blame, which is completely beside the point.

We spend so much time in this life trying to figure out who's at fault. Maybe it's the government's fault, but probably it's our parents' fault. We may have had very confused or absent parents, but the truth of interdependence dictates that our situation can't just be our parents' fault, for the simple fact that our parents had parents. Our grandparents had parents, too, so if we place blame on our ancestry, we may have to go all the way back to the Paleolithic era before we figure out where the first screwup occurred from which human society became a tragic comedy of errors.

When we stay in touch with interdependence, we also stay in touch with the larger systemic forces of greed and hatred that oppress whole groups of people on this planet. It does not weaken the work of caring about social justice to also say that we need to take responsibility for the conditioning in our own heart and mind and how we as individuals react to circumstances.

When we stop asking the question "Whose fault is it?" and start asking the question "How can I work with this now?" then we are truly stepping onto the path of taking responsibility for our karma. When we move beyond the materialistic view, and also overcome a "shame and blame" way of exploring the topic, karma becomes a way to take responsibility for our true home. Acknowledging karma is meant to both empower and challenge us simultaneously, to invite us to open our eyes to the fact that our experience of events is rarely pure and straightforward: perception is usually filtered through our habitual reactions and the biased scripts and story lines to which we have become numb.

In the classical teachings on the journey of self-awareness (Hinayana in the Tibetan system), taking responsibility for one's own karma is called "renunciation," rising above and renouncing samsara, the cycles of mindless habit. Renunciation is an attitude slowly cultivated over time, a commitment that begins as an intellectual understanding: we first gain some idea that the commuter's story leads nowhere but around and around, and we slowly come to realize that commuting through life objectifying and grasping after home is not going to help us or anyone else. Renunciation is a negative phrase for overcoming a habit of not taking responsibility for our karma. But for every negative phrase in Buddhism, there is also a positive approach. For me, the best positive language for describing renunciation is "taking responsibility for our true home, our own mind." In this way, we use the language of empowerment, rather than negation, to describe what this path is really about.

If we are able to take responsibility for our own mind, then we can work with whatever life throws at us without resentment or blame, and with the curiosity and self-care that are necessary for mindfulness to develop in all aspects of life. On this basis, we can also help others.

Before we talk about the present moment, though, we have to look at the past. What follows is a fairly detailed explanation from the Buddhist tradition of the earliest framework for examining a karmic pattern. This twelve-step process is known as the twelve *nidanas*, or twelve links in the chain of habitual cause and effect. These twelve stages divide into the past, present, and future of a habitual pattern or karmic act.

THE TWELVE STEPS OF KARMA
(HABITUAL PATTERNS)

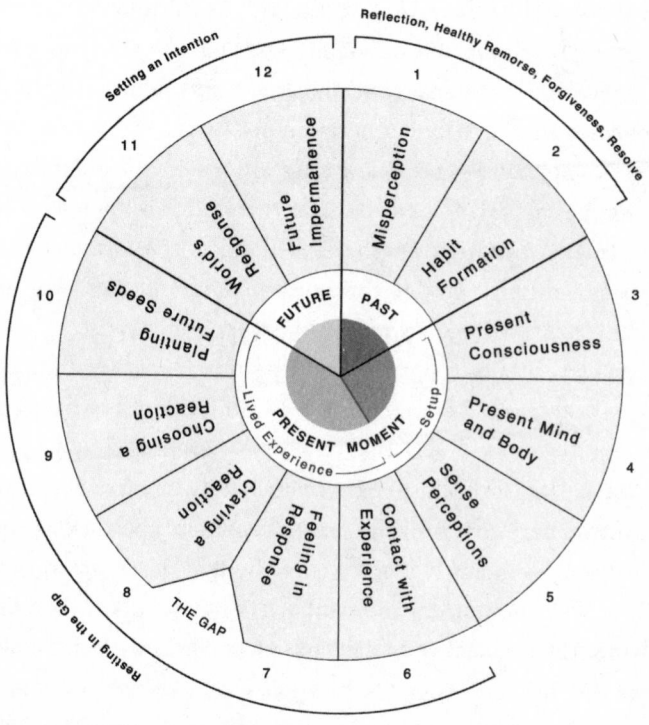

© SETH FREEDMAN

KNOWING THE PAST: REFLECTION
ON OUR STORY

A crucial question arises on the journey of self-awareness: If we seek some kind of transformation in our present and future, then how important is understanding the story of what happened in our past? Western psychologies—especially psychoanalysis, attachment theory, and related disciplines—place great importance on learning about the relational histories that dominated our early development, and seeing how those patterns might play out in the present. In Buddhist terms, we can think of these examinations as knowing the roots of our karma—our habitual conditioning—and knowing how those root narratives and relationships affect our current ability to feel at home in our own heartmind.

At first glance, placing a strong emphasis on understanding our past story might seem outside the Buddhist paradigm, because Buddhist practice emphasizes working directly with the experience and behaviors of the present moment over everything else. But, from the standpoint of interdependent cause and effect, this separation between understanding our past story and experiencing the present fully is a false separation, one that needs to be overcome.

It's true that Buddhist practice rightfully emphasizes mindful recognition and action in the present moment, because the present moment is the only place where the real power to work with our life lies. The present moment will always be key, because in truth it is the only thing that exists. However, the Buddha clearly taught—in his very early teachings on karma—that understanding how the past affects our mind is the foundation for seeing how we experience ourselves now. Therefore, Buddhist practice offers many methods and contemplations for reflecting on the past in order to achieve insight, forgiveness, and healing, and more important, to offer us the ability to be ready when our habits strike us right NOW.

The Shambhala teachings also repeatedly emphasize the importance of coming to terms with and even honoring our ancestral lineages, our family histories, our parents, and the culture in which we were raised. In Shambhala, honoring our human past is a central endeavor. We honor our lineages in order to heal our wounds, as well as to gain confidence in our humanity, and to pass that confidence—along with perhaps just a tiny bit less neurosis and self-sabotage—on to future generations.

In short, while our power to act always lies in the present moment, that power is always based on understanding what came before. But what happens if we dwell on the story of our past, spending all our time recounting the details of our history to anyone who will listen? For a practitioner, the main problem with dwelling too much on the past is that it can lead to an obsession with a certain story line, a kind of internal screenwriter's fixation that could take us away from working directly with our experience in the present moment. Instead, if we reflect on the past with the clear intention to illuminate our experience in the present, and we learn, through both our own meditation practice and guidance from others, how to let go of our tight grip on the past narrative at the exact point the mind begins to fixate on it, then our understanding of the relation between past and present can come into balance and harmony.

The teachings on karma demonstrate a very important point about the past: the fundamental force behind our conditioning isn't stupidity or evil, nor is it a flaw in our genetic design. We adopt habitual patterns to begin with as the result of misperception, or a lack of awareness.

If we view the root of the problem as a misperception about the nature of experience, then forgiveness is always possible. We can rise out of feeling ashamed at our habitual confusion. According to the tradition, confusion has happened to every sentient being that has ever existed. We have to forgive ourselves for being stuck in habits and addictions, for being caught up in commute. Working with karma is something that everyone has to go through; none of us are free of conditioning.

If there were really such an immaculate birth, a person born without karma, that person wouldn't serve much purpose as an example for those of us who have things we need to work though. Having something to work through is actually something to celebrate; having karma is almost a synonym for being human. For this reason, as he was developing the Shambhala teachings, Chogyam Trungpa Rinpoche gave a very hopeful and optimistic spin to the notion of karma and habitual patterns of behavior, referring to the totality of our karma as our "cocoon."

Many psychological traditions have noticed that a given behavior pattern was originally a helpful strategy for survival, a strategy that may no longer apply in the present. If you were bullied in the seventh grade, there might be a block in your hometown or city where the bullies used to wait for you, and even as an adult your sense memories might cause you to hesitate before walking confidently down that block. This is definitely true for me, having grown up in New York City. Thus, we have to acknowledge that every habit contains a kind of protective intelligence, a wisdom that somehow got frozen in a bygone time.

The silk moth uses a cocoon for protection during a necessary period of transformation, until it's ready to emerge. Seeing karma as a cocoon is a beautiful way to slowly make friends with even the darkest parts of our habits, to understand the unfolding process of living, rather than to feel shame that we aren't perfect. In the positive light of the Shambhala teachings, karma is nothing more than the recurrent freezing of our past intelligence, a process that ignores the fluidity of actual experience as well as the truth of impermanence. We never fall in love the same way twice, we never meet the same bully again, and the experience of every cup of coffee is unique. No defensive strategy works the same way more than once. However, in order to feel safe and at home in our experience, we try to use our karmic cocoons to control every new moment. Thus, we reify karma by solidifying habitual strategies, strategies that preemptively filter our perceptions and manipulate our reaction to whatever happens. This is understandable—who, ever, in the history of this universe or any other, has not wanted to feel safe? Who wants to get bullied? Given the groundless nature of life, attempting to feel safe is the smartest thing a sentient being can do. So, while examining our habits may give us a painful doorway onto our harmful histories, it also gives us a chance to see that our thoughts and actions are actually made of a kind of innate intelligence.

The first stage in every cycle of karmic habituation is called *avidya*, a word that often gets translated as "ignorance," but that really means something like "without knowledge" or "lacking awareness." "Misperception" is my preferred translation. What is the nature of our misperception? Why did we misperceive in the first place?

In many mythologies, gods are invoked to explain the origin of various aspects of our human experience. A Buddhist creation myth, on the other hand, might simply try to tell the origin story of how our confused predicament came about. This story doesn't necessarily occur at the dawn of time, in the midst of the primordial soup, but instead recurs at each moment, and in each lifetime. The karmic story of misperception is the creation tale of how our perceptual process accidentally separates that which is not inherently separate. On the deepest level of consciousness, misperception involves the experience of duality, the misguided separation and isolation of subject and object. In this karmic creation myth, at some point a sentient being misperceives, coming to believe that subject (me) and object (my experiences) are entities that exist independently from each other. In truth, how could these ever be separated? As subjects, we never experience ourselves as isolated from the objects of our experience. Perceiver and perceived always exist together; it's a package deal. But we talk as if "me" and "my experience" are separate all the time and we say strange, nonsensical things like, "A funny thing happened to me today," when, in fact, nothing just *happens* to us. This mode of separating ourselves from our experience is a mistake that occurs on a very deep level of consciousness. It is also a mistake sewn into the fabric of our spoken and written language.

Built upon the mistake of this duality, other problems begin to unfold. This is the basis for how our materialistic tendencies began in the first place, both personally and societally. Once we believe that "me" is separate from "my experience," that "me" is a solid entity to whom things happen, rather than a fluid part of the unending action, we have to start thinking about defending this isolated "me" against the objects we encounter. Thus, we need some basic strategies for survival. We have to start (1) pursuing objects that make "me" feel safe and happy, (2) destroying objects that make "me" feel threatened, and (3) ignoring all other objects of experience, because the first two categories take up all our time and energy. These are the three most basic strategies of habitual reaction, also called the three root poisons, which in different Buddhist traditions are typically translated as either "greed, hatred, and delusion" or "passion, aggression, and ignorance."

I prefer the translations for these poisonous strategies used by the Buddhist psychologist John Welwood, who chose to use verbs rather than nouns. Instead of passion, aggression, and ignorance, he called them grasping, rejecting, and desensitizing, respectively.

After all, when we apply mindfulness, we experience the present moment more as a verb than as a noun, as an action with an intuitive tone and texture that we can begin to recognize. If we can familiarize ourselves with how these defensive strategies feel, we discover a doorway to understanding our deep-seeded patterns of confusion. The important thing in working with karma is to get to the level of awareness, through meditation and reflection, where we can actually begin to feel these reactions as they arise, and slowly over time develop the wisdom to know what to do when they come about. We have to get to the point where, when we arrive at the block where the bullies used to wait for us, we recognize how we tighten up and begin to walk in another direction, or else freeze.

Using verbs removes these three confused strategies from the realm of religious commandment and turns them into emotional, embodied experiences we can witness happening in the present moment, reactions that we can pay attention to as mechanisms of the mind. If we can begin to see how the reactions of grasping, rejecting, and desensitizing actually function in our own mind and body, we will already be a long way toward feeling more at home in our own being, rather than constantly being taken by surprise when our conditioned reactions are triggered.

Based on this primary misperception—*avidya*—and based on the millions of different subcategories of these three confused strategies, we develop a particular habitual pattern for responding to similar moments in the future. This is the second step in the cycle of a karmic pattern—habit formation (*samskara*). These first two steps, misperception and the resulting habit formation, prime our mind to respond to situations in the present moment.

Back to the seventh-grade bullies. Let's say that, arising out of the initial *misperception* that I needed to always defend the solid "Ethan" against the bullies of experience, that what happened in seventh grade would happen every time I met someone who seemed similarly threatening (step one), I developed *habitual strategies* for how to deal with new bullylike situations (step two), which then mold my *present moment consciousness* (step three, *vijnana*), which becomes embedded in my *present mind and body* (step four, *namarupa*), and even predisposes and biases the fields of *present sense perceptions* based on the past habit (step five, *ayatana*). Steps three, four, and five—which happen pretty much simultaneously—describe how our mind and body are "primed" to perceive based on our past karmic experiences. Taken together, they describe the conditioned setup of our consciousness as we face a new experience in the present moment, which is described in steps six through ten.

What practices are useful in helping us to reflect on our past karma? Forgiveness and gentleness are key. Whether we look at a recent habit, like the cigarettes we started smoking last week when things got too stressful, or a longer-term habit, like our anxiety around anyone with the same jawline as that old bully, these are strategies that have been slowly ingrained in our consciousness, and our nervous systems, for a long time. For Buddhists, the ancient narrative of reincarnation offers even more support for this forgiving and gentle approach, as long as we don't use it to solidify a story about previous existences. Who cares if I was Cleopatra or Claude Monet or Joe Shmoe in a past life? Here's why I think reincarnation might be important: it's an invitation to greatly increase the scope of time in which we got caught up in negative patterns and defensive strategies. If I think a negative thought pattern started only recently (e.g., the recurring thought "I suck at writing" that still visits each time I sit down to write), it might be harder to forgive myself for not getting free from those thoughts immediately. But if I think I've been caught in similar patterns for many cycles of consciousness (i.e., the recurring thought, "I suck at fill in the blank" reiterating itself as the mind reiterates itself across the expression of many lifetimes), I might give myself a break, which might actually be the most helpful thing for my writing.

Again, karma is not just something that we can liberate ourselves from immediately. If we didn't get into our habits quickly, how can we get out of them instantaneously? Of course, some of the most popular spiritual thinkers promise instant transformations of consciousness. Let's face it, the promise of sudden liberation—cutting the chains of stuck karma—is much more marketable than presenting tools for a slow, gradual, lifelong process. It's just a little harder to catch people's attention if what you are saying is, "Show up to your various practices every day of your life and look for tiny incremental openings in your awareness and behavior, and celebrate those tiny victories." It's also a much more honest approach to transformation.

Yes, sudden shifts are always possible, and there are many techniques in Buddhism for purifications of consciousness that might lead occasionally to quick changes, a feeling of clicking into a new sweet spot in how we are approaching our life, but those sudden shifts only come if we have laid the groundwork with quite a lot of contextual understanding and consistent development. I remember being at a workshop with Pema Chödrön, when she was asked whether the path of awakening was sudden or gradual. She had this wry look on her face when she answered the questioner: "Gee, that's funny. I've always thought that 'sudden' was the result of a heck of a lot of 'gradual.'"

In encountering our past, two contemplative meditations we can use involve, first, replacing guilt and shame with a healthy remorse, and second, practicing forgiveness.

In this light, the contemplative practices of reflection that involve confronting our past also involve forgiveness and healing. They consist of understanding the complex causes and conditions that led to our current state of confusion, in order to develop compassion toward our own history, as well as toward our familial and societal ancestries. In so doing, the poisonous influences of guilt and shame are slowly replaced with a positive sense of remorse toward our negative habitual patterns. Healthy remorse is what happens when we can honestly acknowledge our own confusion and mistakes along the path without believing those mistakes somehow doom us. While guilt and shame turn us into frozen, insecure, and incapable beings with no path forward, healthy remorse acknowledges confusion and mistakes with a lighthearted-ness that actually gives us the means to shift in the present and future. Shame says, "I'm fundamentally broken," whereas remorse says, "I'm whole, and yet I've made some mistakes." Guilt says, "I can never change," whereas remorse just says, "Oops!" "Oops" may be my all-time favorite word in the English language, and it's not even a real word. If we aren't willing to make a lot of mistakes, maybe even some big ones, then we aren't really willing to be students of life and students of self-awareness.

MINDING THE GAP: VULNERABILITY AND THE PRESENT MOMENT

You'd be hard-pressed to find a person who wouldn't agree that life would be better if we could each be more "present." However, when we discuss why that's the case, even those of us who have been meditating a long time tend to get a bit vague in our explanations. There are actually quite a lot of reasons we want to be more present, more able to turn our attention at will to what is going on now. Often, in the Shambhala teachings, we frame the importance of the present moment in terms of appreciating the vividness and aesthetic beauty of now. This is why the covers of many meditation books are filled with pictures of nature, like autumn leaves falling onto a path, or a beautiful pond and trees. From the very simple point of view of appreciation, when we slow down and actually acknowledge the treasure trove of our sense perceptions, our experience deepens and we often almost instantly begin to feel more at home, as an immense gratitude comes flooding back to us. When we learn to return our minds to our sense perceptions, experience takes on a priceless quality. Cocktails in Brooklyn have gotten increasingly expensive, but if you actually tasted each sip fully, they could charge $1,000 for a good margarita, because the experience of flavor is that rich. And likewise, if we tasted each sip fully, we might not need to go grasping after another cocktail and another and another just to keep feeling good about ourselves. One margarita, fully experienced, might just be plenty. From the standpoint of sense perception, being present is about realizing that we have already inherited, with our human anatomy, an unbelievably rich apparatus for appreciating our experience. If we can just learn how to be fully present for five more sensory experiences a day, the depth of these simple experiences would offer more to celebrate than any expensive vacation we spent scattered and mindless. This mentality of sensory appreciation might be the key to ecological sustainability and responsible consumption, in addition to allowing us to enjoy the magic of being alive. Unfortunately, it is also this appreciation for the present moment's sensory experience that has been most co-opted from contemplative traditions into the language of advertising. It seems that everyone wants to be present with the richness of sensory experience, even Citibank.

The teachings on karma, however, define the importance of being with the present moment in a much more psychological way, one that might not be quite so comfortable to face. From the standpoint of karma, being present is all about trust—trusting *vulnerability*. Being vulnerable doesn't always feel like seeing an inspiring painting or taking a walk in nature. It is often a much more painful and awkward experience, the experience of fully feeling what it's like to step back onto the block where we were once bullied, to step back into a room where our heart was once broken. In the present moment, we might experience the habitual demons of our past in an intense and intimate way. To understand how karma relates to the present moment, we have to talk about something called the "gap." The sixth through tenth of the twelve stages of a karmic pattern describe how our mind functions around this "gap" and how we work with this experience.

Based on our past experiences and how they have primed us for the present moment, in the sixth step our sense faculties come into *contact* (*sparsha*) with a new object of perception. So, let's say that as an adult, I meet someone with the same jawline or voice as my old bully. Whether or not I am presently aware that this is what is happening is another matter (you might just react with an aversion you can't place).

As our conditioned consciousness comes into *contact* with this new experience—this new person who is not the old bully—a *feeling* inevitably arises, which is the seventh step. If we broke down the huge range of possible feelings to its simplest components, as the Buddha did in his earliest teachings on karma and mindfulness, we could say that this feeling is basically either pleasant, unpleasant, or neutral. Of course, the range of possible feelings and impulses in reaction to seeing someone who reminds us of a bully would be much broader than that. Most likely, feelings of fear, nervousness, aversion, or rage would be right there, too.

How we handle this seventh step—*feeling* (*vedana*)—is probably the most important aspect of the twelve-step teaching on karma, because this is the very crux of meeting the present moment directly. This stage also offers a key insight into why mindfulness techniques are so important to our transformation. First of all, how we feel in the present moment is always based on past experience and conditioning. We cannot alter the reality of our feelings right now, not through any method. We can't avoid feeling scared or irritated by that person with the old bully's voice. For that matter, we can't avoid feeling turned on when Cute Person X enters a crowded room, or turned off when Annoying Person Y texts us yet again. We can't make ourselves like music we dislike, just to try to impress someone. Of course, we can pretend we don't feel the way we do, but the practice of mindfulness is all about ending any pretense, at least to ourselves. Our mind is conditioned by the past, and to try to alter what we are feeling right now, especially in the name of being a compassionate spiritual person, is just wishful thinking. This is a crucial realization, because we spend so much of life, and, sadly, so much of our spiritual paths, wishing we were feeling something other than what we are actually feeling in the present moment.

This is especially true when we get caught in a mentality of spiritual materialism, which is all about the pretense of manipulating feelings into more blissful states. Maybe we wish we felt universal love when actually we feel irritation, or we wish we felt devotion to a guru when actually we feel deep doubt, or we long to be surrounded by rainbow explosions of insight when actually all we have right now is a big fat dose of boredom. What if we stopped using all of the energy we spend trying to edit, tailor, and fabricate the right feelings, and converted that effort into awareness—noticing and acknowledging the feelings we actually have? We would save a lot of energy, and we would develop real compassion for ourselves and others. This is the work of mindfulness meditation—the repeated practice of letting go of "should" and embracing "is."

The other crucial aspect of this seventh step of feeling is that it helps us to acknowledge how sensitive all sentient beings are. After all, "sentient" means "possessing the ability to feel." *Feeling* is the defining characteristic of our humanity. The teachings say that the moment of feeling—meaning every moment of feeling— is actually an incredibly intense experience with which to be present. In traditional Buddhist art, each of the twelve karmic stages is depicted by an iconographic image. This moment of feeling, whether sensory or emotional, is depicted as a man stumbling around with an arrow piercing his eyeball. This depiction is used regardless of whether the experience we just came into contact with is one that we like or dislike, one of either attraction or aversion or, for that matter, one of neutrality. Think about that for a minute: even in experiencing a neutral feeling, a "whatever" moment of boredom, you are being pierced in the eye by an arrow! As we become more aware, as we resensitize to our heartmind, we recover an understanding of just how vulnerable to feeling we truly are. We are sensitive beings with sensitive hearts and sensitive nervous systems, and what happens to us in the present moment is intense. Even a simple sip of coffee is an intense experience when we bring our full attention to it. Every car horn affects us deeply. Never mind the more "noteworthy" present-moment experiences, like the moment right after orgasm, the moment we get a standing ovation, or the moment we receive a heartbreaking text.

During and just after the intensity of the impulse of feeling, there is a space—the gap I referred to earlier—where we have not yet chosen how to react. This space is called a "gap" because it's a space of potential freedom placed in between, on the one hand, feeling the intensity of the moment and, on the other, the next steps in the karmic chain of recurring habit—step eight, *craving to react* (*trishna*), which means moving toward a response to what we are experiencing, and then step nine, *choosing a reaction* (*upadana*), by employing one of our old strategies or, alternatively, making a different choice. Maybe, with courage, we just shake the hand of the person who has the bully's voice, rather than avoiding him. Once we react, step ten, *future seeds* of karma are planted (*bhava*). This tenth step means that our choice to shake his hand will condition the way we experience a future encounter with someone "bullylike." The more we are able to inhabit the gap now, the more likely that the seeds we plant will lead us to a more open future experience.

Usually when we think of a gap, we think of empty space. But the gap of the present moment is not a blank space at all; within the gap there is tremendous momentum and powerful energy. It is only called the gap because it represents the space of awareness in between feeling an intense impulse and choosing a reaction to it. Resting in the gap is the most difficult and vulnerable experience we can have, because when we actually show up for the present moment, we become infinitely more intimate with subtle intensity of feeling, both emotionally and physically, as well as with the strong momentum of habitual reactions we have chosen in similar situations in the past. Even if I am many years removed from being bullied, the anxiety and irritation I encounter when I see someone who reminds me of the bully are intense, if I'm willing to make myself available to them. This moment of availability, of trusting the wisdom of not reacting defensively, is what is called resting in the gap.

The gap is not a bliss space, but a courageous space where we stay with what is happening within our mind and nervous system. Resting in the gap is a brave willingness to be vulnerable. It is that moment when we let ourselves feel again what we felt when we were being bullied way back in the day and, for a moment, we dwell there. The gap is where I don't choose my scripted reaction of panicking and stepping away from this new bullylike person, or trying to sarcastically undercut him so that he won't mess with me. In the gap, we literally don't know what happens next, or how the world will respond to us without the rehashed profile we used to carry around. In this vulnerable space, it's sometimes not even clear if my old hashtag (#ME) is going to survive at all.

Without any kind of mindfulness training, this gap probably feels more like a crack in the sidewalk than any space we could actually inhabit with awareness. Without practice, we just rush on from impulse to reaction (steps eight, nine, and ten), forced violently along by what are traditionally called the winds of karma, reifying our habitual pattern without even realizing it. Even with practice we often only notice the gap retroactively, upon reflection, which is especially true if the moment of feeling in question was extra intense or triggering. This is why the practice of reflection is so important. It's also important to note that a master practitioner probably experiences the gap very differently from us. The most ancient tradition of Tibetan Buddhism, the Nyingma, has a very simple way of discussing the difference between enlightened beings (Buddhas) and confused and grasping sentient beings (zombie commuters).

If we boil it all down, there are only two ways to experience the universe in the present moment. Resting in the gap between a habitual impulse and a chosen reaction, we experience the universe based on *trust*. We trust ourselves and we trust the world. Whatever happens next, it's okay—we don't have to force a reaction in order to feel safe. This is how an enlightened being lives. If we always trusted that our mind could fully accommodate each moment, then no experience would ever have to be excluded, and we wouldn't need to defend ourselves against what happens next. Because a Buddha completely trusts her own mind, curiosity comes naturally. A Buddha is actually curious about how the old bully is doing right now! With natural curiosity, the practice of mindfulness becomes effortless. When we actually start to want to be present, we start to care for everybody, so compassion becomes increasingly panoramic. As compassion expands, the mental barbed wire between yourself and your experience dissolves. Once that wall of duality crumbles, nothing can take you away from feeling at home in the universe, and no experience needs to be rejected as unworthy. This is what it really means to feel at home wherever you are.

However, as commuters who are unable to rest in the gap, we necessarily experience the universe based on defensive strategy. The commuter's universe revolves around seeking security and defending against an ever-expanding array of possible threats. Habitual strategy, the force of karma, is what happens when experience becomes something we think we have to defend against. Karma is what we fabricate when we no longer trust the universe.

If we wanted to simplify, it could be said that every technique of Buddhist meditation is preparing us to work with and become more comfortable in this space between feeling and reacting. Techniques of mindfulness-awareness meditation help us to recognize the gap between impulse and reaction, aiding the difficult work of resting within that vulnerable space. Mindfulness also allows us to see how often we escape into all-too-familiar narratives in order to avoid feeling open and vulnerable. All other meditation practices build on the basic qualities of recognition developed in mindfulness-awareness practice.

Analytic meditations serve to clarify our view of the relationship between past and present. They also give us a better map of reality altogether, so that when we experience the next gap, we have a more accurate context for the experience. Techniques of lovingkindness and compassion encourage us to become gentler toward both ourselves and others whenever the intensity of feeling arises, forgiving the fact that we all get caught in patterns to begin with. Compassion meditation helps us to empathize with the truth that every being is subject to confusion, reminding us that we are not alone on our journey and creating a less isolated inner space in which to experience the gap. With compassion, we become infinitely more willing to rest in the gap, because we realize that karma is nobody's fault.

Tantric visualization techniques help us to gain a kind of heroic confidence that we can be much more in touch with our inherent wisdom than we think, so that we approach the gap with a sense of empowerment and capability. Direct meditations upon the nature of mind take us right to the very source code of thought, emotion, and perception. By directly seeing thoughts and habitual impulses as temporary visitors in the home of our awareness, we can learn to trust the gap, so that we can slowly figure out how to act upon our thoughts and emotions only when helpful and necessary.

Sakyong Mipham Rinpoche has developed a very simple and potent meditation technique that he calls "Shambhala Meditation," which begins with the simple practice of "feeling," deeply emphasizing the ability to rest without rejecting or grasping on to whatever we are actually feeling right now. While it sounds exceedingly simple, it is a technique that creates a trusting context for experiencing tenderness and vulnerability, the needed preparation for resting nonreactively in the gap and achieving liberation from past habits.

INTO THE FUTURE: THE PRACTICE
OF SETTING INTENTION

The eleventh and twelfth stages of karma simply remind us that the world will respond to us based on the choices we make after the gap disappears. The eleventh stage refers to the inevitable birth or arising of the *world's response* (*jati*) based on our reaction, a future moment in which we will have to face our karmic conditioning again, based on the reactive seeds that we planted in stages eight through ten. In the future, we will have yet another chance to work with the gap. If we are completely unable to rest in the gap now, then our next experience of habitual mind will be more deeply ingrained. However, if we can glimpse, even for a moment, a nonreactive awareness within the gap, then the next time around we may be able to shift our response, even if only very slightly. The twelfth stage refers to the eventual withering away and *impermanence of any future karmic situation* (*jara marana*). The twelfth stage is a constant reminder of impermanence, the truth that we are never screwed. Rather than something morbid, here "death" means that no future situation is ever fixed. Whatever habits are reified in the present moment, whatever the future outcome of our present practice—or lack thereof—that situation too will be impermanent. Nothing will ever get stuck in place. There will always be another present moment in which we can meet experience fresh and new. And if we miss that next opportunity, there will be yet another moment.

The practice we use to prepare for the future is the setting of intention, because the present moment is always a prelude to a future now. When we set intention, we contemplate what aspects of our experience we want to highlight in the near future. For example, you could simply end a morning meditation by saying, "Today, I want to stay present with my bodily sensations when I feel bullied." By contemplating intention, we are more prepared to work with the next round of experience. We can never work *in* the future—we can work only *for* the future. Working in the future is the mistake made by the commuter, who is always looking at the hopeful promise of a home ahead, and therefore never actually arrives anywhere. Working *for* the future is the practice of setting intention. One of my favorite things my friend and mentor Acharya Eric Spiegel has said is, "If you set an intention, I can't guarantee that what you intend to happen will happen. There are no guarantees. But if you don't set an intention, I can guarantee that it won't happen."

Thus, checking in a little bit every day about our intention, perhaps at the end of a meditation session, is one of the best methods we have for preparing for how karma will arise in the next NOW. We can also prepare for the future by taking our practice up off the meditation seat and into our daily life.

3

COMING HOME 24/7/365
Ethics in Everyday Life

Without a doubt, in the Western world, meditation techniques have been the most popular part of what Buddhism offers. As Buddhist traditions have been increasingly imported and integrated into the Western world since the mid-twentieth century, there has been a growing fascination with meditation practice. The psychological and medical studies of Buddhist offerings, for instance, have almost entirely revolved around investigating the effects of a small range of meditative practices. This fascination with meditation makes sense, because it is the piece of Buddhist teachings that is the newest to our Western educational approach. But the Buddhist path is about much more than just sitting here. True, Buddhism offers extensive and detailed teaching on the nature of mind, and a huge variety of contemplative tools for working with a range of mental obstacles. If you wanted to simply study teachings on the mind as it is experienced in meditation, the tradition offers plenty to do for your entire life. But studying meditation alone is not enough.

Simply put, if you meditate ten minutes a day, what do you do with all the other hours? How do you bring self-awareness to every aspect of your life? Even those of us who meditate quite a lot would be at a severe disadvantage if we only made our path about meditation practice. Personally, when I'm not on retreat, I practice at most an hour to an hour and a half a day. What happens with the other sixteen hours of waking life? Shouldn't I work with my heartmind then? For a committed practitioner, forming a healthy relationship between meditation practice and the cultivation of awareness throughout the day is crucial. Otherwise, the momentum and pace of the rest of our life overwhelms whatever insights we are able to experience through formal meditation. Ideally, a positive feedback relationship grows, a relationship of support and symbiosis between our formal practice and our life in the world. Our life teaches us as much, if not more, about how we can come home to our own heartmind as our sitting practice does. To frame this connection in terms of the video games of my youth, meditation ideally acts as a power-up for our practice throughout the rest of the day.

Meditation allows us to enter a kind of personal laboratory, in order to see our mind in a slightly more settled and clarified way and to prepare for how we are going to live life that day. Our life in the world can then also become a lab for our practice, just a much bigger, less defined lab, with infinitely more moving parts and sentient beings involved. For example, if you notice an addiction to a tech device, when you want to get up and grab your smartphone as you sit in meditation, the insight and awareness developed from feeling this impulse nonreactively can carry over to how you relate to your device throughout the day. In turn, the insight we develop from working mindfully with our device can then help us see more clearly how we latch on to and chase after our thoughts during our next meditation session. This back-and-forth relationship between practice and conduct in daily life constitutes a balanced and consistent approach to cultivating self-awareness. It really doesn't take much on either front: just a little bit of practice, and a little bit of awareness of our actions throughout the day.

Eventually, if we are going to wake up and truly come home to our own heartmind, we have to turn the full scope of our life into a practice space. This doesn't have to start as an all-the-time endeavor, but little by little it is said that our awareness practice can become a constant companion. It could start with observing just three more carefully chosen moments each day, three moments where we are actually contemplating and applying some mindful principles to our thoughts, expressions, and behaviors. This is what happens when we start bringing ethics into our journey of self-awareness. Our practice starts to be with us everywhere.

In its complete form, as traditionally taught, the path of awakening involves eight distinct sections, known as the eightfold path. These eight practices condense into three basic life areas. These areas are (1) study of the mind and study of the world, (2) meditation practice, and (3) daily conduct in life (ethics).

In our lexicon, ethics refers to the principles, beliefs, and practices that govern our behavior in the world. Ethics is about asking the deep questions concerning how we make choices, especially when we don't know definitively what we should do, which is pretty much always. How do we take care of our body? How should we speak to others? Does what you buy promote outcomes you want to support in this world? How do we use technology thoughtfully? Whom do we vote for? Do we vote at all? Because all of these questions affect sentient beings, all of these questions are part of the Buddhist path.

Ethics—our daily conduct—is primarily a practice of self-awareness, because we are fundamentally interested, at this stage, in how our actions affect our personal journey, our own ability to be at home in our own heartmind. At the stage of self-awareness, the practice of ethics is primarily about you. This is not some attempt to be a libertarian; it is an acknowledgment that the path begins with taking responsibility for your own mind. At the same time, the practice of ethics forms a crucial link among the various stages of our experience—the personal, the interpersonal, and the societal. In a way, our daily conduct is both the vehicle for and the passenger on our journey home. First, practicing ethics allows us to extend the healing work of the path beyond the meditation cushion. Further, making conduct a practice allows us to work for the benefit of others in our relationships, which is the topic of this book's second section. Finally, exploring and deeply contemplating what to do and what not to do, what to participate in and what to avoid, what to purchase and what to protest, creates the basis for a systemic, cultural, and even political understanding of the Buddhist path, which will be addressed in the book's final section. Our daily conduct must relate to our views of what we want the larger world to look like, because our own personal life is simply a microcosm of the cultural and political landscape we inhabit.

I find that when the conversation shifts to ethics, people tend to have three basic reactions that complicate the exploration. I've been guilty of having all of them at different times. They seem impossible to avoid, and are each worth examining with two parts seriousness and one part humor and irony.

Often, when we start talking about ethics, we either become (1) apathetic, (2) defensive, or (3) righteously judgmental.

Until a person takes an interest in some basic form of mindfulness and in the cultivation of self-awareness, it's actually pretty hard to see the point of studying ethics. Without awareness, we can't see an immediate correspondence between our actions and their effects, or how our choices affect how we experience our life. It's often hard to see how our choices affect others. When we are caught up in apathy, the world seems like an insurmountable fortress of greed, hatred, and delusion, a dark place where nobody seems to hold themselves accountable for the choices they make. If no one else thinks about the hard questions, why should I?

If you notice yourself getting bored when the conversation turns to ethics, it might be helpful to reconsider what it means to be a contemplative person at all. To be contemplative means we are trying to think deeply about life, to grow more curious about the links between how we experience ourselves and how we act. To be a contemplative is to create a lifelong study of the interdependence between our views and our behaviors. If we want to step onto this path, we need to recapture the original purpose of both human philosophy and human psychology, which is to become a curious person, appreciative of our precious opportunity to be alive, exploring principles that have useful and specific applications. From this standpoint, ethics is no abstraction; there is nothing vague about it. Practicing ethics is about making our life tangibly better, because if we can learn to live fully in our own heartmind throughout the day, every day will feel infinitely more satisfying.

A discussion of ethics can also make us defensive, as though someone is personally attacking our lifestyle. Somebody starts asking simple questions about why we choose to eat meat, or why we hold the political beliefs we hold, and we don't even want to hear the question. I am a Buddhist who occasionally eats meat, although I was a longtime vegetarian. If somebody questions my meat eating as a Buddhist, I shouldn't just shake him off. Each time the question comes up, I should be prepared to explore the topic with the person who asks it. As I should if somebody asks at dinner why I keep looking at my smartphone instead of being present with him. I shouldn't attack the person who questioned me by pointing out that he is often on his phone, too.

We might also become righteous and judgmental as the conversation shifts to ethics. Let's face it—we've all made a ton of mistakes. I could fill other volumes with just a fraction of mine. Our leaders are flawed, too. One of the largest issues we face in the twenty-first century is that it's become so hard to even trust in the idea of decent and honorable leaders. There is so much going on in this world that we don't agree with, and we might not even agree with each other about what's wrong. Because we don't trust the openness of our own heartmind, when the going gets tough, we lose the flexibility that would allow room for mistakes. Without flexibility, we judge and condemn. Without trust in the goodness of the mind, mistakes cease to be occasions for learning. Instead, every mistake that comes before our Supreme Court of Righteousness becomes a condemnation, a death sentence. With this mistrusting mentality, we don't allow space for learning from mistakes, and we certainly don't allow room for the truth that the really hard questions in life almost always fall into gray areas, where righteousness can't help us.

With righteousness, we try for sterilized perfection. We might expect ourselves and everyone else to become vegan, sober, anti-war, ever-smiling, never-biased, cannot-tell-a-lie, one hundred percent ecoconscious consumers, dedicating twenty-five hours a day and eight days a week to charitable causes, willing to give the shirt off our back to anyone who asks for it. When these standards aren't met, we say things like, "Oh my God, I killed a mosquito—what have I done?" or, "I can't believe you would wear that shirt and call yourself a Buddhist!" or, "You work at Goldman who? I can't even deal with you." Or, on the other hand, our friends might learn that we've taken an interest in studying meditation, and launch passive-aggressive barbs like, "Well, that's not very Buddhist of you" when we aren't doing exactly what they want us to do. I remember, throughout my teenage years, heavily judging my parents after their divorce, feeling, completely unfairly, that because they were Buddhists, they should somehow always be able to work things out. Where were my parents' halos??!! Of course, this righteous anger was probably just a defensive posture against resting in the gap, feeling my own sadness that I didn't have a nuclear family.

In this judgmental trap, we become unfairly angry at others, pissed off at the world, and full of secret shame and guilt toward our own inevitable mistakes. What gets lost? Trust and curiosity. We lose trust in the universe, and we lose curiosity about the process of exploration, which is the basis for any contemplative journey. Eventually, because this kind of righteousness can't sustain the level of acrid energy on which it runs, we will probably become apathetic and tune out the whole conversation on ethics. Apathy, that cynical "whatever" mentality, is usually what happens after righteousness burns itself out. Sometimes this apathetic burnout happens to a whole generation of commuters.

For any of these three habitual reactions to ethics—apathy, defensiveness, or righteousness—the solution is really the same. If we bring the same outlook that we have to formal meditation— making friends with our experience, while slowly working to cultivate positive qualities over a long period of time—then we can introduce curiosity and a sense of exploration to our life. This path is more about engaging in a learning process, being a lifelong student of cause and effect, rather than always doing the "right" thing.

There are many frameworks for taking on the practical contemplation of ethics within the Buddhist tradition. Below is one of the simpler lists, a set of five basic contemplations that in my tradition are usually called the five precepts. When a student formally commits to Buddhist practice, she is asked to make an ongoing commitment to working with these principles. Thich Nhat Hanh calls them the five mindfulness trainings. These guidelines create a general template for a contemplative life, a life of self-awareness and a journey of becoming curious about our habits and their effects.

Working with the Buddhist teachings on conduct, the teacher always has a choice either to emphasize what positive actions should be cultivated and taken up or to emphasize harmful conduct that needs to be given up or refrained from. Sometimes this is called knowing what to "adopt and reject." Typically, in the Hinayana, or self-focused teachings that come from the Tibetan system, the emphasis is on avoiding the negative, on refraining from harmful activities. However, it seems crucial that we learn to positively reinforce our successes, and therefore I choose mostly to emphasize the positive actions to be cultivated in each of these contemplations.

In terms of the actual "do" and "do not do" related to each of these precepts, there are about a thousand different interpretations among Buddhist teachers about what these contemplations actually mean, especially when they touch on harder subjects like eating meat, dating, or the right livelihood. Some teachers have interpretations that are strict and quite specific, while others have interpretations that are vague and more general. I think these precepts are most helpful as general contemplations that we each apply to our own life choices. That way, we avoid the pitfall of trying to live life by a robotic manual, which is impossible anyway. If we take these contemplations to heart, they become questions we ask ourselves day by day, moment by moment, as we try to apply them to what actually happens along our journey. Thinking of them as companions rather than as judgments, we avoid the tendency to burn out on our ethical exploration.

FIVE CONTEMPLATIONS OF ETHICS (PRECEPTS)

The five traditional contemplations of conduct in everyday life are: (1) promoting life, (2) generosity, (3) truthfulness, (4) responsible sexuality, and (5) responsible consumption.

Promoting Life

Promoting life stands in contrast to refraining from the negative action of mindlessly taking life, or killing. While the practical application and debate of this question often involves the consumption of meat, the question is actually much broader than that. In some Eastern traditions, vegetarianism is emphasized, and in others, not so much. Within this contemplation, we turn our thoughts to the basic question of how our habitual aggression causes us to thoughtlessly destroy or hinder the energy of situations around us. We also turn our attention to our participation in larger systems where the lives of sentient beings are disregarded. Instead, how could we help the health of sentient beings, especially human beings, flourish? By engaging in the promotion of life, we are thinking about little things we can do to become a more ecological human being in the deepest sense of what it means to live in harmony with one's environment. We are working against the habitual tendency to reject and destroy that which we believe threatens us.

Generosity

How can we live a life of generosity? This practice of offering stands in contrast to the harmful action of stealing or greedily taking what is not offered to you. We often think of generosity as a practice of charity, of being a great tipper, or of helping those less fortunate than us in some way. However, at the level of self-awareness, each of these practices is meant to help us dwell more fully in our own heart and mind. Here, ironically, the practice of generosity is mainly meant to benefit ourselves.

When we conventionally consider generosity's opposite—greed—we often think about what greed does to others. Activists condemn a greedy global elite that has consumed the world's resources rather than creating a shared and sustainable future. I agree with a lot of the sentiments behind these critiques, but here we are more interested in what greed does to the greedy themselves. Greed keeps us trapped in the commuter's mentality, as it trains our mind to seek safety by mindlessly latching on to passing fixes. Greed decreases our ability to empathize with others, because it inhibits our ability to even see them, and greed keeps the bar for our basic comfort level moving ever higher and higher. For any human, empathy is the very basis of mental health, and greed directly obstructs our ability to experience empathy and, therefore, love. When we practice generosity, what we are fundamentally doing from the standpoint of self-awareness is letting go of fixation on objects: again and again, we practice relaxing our tendency to objectify home somewhere "out there."

On an interpersonal level, it is pretty clear that practicing generosity and making offerings whenever we can opens up our human relationships to a whole new level of shared appreciation. It's a fairly simple rule that bringing flowers gets you pretty far in life. On a societal level, every act of letting go undermines the demonstrably false notion that greed is good, either for individuals or for society at large.

It is also important to note that if we think of generosity as letting go rather than as charitable giving, then it becomes a two-way street. Generosity is no martyrdom, no act of ignoring your own needs or value as a human. Generosity is every bit as much about being open to receiving, because one of the ways we avoid being present is by convincing ourselves that we aren't worthy to receive what comes to us. One of the best ways I have found to practice letting go is to actually allow myself to accept a compliment openly when somebody says something positive about me. If someone praises you, just say thank you. It might be the hardest practice of all, and it's actually part of practicing generosity.

Truthfulness

A life of honesty is the third practice. This contemplation asks the question: What does it mean to live a life without deception, a life of authenticity and truthful representation, both to ourselves and to the world? For me, this has been the trickiest and most challenging of all five contemplations. It's often been painful to be a curious student of my own subtle deceptions. However, both internally and externally, honesty is the best tool we have to truly make friends with who we really are. Honesty is the vanguard of self-acceptance. At times we want to hedge our bets on honesty, or we try to shift truths just a little to make people like us or to avoid conflict and hurt feelings. Sometimes we are dishonest just to get what we want. While the practice of human communication will be addressed more fully in the next section of the book, the main aspect of the contemplation of honesty is the feeling that it's actually okay to be who we are, without doubt or hesitation. With that in mind, we can begin to represent ourselves honestly to the world and to each other, saying what we have to say, clearly and straightforwardly.

Responsible Sexuality

The fourth ethical contemplation asks us to consider a mindful and compassionate approach to sexuality. Unfortunately, much of the teaching on how to use the energy of sexual relationships has historically been given by monastic practitioners who chose to no longer engage in them. This is sort of like asking an accountant to teach you how to paint. You might get lucky and end up with an accountant who is a great painter, but it's probably better to ask someone you know has the kind of experience you are seeking help with.

Any relevant approach to sexuality would have to fully acknowledge the diverse scope of modern sexual relationships and identities, and also include an examination of how our society commodifies sexuality through entertainment and pornography. There is no traditional Buddhist teaching, for example, on the appropriate use of Internet porn. The main guideline on the journey of self-awareness as it applies to our ethical life is to always "minimize harm." If we actually bring this intention—both to minimize harm and to help others—into our sex life, a whole new set of questions arises. Again, these are personal questions of practice and contemplation, not rules written in stone. The fundamental question is much deeper than those about engaging only in longterm relationships or discussing the spiritual validity of one-night stands. The fundamental question is one of manipulation and grasping. A one-night stand isn't problematic because it happens out of wedlock. From the standpoint of karma, a one-night stand can be destructive if it causes us to solidify our habit of fixating on other beings as merely objects of our pleasure. In fixating on sexual objects, we avoid connecting with our own awareness and we also manipulate the other person, and this is what causes harm. But it's also possible to spend the night with someone without falling into this trap. At the very least, we might consider that every sexual relationship is a relationship of cause and effect. There may be such a thing as sex without commitment, but there is no such thing as "casual" sex, if we think of "casual" as meaning "without effect." There is always energy exchanged, and we should always pay close attention to how we use that sexual energy.

Responsible Consumption

Responsible consumption is the corollary to the practice of re-fraining from harmful intoxicants. What, then, is an intoxicant? In the ancient teachings, this of course meant alcohol. The list of possible ways to escape your own mind through intoxication was pretty short back then. Now, to limit the discussion to only alcohol would be to ignore the truth that a huge piece of modern life is all about escapism and intoxication. This doesn't mean that the discussion of alcohol is moot or passé. We live in a deeply alcoholic society, and I know many people on the path of meditation for whom the appropriate number of alcoholic beverages is zero. But I also know some people—like myself—for whom that's not the case. I also know quite a lot of people who are addicted to their technological devices, something that up until just a few years ago no spiritual or psychological teachings were able to ad-dress at all. With this contemplation, I would recommend an hon-est assessment of one substance or activity to which you feel a small level of addiction, and practice actually relinquishing its usage for a short period. With mindful periods of restraint—perhaps a weekend without our smartphones—we train our minds not to rely so heavily on quick fixes. By practicing responsible consumption, we become intimately familiar with the destructiveness of consumerism, and begin to truly witness how consumerism arises from our inability to rest comfortably with our own mind.

WORKING WITH ETHICS IN EVERYDAY LIFE

The five ethical contemplations above are huge, so broad that we could spend a lifetime figuring out how to put them into practice.

Day by day, moment by moment, so as not to feel overwhelmed, it might be more helpful to think of just one of them at a time. I would suggest that every day or every week, you think of one specific application of just one of the five areas above, such as the mindful usage of your tech devices or what honesty really means for you in a difficult conversation you need to have. Choose something that is relevant, and also that is manageable, meaning that your level of judgment or shame around the given activity is not so great that you can't feel a sense of humor at your perceived mistakes. Just as you might use the breath as an anchor in mindfulness meditation, you can also create anchors for returning your mind to the present and noticing when you get caught up in evading the moment. This could be as simple as returning your attention to your body when you notice yourself itching to look at your device again. If we turn ethics into a mindfulness practice, we can avoid the extremes of defensiveness and righteous judgment, and avoid giving up the entire process by caving in to apathy.

If we take on one of these contemplations each day, and think about one specific application in our behaviors or actions, applying the contemplation to even three simple moments each day, the benefits will be huge. If we can do that, then our practice of self-awareness will truly become a 24/7/365 companion. Slowly, the path becomes completely integrated with life, and a curious awareness begins to touch everything we do.

4

BEING HUMAN

Buddha Nature and the Cocoon

It is not that the ego disappears, but that the belief in the ego's solidity, the identification with ego's representations, is abandoned in the realization of egolessness.

—MARK EPSTEIN

That which knows confusion *cannot* be confused.

—CHOGYAM TRUNGPA RINPOCHE

Classic Buddhist tales of the journey of awakening hint at the irony of our commuter's situation. When they describe the nature of the human mind, texts sometimes tell the story of a poor man who doesn't know there is a treasure chest buried right beneath his dilapidated little house. He has to go on a crazy trip to find enough resources to scrape together his survival, only to eventually return home and accidentally discover the treasure buried where he sits. So, with our sense of irony intact, a question arises: Who, exactly, is engaging in this "journey" of awareness? Who or what are we at our core? What do we think our home— our very humanity—is made of to begin with?

With no exaggeration, your view of human nature is perhaps the most important view you hold. What we believe about the nature of humanity actually lies beneath our spiritual views, our political views, and even our aesthetic views. Our idea of human nature has a tremendous impact on how we participate in our world. For example, philosopher Thomas Hobbes's seventeenth-century statement of his tragically ominous belief that humanity's natural, uninterrupted state is "a war of all against all" had a tremendous impact on the later economic thinkers who shaped the ruggedly competitive economic philosophies that guide so much of the contemporary world. What we believe about human nature is always the deepest script from which our expressed thoughts and actions are born.

A "view" is the Buddhist term for the basic coding, or framework, from which our thoughts, expressions, and finally actions in the world are derived. A Sanskrit word for view, *drshti*, literally means our "gaze." The crucial aspect of view is realizing that how we look at a situation, how we choose to gaze upon reality, deeply affects what we actually see.

When we have only a commuter's relationship to our own mind, we don't always have direct access to the views that we hold. Even with practice, seeing our own views clearly takes a very long time. Rarely do human beings directly express their views of human nature. It's not often that we just say, point-blank, whether we think humans are, at heart, basically good or originally sinful. What we directly experience are our conscious thoughts, which often contain fragments of underlying views. For example, after sending a message to someone asking her out on a date, you might directly think a negative thought like, "She's probably not getting back to me because she doesn't want to go out with me. Why would she go out with me?" More rarely do you think a conscious thought that includes a complete statement of a view of your nature, such as, "My existence is inherently flawed and doomed, I am a cosmic f-ckup, my whole being is based on an original mistake from which I will never recover, when I was born I was already genetically damaged and spiritually broken, and because of all that . . . I'm pretty sure . . . she's not gonna text me back."

These deep—and often pervasively negative—views of our nature may only be revealed to us by examining patterns of conscious thought and behavior over a long period of time. Without meditation, we may occasionally perceive the damage caused by a few self-critical thoughts, or notice some of our sudden and harsh judgments of others, but we rarely put all the puzzle pieces together to see that underlying these thoughts and reactions is a deeply negative—and acquired—view of humanity. Part of the power of meditation and reflection is that, by repeatedly recognizing our consciously expressed thoughts, we have the opportunity to slowly trace back and begin to examine the views from which those thoughts are encoded. Once we have access to our views directly, we can begin to honestly and mindfully weigh those views against our lived experience, to determine which seem accurate, and which seem problematic, false, or just too extreme. Once we know what we believe about ourselves, we can set about examining whether or not it's really true. This ability to put one's views to the test is the most profound outcome of a contemplative life.

The view that human beings are inherently flawed, confused, and aggressive has proliferated throughout human history, across cultures, religions, and countless fields of "secular" inquiry. This view, which Pema Chödrön calls the view of "Basic Badness," has consequently had a huge "invisible hand" in shaping a wide range of systems within which we all live, especially the system of our own heart and mind.

There's no way to avoid the following point: the Shambhala and Buddhist teachings stand in direct and total opposition to a view that human beings are originally sinful and fundamentally flawed. The Shambhala teachings say that human beings, all human beings, are basically good and endowed with inherent wisdom (Buddha nature). Here, "good" does not mean "better than." Good does not stand in relation to "bad," because there is no bad when it comes to human nature. Without comparison, "good" here means whole, pure, and totally worthy of existing. Tragically, many of us don't have trust in the basic goodness of humanity. Even more tragically, so many people I work with believe that basic goodness applies to everyone but themselves. If you have a hard time connecting with your own basic goodness, you are not alone. Far from it. It might be the greatest spiritual challenge of our time.

What are the day-to-day effects of thinking we are fundamentally flawed? If we believe this, then materialistic objectification— i.e., spending as much time as we possibly can getting the hell away from dealing with ourselves—would be the only way to get even temporary relief from a basically flawed design. The logic of materialism extends directly from an underlying view of a sinful and corrupted humanity, even if we don't see it.

The Buddhist and Shambhala traditions push hard in the other direction, using methods of direct experience, as well as complex logical arguments, to contend that the human mind contains inherent wisdom, and that our nature is whole, complete, and worthwhile. Therefore, whatever experiences we have must also be whole, complete, and worthwhile. Thus, basic goodness applies to the mind, as well as to every phenomenon the mind encounters.

If we weren't innately intelligent, then how would we be able to verify any progress along our journey through life? How would we ever know that any spiritual insight we have is legitimate—the real deal? Without innate wisdom, wouldn't any journey along a spiritual path just be a comedy of errors, the blind leading the blind? If we didn't have inherent wisdom, could we recognize wisdom in anyone else? How would we decide who to follow or why? There has to be something already active within us that knows what home really feels like, and that can reliably verify the true experience of being at home in our own awareness. If you fall in love with a teacher because you think that she is an awake and compassionate being, it means you also have that same potential in your own mind. The phrase "it takes one to know one" seems to apply.

As Chogyam Trunga Rinpoche said, the fact that we know we are confused means part of us has never been confused. Let's say you just tried to meditate and totally spaced out for ten straight minutes. It happens to all of us, even us pros. The fact that you know it was about ten minutes means that part of you was present the entire time. When you are lost in thought, what knows you are lost? Something within your heart and mind is already fundamentally awake and available. Something within you is never lost in commute.

This means we already possess the inherent ability to understand our dilemma and experience the freedom that comes from living in our awareness. If not, we truly would be screwed, and any spiritual fix would just be a façade, a cosmetic surgery to buy a doomed patient a little more time to go through the motions. But we are not doomed. This innate capability to see clearly, sewn into the fabric of awareness itself, is the basis of our intelligence and our ability to feel compassion for the plight of others.

This potential, the fact that "that which knows confusion *cannot* be confused," is called Buddha nature. Traditionally, when Buddha nature is discussed, it is referred to as a seedlike quality of awareness, a kind of potential energy of consciousness, a basic soil from which powerful qualities can slowly flourish. The fruit of this potential energy, the actual substance that flowers, is called *bodhicitta. Bodhi* is another word for "awake" and *citta* is the Sanskrit word that I have been translating as "heartmind." Chogyam Trunga Rinpoche referred to the potential to connect with this awakened energy of consciousness as our "enlightened genes." Again, Buddha nature and *bodhicitta* are descriptions of the mind. Basic goodness is a description of the mind and all phenomena.

For each of us who engages in this practice, there are moments along the path where we catch glimpses of our own awakened nature, and actually begin to believe in our own capabilities. Taken together, these glimpses build trust in the journey, and give us great boosts of energy to keep showing up to the present moment, showing up to our practice, and showing up to our life.

Just a warning about glimpsing your own awakened nature: it's really not that big a deal. Sorry. There are rarely halos or fireworks involved in these powerful moments. Usually, they are just moments where we notice our ability to handle our own mind differently from how we used to. Momentarily, we experience ourselves as capable of dealing with our feelings, whereas once we felt inadequate and overwhelmed by whatever emotions we experienced. As our practice develops, we begin to string these moments of awareness together until they eventually become continuous.

I remember a moment for myself, maybe the most powerful experience of glimpsing my own awakened nature that I've ever had, a moment where an insight about my own awareness led me home in a deep and clear way.

It's about five years ago, fifteen years after my committed meditation path began, and eight years since I embarked on the strange path of teaching Buddhism. I am sitting on an airplane around 2:00 a.m., somewhere over one of the Dakota states. The flight is an overnight red-eye, carrying us back to New York from the West Coast. I have been on the West Coast for a while, teaching people as best I could what my tradition has to offer about dealing with your own mind, and helping others. Before takeoff, all the TVs in the airport played a cable news channel on mute, showing images of an earth gone crazy, a surreally beautiful yet broken world, reported on by people who seemed shiny yet unhappy.

There is a couple sitting next to me in our row, and I gleaned just before takeoff that they are headed off to their honeymoon, somewhere in the Caribbean, with a brief morning layover in the fabulously romantic Newark International Airport. Now, two hours into the flight, they are already arguing with each other in the dimmed cabin light, throwing back and forth the kind of passive-aggressive whispers that make me fear their marriage may already be doomed. My flight will land at 6:03 a.m. Eastern time. I am wondering if there is anyone I can text when the wheels touch down. Having recently gone through a breakup I didn't initiate, I realize there's no one there, not at that hour, at least. I have dear friends, I have great parents, but none of them will respond to the sound of their phone rustling at 6:00 a.m.

There are various markers of loneliness that the modern world offers for all us weary commuters, but perhaps the greatest one is realizing there's absolutely no one there for you to text. If you have no one to text, then you are truly alone. I am groundless at thirty-five thousand feet, feeling tremendously alone.

A wave of intense sadness crests in my body, and I feel the tears creeping out. I feel my deeply habitual resistance to actually letting myself feel. But I let go of that, and I am crying now, turning this flight into a literal red-eye. The sad waves go on for a while, longer than any grown man would hope to cry on a United Airlines Airbus. Truthfully, this might be the most intense sadness I have ever experienced.

Of course, I would like to say the saddest moment I experienced came at the most politically correct time to feel sad. You know, a moment of deep grief at the loss of a teacher, or a moment witnessing the insanity of war, or a moment confronting the horrors of systemic poverty, or mourning the heroic death of one of our great saints, like Nelson Mandela. One of those times when people of good conscience are supposed to be sad, when heroic tears are appropriate. Because of the work I do, I hear stories daily of people's desperation, traumas, and grief. I see torments on the news I may never have to face. There are real problems in the world, and I'm still caught up in my own petty melodrama?

The experience of genuine sadness is never quantifiable. There is no chart dictating the correct frequency of feeling, the measured serving of grief proportionate to the event at hand. If there is one thing this path has taught me, it is the truth that every single experience is valid. Instead of judging whether or not my suffering is deep enough to qualify as legitimate suffering, I decide to work with the moment as it is.

I am sitting now. Sitting up tall in my seat, extra tall amongst all the weary travelers, their seats pushed back to the maximum, so they can try to sleep. I'm placing my attention on my breath and my heart center, grounding my body in the middle of the sky. There are many techniques I could use right now, many that the tradition offers. Instead, I choose to just sit and feel. Feel my own vulnerability, feel my own openness, feel myself soaring through the air, uncertain about what home even means right now. After all, every breath I have ever followed, every lovingkindness meditation I have ever done, every mantra I have ever recited, have all been preparing me to bravely face simple moments like this one. As I sit, I remember a voice in my head. It is my father's voice, spoken through gentle thoughts. The voice is transmitting the old

Tibetan lama's words, and therefore transmitting an entire lineage of wisdom. The voice reminds me of one simple truth that carries me through the rest of the flight:

I live in the center of my awareness.

When my flight touches down, during a gray and nondescript New Jersey sunrise, I don't feel any less sad. But I do feel open, thankful for this wacky human life, and ready to deal with whatever comes now. This feeling, that life is truly workable, lasts all the way until . . . the next time I forget. This is the experience of *bodhicitta*, awakened heartmind.

Every time we remember to live for a moment in the center of our awareness, especially during or after difficult emotional situations, we are connecting with the very basis of our awakened mind. Fundamentally, *bodhicitta* can gently witness and accommodate any experience that arises in the mind. It is an open and unshakeable awareness. To borrow a phrase from Jacques Derrida and Heidegger, *bodhicitta* reminds us that we are "always already" okay. In relationships, *bodhicitta* is what allows us to actively care for ourselves, and nurture others. *Bodhicitta* is the ultimate validation of human experience, whether our current experience is pleasant or painful.

When we live in our awareness this way, we live within a kind of normalized profundity that we don't need to construct. We don't go chasing sadness, but when it visits our home, we realize that there is honesty and deep love within that tenderness. We don't go provoking anger, but when it arrives, we realize that it is a valid mind state that can lead to the correcting of an injustice. The same could be said for how we could experience desire, jealousy, or any other emotion we have a hard time making room for. It really is as simple, sometimes, as sitting up and being present for a difficult moment when your habitual mind wants to cave in to doubt and habit. Even at thirty-five thousand feet.

UNDERSTANDING THE "EGO"
AND THE COCOON

At the same time that we discuss basic goodness, Buddha nature, and *bodhicitta*, we also need to discuss the acquired views that obscure or compromise our ability to live fully within our awareness. We need to talk about confused notions of who we are, mistaken views of the self. To do so, we need to discuss one of the most misunderstood ideas in all of Buddhism. This is the Sanskrit concept of *anatman*, often translated as "egolessness" and sometimes as "nonself." If we misunderstand nonself, we might think that there's actually no person who exists, no heartmind to ever come home to. However, the teachings on *anatman* in no way contradict our existence, or the fact that we each have a personality, preferences, and individuality. Instead, *anatman* delivers a critique of a particular way of viewing the self, a mistake with huge consequences for how we experience joy and suffering.

The fact that we exist is pretty obvious. I am Ethan (for now) and it's nice to meet you. In fact, our "existence" is the very basis of this journey. To claim anything else would be to engage in the kinds of strange sophistries that always made my head hurt, the brainiac arguments, stripped of any clear relevance to experience, that can turn people off from studying Buddhism altogether. To me, Buddhist teachings are only meaningful if they positively inform the way we live our life.

But here's the question about existence: What is the *nature* of our existence, and have we adopted harmful views about who we are?

A lot of the brain-twisting wordplay that arises in Buddhist philosophy has to do with a misunderstanding of the word that gets translated as "existence." If we want to understand what is actually meant by nonself, we have to understand how Buddhist philosophy is defining the meaning of "existence," because it is a specific view of existence that Buddhist thought critiques.

When normal people say they exist, what they mean is pretty straightforward. But the Sanskrit word for "existence," *svabhava*, means something more like "independent existence," or "existence from its own side." It literally means something like "self-emerging, self-becoming." *Svabhava* refers to the impossible idea of an existence without context. What the Buddhist teachings remind us is that our sense of self never arises separately from the defining contexts of interdependence and impermanence. If we try to solidify the self, to make it permanent, or try to isolate the self from its relational context, then we run into big problems. These moments of stuckness, these moments of "frozen" self, are the basis for all our defensive karmic strategies. From this freezing of "me," the entire human history of materialism arises.

Buddhist schools of philosophy critique this notion of permanent and independent existence pretty heavily, and for good reason. The teachings from the middle-way (*madyamaka*) philosophical system say that the self cannot exist in terms of the following three conditions. It cannot be (1) permanent, (2) independent of context, or (3) reducible to a singular entity. The fact that we, as human beings, never meet any of these three conditions is actually pretty easy to establish, at least logically and in a calm moment, free from the trigger of a habitual reaction. However, we study and contemplate the truth of nonself not to be logical in moments of quiet reflection, but to prepare for moments of stuckness and conflict in the heat of daily life. We study philosophy in order to slowly learn to recognize and transform the moments where we are habitually triggered, moments where we cannot live within our own awareness. In these moments of solidification, logical clarity usually goes out the window, leaving us to react as if we existed without context, as if we were permanent. In these triggered moments, also called *klesha* (afflicted reactions) moments, we basically tell interdependence to go f-ck off.

When thinking about the solidified self, the "ego," I often get the image in my head of the Stay Puft Marshmallow Man from the classic movie *Ghostbusters*, who comes to life and runs amok, unleashing havoc on New York City. While moments of stuckness usually cause us to experience the self as thick, puffed up, and generally bad for you—just like a marshmallow monster—it's crucial to note that this stuckness is rarely, if ever, a positive feeling, even in the moment we get stuck. Classic texts point to the experience of solid self as having a narrative of extreme self-importance, a feeling of being at the center of the universe, somehow better than everyone else. While it is true that moments of solidification make us feel at the center of everything, in my experience, as well as in the experience of almost everyone I work with, we feel insecurity and inadequacy when our sense of self solidifies. Solid self, as one student put it, is like seeing yourself as the "piece of shit at the center of the universe."

The experience of self-as-process, or *anatman*, which we glimpse when we live in our awareness, usually has a harmonious balance of humility and confidence. We are humble because we realize there is actually no center of the universe, and we are confident because we know we are capable of meeting the present moment adequately. It's usually the case that if you feel good about yourself, if you feel you are genuine and authentic, then you are experiencing this fluid self, the self-as-process, not as a marshmallow monster. Sometimes Sakyong Mipham Rinpoche refers to the recognition of "egolessness" as having a healthy sense of self. While this may appear to be a contradiction in terms, it illustrates a crucial point regarding how we tend to feel about ourselves when we solidify a self-image, and how healthy and balanced we feel when our sense of self is more fluid.

For the sake of distinction, we need a word to describe the totality of our habits, our afflicted or obscured sense of solid self, that which we are trying to bring to light and over time, let dissolve. Sometimes spiritual thinkers use the word "ego" to describe the source of our problem. The Buddhist teachings also use the Sanskrit word *atman* to refer to the fictional self, the self that we keep imagining exists permanently, outside of any context.

However, egolessness means that in those triggered moments, we are reacting to something that isn't really there. So, a massive linguistic problem arises when we refer to the "ego" as an entity that does really exist in Buddhist terms—imagining "ego" as some problem to be overcome or destroyed—because the Buddha's whole teaching was that he could never find such a solid entity, no matter how hard he looked. Using the word "ego," we also run into other problems in conversations with Western psychology, because the meaning of "ego" as understood in Buddhism is completely different from its meaning in the Freudian triad of id, ego, and superego.

Language matters if it leads to confusion about how we view ourselves. In this case, language matters quite a lot. Viewing "ego" as something to destroy, on the one hand, and gently seeing that solid self never ever existed, on the other hand, can lead us down two very different spiritual paths. The first is a path of self-aggression and chasing ghosts. The second is a journey of awareness that leads us back to a healthy sense of self experienced in context, a self understood as a process, not as a statue. If we try to destroy the ego, we proceed from a nonsensical premise that Buddha never taught. It's sort of like saying "My unicorn is a total freak, a complete jerk, and it's causing me tremendous problems. I need to kill it. Sorry, unicorn."

The Buddhist psychologist Mark Epstein makes a valuable distinction between the fictional "solid self" and the "self-as-process" by referring to the first as our "representational" ego. The fictional ego is representational because it solidifies self-images as defensive patterns of karma.

On the other hand, self-as-process can be seen as including a more functional or contextually existing aspect of who we are. In other words, Buddhism only critiques the stuck self-image, not the functioning, feeling, experiencing aspect of personality. If we are going to study Buddhism and use the word "ego" to describe the mind, making this distinction will avoid a lot of confusion, and will prevent a lot of unnecessary unicorn abuse.

Chogyam Trunga Rinpoche seemed to see this linguistic problem and came up with a beautiful and poetic analogy for the solidified or representational sense of self, the sum total of our habitually triggered reactions. Instead of referring to it as "ego," as we discussed in chapter 2, he called it our cocoon.

Again, calling the stuckness of habitual reactions a cocoon puts a positive spin on a deeply entrenched problem. A cocoon is a protective space, a type of temporary home, created by a silkworm during its journey to maturity, a space in which to grow and transform. If the silkworm stays in this space too long, problems arise. The worm never faces the world, it never matures, it never grows up. This is what a stuck self-image does to our ability to live in the center of our awareness.

At the same time, the cocoon is woven out of silk. This analogy offers an insight into how an innately wise and capable mind (Buddha nature) can coexist with deep layers of habitual confusion. Wisdom and confusion can coexist because the cocoon is made out of moments of frozen wisdom, moments of innate intelligence that harden and ossify into habits. Meanwhile, the material of the mind never ceases to be silken.

It's like what happens when you put a pair of headphone earbuds in your pocket. You pull your headphones out a few hours later and they are tied in insane knots. Amazingly, it almost seems like there are more knots than there would be if you tied your headphones into knots on purpose! But we don't need a new set of headphones. We just simply need to untie the knots and the music is beautiful once again.

BECOMING A WARRIOR

For me, the moment of the red-eye was a profoundly no-big-deal culmination of years of practice. It was also the culmination of helpful feedback from mentors, teachers, therapists, students, and friends. The moment we realize that it really is possible to live in our awareness could also be called a moment of warriorship, a heroic word that reflects a Tibetan concept of bravery. The key to being a warrior is being brave enough to repeatedly look honestly at your own heartmind, to be fearless enough to keep challenging your own negative views of who you are. If we are willing to begin to feel fully who we are, if we are willing to begin to challenge millennia of negative views about human nature, and if we are willing to accept that we are actually wise and capable, then we can begin to lift our eyes and extend our practice of awakening toward others as well.

PART II

The Journey of Relationships

There's a gap where we meet
Where I end and you begin

—RADIOHEAD

5

WHERE I END
AND YOU BEGIN

I have a little theory about enlightenment. If you were all alone in an alternate universe (population: you), you could get enlightened quickly, if you set your intention. Your life would be greatly simplified. There would be no border disputes, no angry divorces, no revenge narratives starring Clint Eastwood. Facebook would be extremely boring, with a total of 0 friends to keep tabs on. Voyeurism would be dead. It would be a clean and simple universe, free from the messy entanglements that other sentient beings bring along with them. Here's the reason I think enlightenment would be simpler in this impossible universe: whenever any stuff came up, you would immediately know whose stuff it was. The mechanics of working with your karma would become obvious. You would learn the rules of your own mind quickly.

It would also be much simpler if we lived in a universe where other people's actions were completely predictable. How easy would life be if people always did what we expected them to do or, even better, what we wanted them to do. One movie often held up as a contemporary Buddhist narrative is *Groundhog Day*. In this movie, Bill Murray's character is forced to relive the same day over and over and over again, until he figures out how to be a decent and helpful human being, and until he learns a lesson about love. It's considered a Buddhist narrative because of the cyclical experiences that Bill's character faces. Stuck in a time loop, he goes through one day's confused moments again and again, until he figures out how to do something different, how to shift his reactions to situations as the day's events become more and more predictable, literally like clockwork. In that sense, it's quite a Buddhist narrative indeed, with the day's repetition being an allegory for samsara, the cyclical patterns of karmic confusion that cause us to commute over and over and over again through the same schemes of behavior.

With apologies to Bill Murray fans, *Groundhog Day* is a Buddhist narrative only in the most idealized sense, because the hero can always predict that everybody else is going to do the exact same thing they did on the previous "today" each time he sees them. This predictability of others' behavior would make our journey of self-awareness much easier. But experience isn't ever a perfect circle, and neither is samsara. The same moment never happens twice, people never do quite exactly what we expect them to; it's just that our karmic patterns tend to condition fresh moments with a hauntingly repetitive familiarity, a been-there-done-that feeling of commuter's dissatisfaction. Samsara is cyclical, yet never a perfect circle.

Stepping onto this path, you are confronted very quickly by the untidy and complicated reality of other human beings. We can never escape our relationships. For many of us, difficulties in relationships are what launch us onto the path of self-awareness to begin with. Sakyong Mipham Rinpoche likes to call this realization—that the path of awakening isn't just a personal journey but a shared one—the "great switcheroo." At first we think the path of coming home to our own awareness is all about "me." There's no shame in practicing for reasons of self-care. This is the initial reason that almost everybody I know has taken up a meditation practice, to learn more about ourselves and to get some respite from others, a chance to reflect, in isolation from our relationships.

However, we are quickly forced to realize that it is impossible to isolate ourselves from our relationships. Our universe is structured relationally, and therefore our state of mind—our very sense of who we are—is constructed in terms of our relationships to other sentient beings. With this realization, the journey necessarily evolves beyond just "me."

Moving from a more focused approach to self-awareness and our own personal karma to a more relational approach to how we interact with others is referred to as the transition from the Hinayana* (narrow vehicle) to the Mahayana (expansive vehicle) within the historically Tibetan tradition. The journey of relationships is not a better path—it's just a natural broadening of the scope of our practice.

In the ancient system of Indian and Tibetan Buddhism, this transition is usually marked by a description of the practitioner's

---

*There is an alternate usage of the word "Hinayana"—sometimes later schools of Buddhism used the term as a negative designation of earlier schools of practice, referring to them as "lesser." Here, Hinayana refers only to the first stage of teachings within the Indo-Tibetan and Shambhala approaches, and has no correlation with earlier Buddhist schools. Many teachings of the early Buddhist schools (such as lovingkindness and compassion) reappear in the Tibetan system within the Mahayana body of teachings, demonstrating that there isn't a clear correlation between Hinayana as used in the Tibetan system and the ideas of the Pali and Theravadan systems. As used in this book, Hinayana simply refers to teachings on self-awareness, and Mahayana refers to teachings on relationships.

relative maturity. The idea is that as we become more familiar with our mind, we become more and more able to be present for others. This approach is reminiscent of airplane safety warnings that say, "Adjust your own mask before assisting others." Once you do adjust your own mask, it becomes your responsibility to help others.

Perhaps a good visual analogy for this maturation from self-awareness to relational awareness, from Hinayana to Mahayana, is the image of water overflowing the way the spaces in an ice-cube tray fill up with water. We could think of the water as the cultivation of our positive qualities of self-care and mindfulness. Once one compartment fills, the sanity and compassion developed naturally overflows to others. From this standpoint, if we don't raise our gaze and see other beings, we aren't taking full responsibility for interdependence. Personal responsibility for karma only carries us so far. It helps us to see our own mind more clearly, and as a result of this we begin to experience the lack of true isolation between ourselves and others. We start to pay attention to others, because we don't need so much work ourselves. We have become decent and lower-maintenance human beings. At this point, traditionally, the journey of relationships—the Mahayana path—begins. The being who has devoted his practice to staying fully present in relationships is called the bodhisattva, one who is practicing awakening in relationship to everyone else.

However, this inside-out approach is a little too linear and idealized. It's never the case that a person feels he has perfected working with his own karma before he takes on the Mahayana practices of staying present in relationships. It's not like you get a black belt in self-awareness before moving on to relationships. It's much more akin to the idea that you should take a beginners' yoga class before moving on to an intermediate or advanced class. Taking an intermediate class does not mean you have mastered the basics—it just means you feel ready to build upon them.

We always have to return, again and again, to the foundation of self-awareness and personal accountability for our heartmind. While some ability to take responsibility for our own mind has to be present in order to really turn our attention to relationships, we quickly realize that even our personal self-image is a relational entity. When we actually look into our identity, we see that our sense of self has always been crafted in relationships. In the first stage of the path, we narrow down the scope of reality to focus on our own mind, because our own experience is all we can witness directly and take responsibility for. But quickly we realize that to isolate self-awareness from an exploration of our interdependent human relationships is only an approximation of reality.

Within so many of the investigations of Western psychology— such as attachment theory—our sense of our own mind is conditioned by the nature of formative relationships from a very early age. According to traditional Buddhist causality, our sense of self might even be conditioned by relationships we can't remember, from earlier versions of our consciousness (i.e., from our relationships in past lives). I don't know if you believe in reincarnation (for me, it's an open question), but no matter which lens we look through, our sense of self has been relational for a very long time. If we view Mahayana practices as further nurturing the work of self-awareness, then the journey of relationships is not overwhelming, and it's not about self-sacrifice or martyrdom. The bodhisattva's path is simply a more evolved form of self-care. This is the "outside-in" approach to the Mahayana journey. By making our relationships part of our path, we learn on a much deeper level what it means to heal our own karmic wounds.

This outside-in approach isn't just a theory; this is necessarily what happens as our practice moves off the cushion or mat. There's always a moment—both painful and insightful—where we realize that self-awareness without the context of relationships is simply not enough for us to fully awaken. There is no technical term for this moment. I like to call it "A Bad Moment after a Great Meditation."

I haven't met a committed practitioner who hasn't observed this phenomenon in some way. Here's how it goes: for once, you have a great and peaceful session of meditation practice. The bell chimes, and you feel balanced, confident, and momentarily not overwhelmed by the daily grind of being who you are. During the session, you were present and conscious of a good deal of the experience that transpired. You felt capable and confident. The "oy vey" sigh of your life lightened up, and you even felt your muscles relaxing. Everything that arose in your mind felt manageable. You really did come home to yourself, and your spot on earth was a basically good place to be. You even wished, without it feeling fake or cheesy, that all beings could have happiness.

And now, suddenly, only minutes later your phone rings, and it's your wicked stepmother (insert your own personal nemesis here). Just the sound of that voice pushes a button somewhere, somewhere you can't even reach yourself, and you suddenly feel like an old robot with an attitude problem. Without your control, you hear the scripted sarcasm and aggression emanating from your voice. Before you can blink, you say something careless, and all your peace and compassion from meditation evaporate before your eyes. Your wish for all beings to have happiness collapses under the irritation of the one being you just can't stand. Your practice suddenly feels like it's regressing or, even worse, it feels pointless.

If this scenario has ever happened to you, it's not a message that you should give up on worldly life and head for the nearest cave. It's an insight into the relational nature of personal experience, and a mandate for our practice to include our relationships. These tough moments don't happen because our difficult relationships stand in the way of our journey home. These trying moments occur because our relationships *are* the path. According to tradition, it's only through a full engagement with our relationships that the cultivation of awakened heartmind, *bodhicitta*, really takes off. At a certain point that arises in the organic flow of working with our minds, we realize that if we are going to fully live in awareness, we have to work to heal our relationship to other beings. The places we are stuck always involve our sense of who we are in relationship to others, and that's exactly where we need to take our practice.

To go on this journey of *bodhicitta* means to hold an apparent contradiction in mind: the apparent contradiction between personal responsibility for our experience on the one hand, and interdependence on the other hand (a contradiction we will discuss more in chapter 13). My favorite F. Scott Fitzgerald quote is: "The test of a first-rate intelligence is the ability to hold two opposed ideas in mind at the same time and still retain the ability to function." This is a perfect description of how to visualize this path; in reality, each being is distinct—each with our own mind, heart, and karma—but, at the same time, we do not exist separately from each other. If we fully embrace the apparent contradiction that we are distinct from others yet interdependent with them, then we realize that in order to fully awaken ourselves, we need to heal our relationship to others. This doesn't mean enabling other people's negative habits; it means healing their effects on our own consciousness. This healing brings our mind into harmony with interdependence, and therefore, into harmony with reality. Cultivating *bodhicitta* is realizing the union of our aloneness and our interdependence, and being willing to work with the apparent contradiction between them.

Bodhicitta is typically divided into two aspects: first, its unconditional quality, meaning how it manifests regardless of time or place, and second, how it manifests as a compassionate force in human relationships, which is its relative or relational aspect.

ULTIMATE *BODHICITTA*: AVAILABILITY AND OPENNESS

There are many words in the Buddhist tradition that point to the ultimate or unconditioned level of experience. Whenever you see a word in a Buddhist text like "absolute," "unconditional," "fundamental," "basic," "primordial," "original," "timeless," or "unchanging," the word is pointing to a particular facet of ultimate truth. Some words in this category, like "ultimate" or "basic," take an affirmative approach. These words point out what *is* present in ultimate truth, what qualities exist in all phenomena.

Some words for "ultimate," such as "unconditional" or "timeless," take a negating approach, pointing out that these qualities exist regardless of conditions or linear time. Whether affirmative or negating, this absolute level of *bodhicitta* refers to the fundamentally indestructible quality of awareness as our true home.

When we talk about ultimate *bodhicitta*, we are making quite a powerful claim about the essence of the human mind. This claim pushes back against many recent developments in postmodern Western thought. As Rebecca Solnit writes: "Since postmodernism reshaped the intellectual landscape, it has been problematic to even use the term 'human nature,' with its implication of a stable and universal human essence."* While Buddhism

---

A Paradise Built in Hell, p. 8: In this book Solnit explores how an optimistic view of human nature competes with a Hobbesian view of selfish humanity after disaster strikes a city or region.

has a strong interest in the many subjective and cultural aspects of experience that postmodern thought also mulls, Mahayana Buddhism also provocatively proposes that there are aspects of experience, aspects of consciousness itself, that are not beholden to any specific causes and conditions. Ultimate *bodhicitta*, the basic nature of awareness as open and accommodating no matter what, is one example. In this way, Mahayana teachings can be thought of as post-postmodern, because even after all of our deconstructions of a so-called "objective" reality (insights that are also strongly utilized in Buddhist teachings on emptiness), there remains an awareness that stays watchfully open to experience, noticing and knowing whatever happens. This claim—that awareness itself is unconditioned at its base, and therefore is the only place we can really call home—is a radically optimistic claim. The only way to put this claim to the test is to work with one's mind and see that we are always noticing what is happening, even if what is happening feels deeply confused. That which knows confusion cannot be confused.

While you can't really describe unconditional awareness, you can talk around it in a way that might dig beneath language and spark a preconceptual understanding. The words we use, like "unconditional," are a linguistic attempt to signify the innate aspect of an experience that's unmanipulated by circumstance. When the teachings turn to the language of ultimate truth in this way, they are no longer talking about a quality we need to cultivate or build. Developing or cultivating qualities is all about creating the likely conditions for something positive to happen, which is why the gardening analogy is used. Mental muscles like mindfulness and compassion need to be cultivated, the way good health needs to be cultivated, the way root vegetables need to be cultivated. Ultimate *bodhicitta* and basic goodness, however, always already are.

The fact that open awareness is an unconditioned quality does not mean that we don't have to do anything. There is still something we must do to connect with ultimate *bodhicitta*. The practice is one of tuning in, getting in touch with a certain mode of awareness already embedded in our consciousness.

Working with ultimate *bodhicitta* is almost like setting an old-style radio dial to the right frequency on a long road trip. In meditation, you have to keep slightly adjusting and retuning the dial to align with the right frequency, because the relative position of the antenna keeps changing and shifting as you move through life. During those brief moments on the road when we feel tuned in, the music is sweet and we come to life. If the right song plays, others might even sing along. With this attunement, we connect with the open and unconditioned aspect of our being, a basic space of awareness that does not see the self as solid, and therefore does not regard others as either commodities or threats to our own short-sighted satisfaction.

While we can't describe this ultimate space of awareness with words, we can always talk about the experience, and it is said that great masters can point it out to us in a way that helps us tune in to the right frequency, holding our attention in the proper balance. The first time Buddha taught about ultimate *bodhicitta*, he merely held up a flower as a way to point out unconditional awareness to one of his most attuned students, Mahākāśyapa, who never lost the signal after that moment.

The best way I've found to describe this space in my own being is in relationship to emotions. This kind of openness and accommodation is a space where it no longer feels like our own emotions are attacking us like space invaders. Emotions, from the standpoint of ultimate *bodhicitta*, are simply guests in our home, very welcome guests. From the standpoint of sensory and bodily experience, emotions are just a sixth type of sense perception, containing their own information and beauty that don't need to be either indulged or rejected. When we are open, our own feelings are no longer attacking us, which also means that other people are not threatening us. After all, the only way another person can ever threaten our consciousness on this fundamental level is to make us feel something we don't want to feel. If we are no longer resistant to our own awareness and what enters it, we don't have to feel threatened by emotions, and we can relate to anyone. Ultimate *bodhicitta* doesn't take sides; it doesn't create emotional cliques.

After much hard work along his path, the Buddha himself described the memory of such a moment of ultimate *bodhicitta*. He remembered this moment when he was thirty-five, several months before his full enlightenment experience, and it supposedly helped transform his relationship to his practice. After much struggle, with years of extreme effort, he suddenly recalled a simple moment as a boy, sitting under the tree in one of his father's fields, watching workers plow the fields. It was a moment of spontaneous attunement with himself and with all beings. It was a moment where he didn't have to make any effort at all to be present. This memory allowed him to trust that he didn't have to *earn* his place in the present moment through some struggle or discipline. He now had the confidence to relax fully without losing his awareness. This is what tuning in to *bodhicitta* feels like.

RELATIONAL *BODHICITTA*: CARE AND CONNECTION

On its relative or relational level, *bodhicitta* manifests as our capability to care for and connect with specific beings. Relational *bodhicitta* takes the universal openness of ultimate *bodhicitta* and directs it at specific beings. After all, we don't really experience the abstraction called "all beings." We only really encounter the beings we have specific relationships with.

I am constantly fascinated by reading modern neuroscience's discoveries about the relational and empathetic mappings of our brains, and always try to see a link between the insights of modern neuroscience and *bodhicitta*. I have often thought that the theory of "mirror neurons" is one major biological explanation of *bodhicitta*'s relational aspect. Mirror neurons are what scientists believe might allow us to learn and mimic the behavior of other beings, as well as to share the feelings of others, which forms the basis for empathy and compassion.

Relative *bodhicitta* is what allows us to generate empathy and compassion for the subjective experience of another person, to take interest and eventually feel love. It is what allows us to feel pain when somebody we care for is also in pain. Relative *bodhicitta* is what motivates you to bring flowers with you, and what makes your tear ducts something more than just tools for cleaning out your eyes.

We cultivate relative *bodhicitta* by engaging in a variety of practices both on and off the cushion. It is very important to note that the body of teachings based on ethics, or based on taking our practice off the mat or cushion, expands greatly in the Mahayana journey. One of the main ways we engage in relative *bodhicitta* is through the six transcendent practices, or the six *paramitas*. These are generosity, discipline (staying present with relationships), patience (dealing with anger both in oneself and others), rousing energy and effort, meditation, and wisdom (knowing what is real and what isn't).*

---

* In my first book, *One City: A Declaration of Interdependence*, I go much deeper into a contemporary discussion of the six *paramitas*.

THE ROLE OF MEDITATION IN THE JOURNEY OF RELATIONSHIPS

In Mahayana meditations on compassion, we work carefully with healing our self-image, as well as our image of other people we are in relationship with. From the standpoint of the confused commuter, our habit of materialism has also affected our interactions with other people. Without paying attention, we have objectified so many of our human relationships. Unknowingly, we use others as merely the vessels of our own instant gratification. In compassion meditations, we begin to imaginatively push ourselves across the malleable line between self and other, a boundary we can't actually cross. Within these meditations, our relationships are viewed from the perspective of a mental play space. Within the arena of our own ideas of who other people are, we begin to think about how others experience happiness and suffering. After compassion meditation, we try to apply this same curiosity to our daily interactions. We don't just ride the train; we try to actually inhabit the experience of the conductor. We don't just make a film; we try to imagine the experience of the audience. We don't just vote; we try to remember that the family of the person we aren't voting for just wants to be happy, like everyone else.

Still within our own subjective experience, we no longer just see other people as actors in the melodrama of our life, but as full subjects in their own right. We use the meditation cushion to prepare for relationships with a more panoramic view, by coming home to the messy truth that, yes, there are other sentient beings. From our seat, we reach across the very limits of our own subjectivity and try to test the boundaries of where "I" end and "You" begin. We do these practices again and again, because we constantly forget this truth—the truth of multiple subjectivities—and our mind slips back into objectifying others, commuting through our relationships mindlessly. By repeating these practices over and over, we come to deeply respect the truth that every human being has his own road home.

Within the relational practices of various Buddhist traditions, from the earliest teachings of Siddhartha up to modern times, there are many meditations for preparing and intending to be openhearted and compassionate within our relationships. The two most well-known of these various techniques are *metta* and *tonglen*. *Metta* is the best-known name, from the ancient Buddhist language of Pali, for lovingkindness meditation. *Tonglen* is Tibetan for "sending and receiving," a more intensive practice that fully utilizes our bodily awareness alongside our imagination as a way to offer healing interdependently with another suffering being.

With Mahayana meditation, we feel both how our relationships can inspire us and how our relationships tend to trigger stuck karmic reactions. Relational meditations involve visualizations of many different people—our heroes, ourselves, people we love, unknown people, difficult people, and possibly (eventually) even abusive people.

The notion of compassion meditation—a practice executed in private in order to generate good vibes for relationships—may seem like a contradiction in terms. However, a crucial aspect of relational *bodhicitta* is called intentional or aspirational *bodhicitta*. This type of inner work is about embedding caring intention within our thoughts and reactions to people. Intentional *bodhicitta* practice through *tonglen* or *metta* practice is about turning up the volume on thoughts and feelings of interest and empathy for the people we meet throughout the day, so that caring thoughts begin to first compete with and eventually overtake the judgmental thoughts that tend to reify our sense of isolation and mistrust.

We all know what it's like to be out in public and to be internally judging people while worrying that they are silently dissing us back. We comment on their clothes, judge their style, roll our eyes at what they say and what accent they use to say it, existing in a state of constant annoyance. Wouldn't it be nice if in at least equal measure to the thoughts like, "I can't believe he's wearing that hat" or "Her voice is so damn annoying," we could generate more thoughts like, "I hope she's sleeping well" or "I wonder how his sister's doing?" This is what intentional *bodhicitta* through meditation helps us to do on a moment-by-moment, day-by-day basis.

My father likes to say that the compassion practices of *metta* and *tonglen* are about slowly "changing your Freudian slip." If we practice compassion repeatedly on the cushion, the next time we see somebody struggling on the street, instead of waiting for someone else to take care of the person, we might instinctively step toward the situation. This attitude of moving toward others and remaining curious and available is the direct result of cultivating *bodhicitta*. *Bodhicitta* isn't a Buddhist thing at all, really. It's just what happens when the human heart comes back to life.

One of the things I love about the Buddhist teachings is the down-to-earth and scientific approach they take. One of my teachers and friends, Dzogchen Ponlop Rinpoche, likes to refer to it as a "science of the mind." While this is completely true for what compassion meditations do to our nervous systems and brains, we might also leave some room for a little touch of mysticism about the effects of generating a positive and nurturing attitude. From the more mystical or energetic standpoint, we might ask if doing the meditations of compassion actually has a real and immediate effect, not only in setting intention or creating aspirations for "real" life in the future. Many healers believe that thoughts of positivity have actual health effects in the physical universe, both on the subject and recipients of such practices. One of my dear friends and teachers, Sharon Salzberg, lists eleven traditional results of *metta* in her book *Lovingkindness*, and the list includes some pretty far-out outcomes, such as receiving the protection of invisible beings. Sharon is a very down-to-earth lady, so I don't think she listed these effects to sound like a character from a Harry Potter book. Perhaps the best approach to a meditation upon compassion is to view the outcome as primarily intentional and psychological in terms of how we subsequently interact with the beings in our life *after* meditation practice, while still leaving just a little room for mysticism. After all, each age of world history so far has witnessed the human arrogance of believing that the technological understanding of the day constituted the limits of all reality, only later to find that as technology increased we discovered that things which were previously fairy tales were actually just observable science. Maybe doing compassion meditation helps the recipient in invisible ways, right here and now.

6

EARS, MOUTH, AND FINGERTIPS
Communicating with Mindfulness

Restoring communication is an urgent task.

—THICH NHAT HANH,
The Heart of the Buddha's Teachings

L et's talk about communicating. How do we understand communication as a practice in the Buddhist teachings? Before we get into it, let's just take a moment to be clear about the inherent difficulty of two subjective beings communicating with each other. Think about this: How crazy is it, really, that two people ever understand each other at all? Consider how miraculous any conversation you've ever had has been: every time you try to speak to another person, even a person who knows you very well, the process is so delicate and tenuous that it's a miracle it ever works.

First, in order to speak, you have to reach down below your words, down into a prelanguage soup of memories, perceptions, thoughts, and emotions. And from that soup of messily categorized and amorphous experiences, you somehow find syllabic phrases that best represent the things you want to convey right now. Then you turn those memorized syllables into vocal cord vibrations,

vibrations that are quite literally tiny movements of air, and those vibrations travel with great fragility across physical space. Then, the vibrations funnel into these cute, weird-shaped little holes on the sides of the other person's head called "ears." At that point, the other person's brain determines what these vibrations mean based on her own past associations and experiences, experiences that are always incalculably distinct from your own, encapsulated within the subjectivity of a very different human experience. Then the other person has to reach down into, and somehow connect with, her own soup of feelings, memories, and emotions to see if what your vocal cords just emitted resonates with her own lived experience. If, somehow, this has all gone well and succeeded, the other person nods at you approvingly and says something like, "I know what you mean!"

Given this tenuous situation, we should have compassion for the truth that a lot of the time human communication—really understanding another human being and having him understand you in return—is difficult at best. We should also have a lot of compassion for the fact that miscommunication will almost always happen if we don't apply mindfulness to this fragile process.

The Buddhist tradition has many different teachings on speech and expression. What we even mean by the word "speech" in the twenty-first century is so much broader than it was when these teachings on appropriate or skillful speech were first offered in the ancient world. When the Buddha first taught a series of practices called "right speech" (also translated as "helpful or appropriate speech"), he was referring only to the act of verbally expressing yourself with another person in face-to-face exchanges. In sixth century B.C.E. Asia, verbal interactions in person were the only option for conveying what you had to say—it would still be several centuries before the advent of paper and the written word. In many tribal cultures and smaller societies, you probably only spoke a little bit each day. Each expression, as well as the body language that you used, was of utmost importance. People probably planned each interaction with care.

Now, we have incomprehensibly advanced devices that give us literally dozens of ways to express ourselves widely to many "friends" and "followers," instantaneously. Those devices are themselves evolving their own modes of expression at an exponential pace. I hesitate to even mention the name of a specific device here, for fear that, by the time you read this, it will be so antiquated, so limited in its possibilities for facilitating human communication, that you will laugh at me and call me "old school" for even saying its name. What the hell is an iPhone, anyway?

THE PRACTICE OF LISTENING TO OTHERS

When one of my favorite Buddhist writers and teachers, the Vietnamese master Thich Nhat Hanh, discusses the traditional practice of right speech, he actually talks about listening first, sometimes at great length. In the core curriculum of the Shambhala path, we repeatedly emphasize practices of communication done in pairs, where listening is treated as a form of mindfulness meditation. These exercises are deceptively powerful. Taken as an ongoing practice of relationship, listening deeply can mimic the structure of what our mind is doing within sitting meditation. Being a good listener involves the same cognitive structure as a foundational technique like mindfulness of the breath. When your mind wanders, you use awareness to note that you are lost and then come back to being present for the other person, just as we return our mind to the breath during meditation. It's as simple as that. Building the skill of coming back through working with our breath can help us extend the skill of being present with another person.

With listening, we are actually trying to be present with what arises first, and then second, expressing or creating something that isn't there yet. The ground of expression is actually accommodating what's already there—being receptive to another person's experience before we chime in.

Any true human communication means we have developed a genuine two-way street of listening and speaking. We are generally the most mindful when we approach the process in that order: first, listening, and then, speaking. Of course, in any conversation somebody has to speak first. We shouldn't just sit in complacent silence with another person out of awkward deference. Listening first refers only to the mindful attitude we take in communication. You probably know from experience that there are some people who, if you let them speak first, won't allow you to get a word in edgewise. Sometimes, you have to be the first one to speak.

FOUR OBSTACLES TO LISTENING WELL

In recent years, even though I still do many types of meditation, listening is perhaps the practice I have committed to the most. And it is not easy; it still feels like a weak point for me. But what makes listening well so hard? Below are four obstacles to listening well to another human being. Again, whenever we spot an obstacle, we don't have to judge ourselves. Instead, we can honor the obstacle as a realization of the place our practice can go next. Obstacles are merely tools for learning. The entire path is about spotting obstacles and learning to work well with them. In studying many different teachings on communication and in my own path of listening, especially in difficult conversations, these four obstacles have consistently demonstrated themselves as the most fruitful to investigate.

Distraction

The first reason it is hard to listen is the first reason sitting meditation is so uncomfortable: we are distracted a lot of the time. Some of this is personal, sure, but so much of it is environmental and cultural. Sharon Salzberg points to Linda Stone's haunting phrase "continuous partial attention" as a description of the difficulty we have with concentration in meditation, given our twenty-first-century lives. Continuous partial attention—the idea that we are never fully grounded in any one aspect of modern life—is the downside of our attempt to multitask throughout the day. Buddhist teachers have actually been discussing this phenomenon for centuries. One of the most interesting analogies in traditional Buddhist teachings on mindfulness is that of "monkey mind," a mind that is always painfully leaping from object to object without any real rapport with or choice in where we go next. In the twenty-first-century version of this image, the monkey has a smartphone and a computer with seventeen windows open simultaneously, and probably just chugged a few too many energy drinks.

Sadly, our continuous partial attention extends to the way we are present in conversation with other human beings. One of the basic facts of the cultivation of mindfulness is that in order for the mind to familiarize itself with any object of attention, it must be able to stabilize on the object for a period of time. Learning requires familiarization, and familiarization requires a settled placement of mind upon an object. So, what happens when the object of mindfulness is another person? How is monkey mind a factor when listening?

One of the major downsides of being able to communicate

with many people at once is that we are rarely focused on one person anymore. These days, much of our life is spent in a strange limbo: we are in the physical presence of some people, while simultaneously in the virtual presence of others. For example, we are having a meeting with one person while having a text exchange with two others. This split screen between physical and virtual reality creates an odd sort of purgatory for our awareness. I find myself in this dilemma all the time. What's even more difficult is that the cultural expectations of being able to get someone's attention increase with each development in technology. I have often found loved ones complaining that I spend too much time on my smartphone, only to also complain that I haven't used the same smartphone to get back to them quickly enough. Rock, meet hard place. Sometimes, when I get completely frustrated, I find myself momentarily wishing relationships had an "unsubscribe" button.

The truth is, our in-person relationships and our virtual exchanges create an ongoing tension. Physical reality and virtual reality are locked in a twenty-first-century tug-of-war. The answer is not to destroy our technology and go back to some pre-virtual paradise—the answer is to turn communication into a mindfulness practice. We need to know the guidelines for when we are physically present with someone, and when we are virtually present with someone, and to create principles around each of those periods of communication, so that we engage in each more fully.

In meditation, we cannot simply "kill the monkey" of our monkey mind. All we can do is try to be present with it, and offer the monkey a comfortable home to eventually learn to settle within. The monkey isn't a problem—it's a basically good primate. In fact, the monkey can be tamed and trained to attend to life more fully, because the monkey simply represents the active and eternally curious aspect of our cognitive perception. We can, however, create conditions for the monkey to settle by limiting distractions like TV or other technology while we meditate. Similarly, in our human conversations we can't put a sudden end to continuous partial attention. But, just as in meditation, we can create rules and boundaries around being present that can help us experience relationships more completely. Beyond that, compassion meditation allows us to remember why we even care about this person in front of us, which creates the basis for *wanting* to be present with another human being. On that basis, putting my device away during dinner has been one of the most important spiritual choices I've ever made.

Fear of Pain

A second obstacle to listening is the anxiety that what we are going to hear is going to be painful to us. This wariness about uncomfortable exchanges produces evasive maneuvers around the act of listening, countless ways we anesthetize ourselves against really hearing somebody out. There are many subcategories of this type of avoidance. Maybe we just think the person in front of us has a completely unreasonable point of view, like she believes global warming is a hoax while we know it is crushing the planet's ecosystem and endangering our very survival. Or maybe you fear that your sister is going to claim that a family argument was really your fault, that you're the one to blame for what went down at Christmas. And who has ever enjoyed receiving a detailed explanation for why someone has fallen out of love with you? Listening closely to that just seems like masochism. So, as a shield against potential or expected pain, we find ways to not even hear what is being said.

This brings us back to the teachings on karma, how we must be willing to trust that we can live in our awareness, even in difficult moments, and that we can resensitize ourselves beyond our avoidance. The numbed-out evasion of painful communication comes from a lack of confidence that we can accommodate the feelings that arise in our body and mind during difficult exchanges. The need to avoid difficult communications also comes from an ingrained false perception—the immature wish that we could live without pain. But some level of pain, both physical and emotional, is inevitable for us humans. While suffering is (eventually) optional, pain is not. The pain of disagreement within human relationships will last until the end of the human race, because of the inherent friction involved when multiple subjective beings try to share their experience through communication. Painful communication is part of the very structure of multiple beings relating to one another.

Again, here, technology plays a major role in enabling our attempt to avoid potentially painful communications. It has become all too easy to avoid a face-to-face meeting by leaving a phone message, to avoid a phone call by sending a text message, to avoid a text message by sending an e-mail, to avoid an e-mail by pretending it went to the wrong folder, and to avoid any connection at all by blocking the other person on our social network. Of course, boundaries are important, especially if we feel like we have already completed the communication that needed to happen or if we feel mistreated by another person's actions or way of expressing himself. But often, we use technology to avoid painful moments before we even know what the moment will look like, choosing to live in fear rather than to show up and be brave. Like coming back to the present moment in meditation, gently encouraging ourselves to stay present with difficult communications may build our confidence that we don't have to be so evasive with others in life. We can build the trust that whenever a potentially difficult communication is necessary, we can handle it.

Wanting to Tell Your Own Story

This is where the obstacles to listening get increasingly interesting. While the other person is sharing her experience, the act of listening sparks the memory of a story from your own experience. She is telling you about the play she just saw, and you interrupt before she's done, telling her all about the musical you starred in during high school. There is usually a very positive intention behind this interruption; it is the attempt to relate another's experience to your own. But there is also a big downside to it, because, in telling your own story prematurely, you hijack the other person's opportunity, destroying trust in the process of sharing experience. Interrupting another person's expression and blurting out your own, instead of creating connection and camaraderie, can accidentally obliterate the space necessary for real connection to begin.

Wanting to Give Advice

This is the most subtle and tricky obstacle to listening well. This is where our intention to help, to be a bodhisattva and to be present for another person, goes haywire. Because I am often in a position where people ask me for advice, I find myself highly susceptible to this trap.

Traditionally, it is considered inappropriate to offer your suggestions unless they are asked for, either explicitly or implicitly. For a dharma teacher, the tradition warns against teaching when you have not been requested to do so. As a friend, lover, or peer, we should apply this same wariness to our need to give advice. Of course, when our opinion is asked for, then it wouldn't be compassionate to withhold. But we should wait until advice is requested.

One problem with giving advice too quickly is that we may not have listened fully to what the other person said, and our advice may come before we really understand the situation. Learning to listen fully can help us out of the trap of giving advice out of place. We should also always be clear whether the person is asking us for help, because much of the time all another person wants is to be heard and to feel heard, to feel like she is able to share her subjective experience with another sentient being.

If we apply the teachings on karma, paying attention to these obstacles helps us to insert the needed speed bump before we start expressing ourselves. Awareness of these obstacles helps us mind the karmic gap during communication. It is within this gap of listening that insight can arise, so that when we shift from listening to speaking, we have a better understanding of what really needs to be said.

FOUR ASPECTS OF MINDFUL EXPRESSION

Once we realize that we have to work with listening as part of the practice of communication, the discussion shifts to how we express ourselves. These four teachings on mindful speech and expression come straight from the Buddha himself.

Honesty

We already looked at honesty as an underlying ethical contemplation for life in chapter 3. In the Buddhist teachings on appropriate speech, the first lesson is always to try to express ourselves truthfully, without twisting the meaning of what we are saying. This does not mean we have to disclose everything to everyone. When we choose to share things, the question is whether we can do so without changing or sugar-coating what we are saying. For me, the most important aspect of this piece of skillful speech is the willingness to be open and authentic. It's certainly not an easy task, as we tend to spend so much of life being quasi-honest. Maybe we construct a résumé that says we are fluent in French when really what we mean is we speak it a little bit. We blame being late on traffic, when really we should've left home earlier. When somebody asks us how we are feeling, instead of saying we are feeling overwhelmed by life, we say "fine." We tell somebody we just aren't ready for a relationship right now, when what we really mean is that we aren't ready for a relationship with him or her. Is it possible, when expressing ourselves, to notice all the twists and changes we apply to the truth to attempt to make it more palatable? Is it possible to say what we have to say without manipulating it?

Speaking Kindly

Once we decide to express ourselves, we need to keep in mind the guideline to express the truth gently, without unnecessary harshness. In most cases, the truth is a blade that does not need to be sharpened, and we almost never need to twist the knife. Because as a listener we can empathize with the fear that what we hear might hurt, we can also work to apply gentleness when speaking. I often find that when I fall into the trap of speaking too harshly, it is because I don't have enough confidence in the power of my own voice to carry sufficient strength on its own. When you realize that your speech can be powerful, you don't need to amplify that power by making personal attacks that overgeneralize the specific feedback you are trying to give. If you go to a dharma talk you don't like, instead of saying, "He is the worst public speaker ever," you could just say, "I didn't like that lecture," and people will get the point. In speaking kindly, it also seems crucial to remember that when we decide to criticize, we should always attempt to criticize actions, views, and behaviors, rather than vilifying people.

At the same time, kind speech does not mean avoiding telling the truth. Many times it seems that in an attempt to be polite, we avoid saying anything at all, and therefore we let misperception and confusion go unchecked. We will discuss how compassionate intention can end in confused outcomes more in chapter 8.

Speaking with Harmony in Mind

Gossip is fun. Entire media industries are built upon it. Sometimes, when we gossip about a person, we are just trying to be friendly and keep up with what's going on in the life of somebody we care about. Sometimes we gossip because we look up to or admire the person we are talking about. This is where the phrase "Are your ears burning?" comes from. Sometimes we talk about others because we are concerned about them, worried about their health, or worried about the choices they are making.

Much of the time, however, gossip is just a wedge that serves to divide people and set us against each other. It turns humans into puppets for a cynical critique. In order to notice how gossip becomes divisive speech, we should be aware of our tendency to speak negatively about people when they aren't around. An environment where everyone trashes each other behind their backs isn't going to help anyone wake up. It will quickly become toxic. The Buddha was clear within his ancient community that such a cultural environment would always lead to harmful outcomes, and that individuals should strive to shift the way they speak about each other in such settings so as not to feed a toxic culture.

Speaking When Necessary

When is my voice needed? How do I pick the right time to express myself? Obviously, this is a relative guideline, not meant to get us into a debate about whether it's actually ever truly necessary to speak. On a silent meditation retreat, one of the main insights we have is how often we speak just to fill space and not feel bored. If we recognize how much of our speech is really just commuter's chatter, a need to fill up awkward space, it can lead us to use our language more precisely, more effectively. If we don't tweet every single thing we think, then our words have much more power.

This final guideline also refers to figuring out if it is our place to speak in difficult situations, to share difficult truths or feelings, or to offer difficult feedback. Given that the truth can hurt, we should think about the timing and context for speaking. Sometimes it's not the right time, and sometimes you're just not the right person. You are not always the one with the credible voice required to speak truth to power.

For example, if you are at a friend's house for a holiday, and notice aggressive and dysfunctional family behavior, it might be overstepping your bounds to say something. You're a guest, not a member of the family. But at your own family's table, it might be a misguided attempt at compassion if you remain silent, and the real bravery is in speaking up, saying what you think, gently but firmly. Contemplating timing and context is everything in terms of determining whether or not it is necessary for you to speak. The bodhisattva realizes that all beings want to be seen as being right, but that it's much more important to be helpful. This is quite a painful lesson to learn, especially when we long for some kind of acknowledgment that we are, in fact, seeing a situation clearly, and especially when we think our voice could ease unnecessary suffering.

Given the messy miracles of a life equipped with ears and vocal cords, and all the technology at our disposal, communication is an awkward human dance that will only get increasingly awkward as technology advances. There is nothing like human communication to remind us that we are each living within our own unique subjective experience, each dwelling distinctly in our own mind, yet trying to share a world with many other commuters. Remembering how difficult it is to understand another person's subjective experience and how difficult it is to transmit our own ineffable experience will provide us with the gentleness and compassion to actually allow ourselves to make mistakes in communication.

I have to admit that, even though I speak a lot in public, I have always had an anxiety (a manageable anxiety, but anxiety nonetheless) about expressing myself. Speaking more and more hasn't made this anxiety go away; rather, it's just given me the opportunity to get intimate with my fears about communicating. I spend a fair amount of time wondering if I will say the wrong thing tonight in front of students, confusing or offending people, especially when sharing some supposedly "high and mighty" spiritual teachings. Speaking in public is always a form of tough love, because when you do make a mistake, you hear about it immediately, and from multiple vantage points. At the same time, I've always wanted to be myself when communicating, not shying away from exploring the cultural and political implications of the dharma, and using irony and a sense of humor whenever I can get away with it. I use irony because the act of being human is inherently funny, so the practice of communication should always be laced with a healthy sense of humor. Stand-up comedians and Buddhist teachers both understand this truth.

Listening and speaking have been a great practice. Returning to and reflecting on the above guidelines, especially when I am wary of a difficult conversation, has been invaluable. Still, I am definitely not an expert; in fact, I would probably only rank myself as a yellow-belt communicator, even after years of practicing the martial art of listening.

If we want to make expression a true relational practice, then we need *sangha*, or community. *Sangha* is not just about hanging out with other meditators—it's about building a network of relationships where other people are trying to be mindful like we are, and so also understand and forgive the difficulties involved in these practices. If we have at least a few partners who are also studying communication, then we have the trusting environment we need in order for our practice to grow.

7

SPIRITUAL BYPASSING
What Emptiness Means and What It Doesn't

Spiritual bypassing often adopts a rationale based on using absolute truth to deny or disparage relative truth.

—JOHN WELWOOD

Returning to the subject of living within awareness, we should discuss further the unconditional aspect of awakened mind. It is said that the best way to connect with unconditional or ultimate *bodhicitta* is to connect with emptiness. *Shunyata* in Sanskrit, the study of emptiness becomes relevant when we start to grapple with the reality of just how deeply we grasp on to narratives about our experience. While the concept has several names and is employed differently within the many different Buddhist philosophical schools, the basic point is to examine how reality is actually "empty" of, or lacking, many of the false narratives that the confused mind attributes to it.

The different schools of Buddhist philosophy consider many arguments about the nature of mind and reality in an attempt to deconstruct harmful or confused views. They do this because confused views always eventually lead to destructive actions. These philosophical systems, taken together, operate sort of like the spinal column of the various schools or lineages of practice in Buddhism. While the schools of Buddhist practice go by names like Theravada or Zen or Tantra, the systems of Buddhist philosophy go by names like the Atomists or the Mind-Only system.* These different bodies of philosophy and argumentation are often the skeletal views underlying the various practices we engage in, like meditation and ethics. Each of these philosophical systems approaches the concept of emptiness in a slightly different context, addressing different metaphysical questions and employing slightly different language in order to investigate a certain false view that obstructs perception. Whenever the word "empty" is used, it always refers to the need to deconstruct a problematic story line about reality, the need to release ourselves from the mistaken ideas of a confused and grasping mind.

Emptiness never refers to a nihilistic negation of experience itself (sometimes the word is misguidedly seen as referring to some kind of "void" or black hole for the soul). If human beings recognize emptiness, it's not that they stop having experiences. Rather, they start experiencing things fully, vividly, and directly, without mistaken filters. Thus, emptiness is usually used in conjunction with another word—luminosity—to describe the rich potency that comes from seeing life clearly, empty of false constructs. In other words, if we let go of our confining narratives about what holding a flower means, we end up enjoying the flower much more. This is emptiness-luminosity.

In one early philosophical system, called *Sautrantika*,[†] emptiness is explored to demonstrate that our tendency to generalize our experiences out of convenience never quite holds up to scrutiny.

---

*Called *Vaibashika* and *Yogacara*, respectively, in Sanskrit.
[†] Literally, this means something like the "followers of sutra," or the original discourses of the Buddha.

The way we try to put people into generic categories, like queer or straight, always falls flat, especially when it becomes a lazy excuse for not investigating the real person standing in front of us. Every single moment is a specific, snowflakelike arising; each experience is unique. When we begin to generalize, we stop perceiving specificity, and when we stop perceiving specifically, we stop seeing clearly. When you argue with your partner over dishes in the sink, for example, you might say something out of frustration like, "You always leave them there!" But that "always" is just a generalization. In the realm of phenomena, nothing is always happening. That word, "always," only serves to create a defense against examining the present moment directly, in its specificity. It might not be the first time your partner has left dishes in the sink, but it's also impossible that it's always the case.

When generalizations turn into painful cultural stereotypes and biases, those biased narratives disrupt our ability to see each event as individual, which interrupts our ability to intelligently and compassionately respond to what's happening now. In many cases, our generalizations cause real harm, like somebody shooting a person who looks "suspicious" because he fits a racial profile. Generalization is what leads to oppression. Deconstructing our generalizations is the only way to overcome bias. This is where studying emptiness is intended to lead us—toward the cessation of prejudice.

In another philosophical system, Mind-Only, emptiness refers to the lack of any true separation between perceiver and perceived, or subject and object, which we discussed in the chapter on karma. From the perspective of Mind-Only, which is the underlying philosophy of a great deal of the Shambhala teachings, emptiness serves as a reminder that chasing after home through the objects we experience, while avoiding our own awareness, simply will not work, because we as subjects are "empty" or lacking separation from the objects that our mind perceives. From the standpoint of Mind-Only, when we eat salmon, we don't really experience the salmon as something "out there." We only feel our mind tasting the salmon, inseparable from our awareness. Thus, we need to treat subject and object in a holistic way, not as isolated things.

In another system, *madyamaka* (middle-way) philosophy, emptiness refers to the inability to isolate events and phenomena from one another. This is where the most popular understanding of the notion of interdependence comes from. From this viewpoint, we remember that our actions affect others all the time. This understanding of emptiness overcomes our libertarian tendencies to view the actions of our life as separate, with no effect on others. What we do in the United States directly affects what happens in Canada and Mexico, despite the lines we created in order to claim that we are separate nations. In this way, emptiness is the flip side of the coin of interdependence. If everything is connected, then no event can be isolated.

In the middle-way system, emptiness also refers to the inadequacy of conceptual or linguistic labels to accurately signal or point to direct experience, the lack of a true relationship between the languages we use to signify an experience and the actual experience signified. This is very similar to the thinking of many twentieth-century Western poststructuralist philosophers. From this point of view, the narrative or story line that we use to describe events is always an approximation of signifiers, not a direct experience. As one of my mentors, Acharya Gaylon Ferguson, likes to say, we receive no real nourishment from just saying the word "pear." The word "pear" only points sloppily to the memory of actually tasting one. Whatever way we try to signify "pear" fails to stand in for the actual experience of eating one. When we solidify a narrative about pears and then replay the narrative as a recurring story line in our mind, we actually slip further and further away from a real pear. The further we move from reality, the more we suffer, because eventually we forget what a pear is altogether.

No matter what the approach, the study of emptiness always has the same punch line, which can be summarized in a two-word mantra: LET GO. LET GO. LET GO.

The purpose of letting go is to release our fixation on narratives that stop us from fully opening to the present moment as it is. When we open to the present moment as it is, we relax and tune our mental radio back into the ultimate, unconditioned aspect of *bodhicitta*. Why do we want to be in touch with openness? Simply to make ourselves more available to our human relationships. For the bodhisattva, relationships are where the rubber meets the road. Relationships are what happen when we stop telling stories about the people we know, and start interacting with them directly in the present moment.

Studying emptiness can lead us down two roads. On the first road, emptiness becomes a view that reminds us to stay open and not take ourselves too seriously. Here, emptiness becomes a kind of protection for our path, a philosophical amulet that reminds us not to fixate on ideology to the point where we become materialistic about our ideas. If we take emptiness as a constant reminder to let go of fixation, and treat its various philosophies as a series of methods for interrogating the conceptual barriers we erect between ourselves and others, emptiness leads to a great capacity for love. Studying emptiness can help us to hold our own story lines in a kind of holographic space, which is where true creativity is possible. The image within a holograph is beautiful and meaningful, but not solid. That's the best way to approach the narratives of your own life. This way of working with emptiness softens the hard edges of our mind and lets us experience the curiosity that comes from not turning reality into a series of black-and-white, all-or-nothing propositions. When we make everything about black and white, friend and foe, right and wrong, we turn our ideas into concrete prisons that cannot adequately prepare us for the fluidity of life. Studying emptiness allows us to see that there are multiple subjectivities happening at the same time, and that our subjective experience is not universal truth.

Seeing emptiness, we don't have to fixate on our idea as the only one that matters. This is utterly key to becoming a good communicator, because it allows us to see other points of view. It also helps us to cultivate the patience to deal with disagreements without freaking out and hardening into a tyrant.

On the second road, however, studying emptiness leads to a much darker place. Here, it becomes a spiritual trap, an analytic poison, a kind of linguistic shield. Unfortunately, it's possible to use Buddhist philosophy as a way to avoid being touched by our emotions, which is 180 degrees in the wrong direction. If all we do is deconstruct ideas without engaging in the details of life fully, then emptiness simply becomes a way to win an argument, to perpetually play devil's advocate. If we learn the philosophy of emptiness without attending fully to the details of our human relationships, we will walk around deconstructing everything to the point of paralysis, and lose our ability to engage with people. Instead of learning how to listen well, we will just learn how to argue that the act of listening doesn't really matter because it is all "empty" anyway.

John Welwood coined the phrase "spiritual bypassing" to refer to this dangerous way of using spiritual teachings to sidestep the difficult parts of our journey through relationships. Sadly, much of the ancient language of Buddhism is too easily interpreted in translation to facilitate an escapist and nihilistic point of view. If emptiness is used as a linguistic shield to escape experience, it becomes a poisonous bypass, a way to try to get around dealing with the discomforts of learning to live in our awareness. When Chogyam Trungpa Rinpoche spoke of this harmful tendency, he called it "*shunyata* poisoning."

At first glance, it doesn't seem like numbing out with intellectual defenses is a very good painkiller. Morphine or vodka seem like much better choices. But, often, the narratives we cling to can be a remarkable anesthesia to suppress feeling what we don't want to feel. With spiritual bypassing, "emptiness" itself becomes a new narrative to which we cling. However, the purpose of studying emptiness is not to create a new and improved story line but to liberate us from stuck narratives about ourselves and others.

Within the Tibetan Tantric tradition there is a beautiful visual metaphor for misunderstanding spiritual teachings in this way; for becoming imprisoned rather than liberated by them. In the darkest prison of the mind, all of the walls of our jail cell are made out of spiritual texts and teachings that have become rigid and dogmatic. Even the doors and windows that once brought fresh air have been sealed by texts. The trickiest prison is always an internal one, and the trickiest internal prison is always a spiritual one. Once imprisoned, we can no longer access the fresh perspectives that human relationships bring.

Spiritual bypassing is an idea that hits home for me in a way that is not very easy to accept. Below, I've traced out some theoretical examples of how spiritual bypassing might manifest itself. Hopefully, these can allow us to laugh a little at ourselves as much as they offer challenges to our sense of how genuinely we are practicing. All of them come from either my own experience or the stories of fellow practitioners or students. With any luck, we have a sense of humor about them. I call them "I Might Be Spiritually Bypassing If . . ."

- I have credit card, mortgage, or student loan debt and I avoid opening the envelope, because the numbers on the statement are just abstract symbols, all "empty" anyway.
- I avoid taking care of my body through daily nutrition and exercise, because the body is "just a vessel."
- I refuse to make my bed for exactly the same reason.
- I shy away from any political discussion because the mere thought of actually holding any political positions strikes me as "dualistic."
- I know what the phrase "*Madhyamaka Sautrantika-Svatantrika*" means, but if during tea break at a meditation workshop someone asks how I'm doing, I freak out on him.
- I am completely in love with my spiritual teacher, but wish all of my fellow students would just go away.
- I avoid pursuing creative or entrepreneurial projects that might benefit people, because whatever I might accomplish is "illusory."
- I experience loss, heartbreak, or grief but attempt to dismiss feelings such as sadness, anger, and loneliness as not "truly existing," rather than bringing mindfulness and compassion to the necessary grieving process.
- I sabotage the process of forging intimacy with potential friends or lovers, because I know that any new relationship I enter is just "impermanent" anyway. Why should I call him again? We're all just gonna die, eventually.

Do any of these sound familiar? As Welwood points to in his work, these examples share a common characteristic. They all use some partial insight from teachings on ultimate truth as a means to justify avoiding relational truth.

Sadly, this isn't just a modern phenomenon. Sometimes, in

ancient texts, relative truth is unfortunately relegated to a form of second-class citizenship, treated as a kind of mirage that only "confused" people see. But from the standpoint of the Shambhala teachings, which attempt to move us toward an awakening that fully embraces the details of life in the world, relational truth is actually our prime concern along the journey, because relational truth is always the final arena of our practice. As Dr. Martin Luther King, Jr., said in another context, our entire universe is structured in a relational manner.

Even if we completely realized the ultimate truth of emptiness, we would still have to wake up the next morning and deal with the relationships that make up our life, one simple step at a time. This does not mean that our meditation practice or philosophical study don't matter—they matter quite a lot. But if we only focus on philosophy, or only focus on what deep state of meditative concentration we have achieved, we might just bypass the truly beautiful work of our relationships. Glimpsing emptiness should move us toward, not away from, the details of relationships. After we deconstruct our false views, we are left on the doorstep of our real life, ready to deal with our families, our friends, our coworkers, and, eventually, all beings.

8

A BODHISATTVA'S BOUNDARIES

Compassion, Idiot Compassion,
and Knowing the Difference

The ideal figure of the relational journey, the bodhisattva, can seem like quite an imposing one to emulate. In traditional Buddhism, stories of archetypal bodhisattvas serve a cultural function not unlike many of the comic-book superheroes of our Western culture. When you see a statue of Avalokiteshvara or Tara, male and female bodhisattvas of compassion, you may just as well imagine them with S's on their chest, or wearing a Wonder Woman outfit.

If you commit to staying present with human relationships, if you take the bodhisattva vow, you are taking on quite a formidable task. The traditional texts depicting the bodhisattva's journey don't shy away from intense descriptions of the burden we take on in order to help others. One bodhisattva chant, called the Four Great Vows, originating in the Japanese Zen tradition asks us to proclaim, "Sentient beings are numberless. I vow to save them all."

That statement is not only logistically impossible, it's logically absurd. Even if it made sense given the rules of logic and karma (something like: "There are SO damn many sentient beings! I vow to HELP every single one I come into contact with"), it would still be a massive undertaking. Never mind becoming Superman—sometimes it feels like the tradition is asking us to become Atlas, the Greek god charged with holding the cosmos aloft. In one of my favorite animated movies, *The Incredibles*, Mr. Incredible is a superhero with a bad case of burnout. "No matter how many times you save the world, it always manages to get itself in jeopardy again," Mr. Incredible says anxiously. "Sometimes I wish it would just *stay* saved, you know?"

While it may seem overwhelming, almost everyone I meet considers the bodhisattva vow—the intention to dedicate one's life to helping others and alleviating suffering in whatever way we can—an inspiring ideal. There is never one way to work with such a vow, and so many different livelihood and relationship paths that we could take to benefit others. A painter can be a bodhisattva just as much as a president or pope can. To have such an organizing principle for one's life, for one's relationships, and for one's labor, is tremendously empowering. With such a guiding principle, we move beyond just going through the motions of an isolating commute. Such a vow gives us a sense of purpose and energy for the projects we engage in and the relationships we cultivate.

The bodhisattva ideal is especially inspiring when so many aspects of our civilization seem to be moving away from compassion, generosity, and care for others. In our world, Atlas has quite literally shrugged, and the bizarro bodhisattvas of greed seem to have killed off most of our most compassionate superheroes. "Greed is good," *Wall Street*'s Gordon Gekko famously proclaimed, giving a huge middle finger to bodhisattvas everywhere. We live bombarded by the cultural mantras of selfishness and narcissism, echoing everywhere on invisible speakers, mantras that we know in our hearts are false. Greed is not good—as a mantra, "just looking out for #1" is demonstrably damaging, both psychologically and ethically. It turns a healthy self-awareness into a blinding self-absorption and crushes our empathy. All we end up accumulating is more anxiety, because the objects we accumulate are unstable, and begin to decay the moment we take them into our possession. Greed intensifies the desperation of our commute, while generosity opens us up to what is in front of us, and allows us to relax at home in our own awareness, available for others, too. I am not sure if we need more not-for-profit organizations, but we definitely need more not-for-profit humans, and that is precisely what the bodhisattva agrees to become, because he knows happiness depends on overcoming self-obsession.

If we are going to take on the bodhisattva's journey, we have to find a way to humanize these idealistic archetypes, to make the workload more reasonable for us mere mortals. Otherwise, we will quickly associate the bodhisattva path with a weighty obligation, a form of bitter martyrdom, a new way to beat ourselves up. This road only leads to disheartenment. Discouraged by both our own limitations and by the troubled state of the world, we might look around us and begin to wonder why we ever signed up to help anyone anyway, when narcissism seems to be much more culturally lucrative. We might not shrug off the entire cosmos, but we will shrug off the burden of our human relationships, shrinking back into isolation and self-preservation.

To avoid burnout, we need a much more balanced approach to the bodhisattva's journey. Most of all, if we are going to make the path workable, we need to spot the obstacle that Chogyam Trungpa Rinpoche called "idiot compassion."

Spiritual bypassing often involves using ultimate truth as an excuse for suppressing our human emotions. In a similar way, idiot compassion involves using the bodhisattva's idealistic mandate to help others as a means to avoid what we are actually feeling. But there is always something our emotions can show us about the present moment. When we are able to rest in the gap—feeling our emotions without reacting to them carelessly—they become a kind of Spidey Sense, a trustworthy radar. They constantly lend us information about how the present moment strikes us, information that we can learn to apply intuitively and skillfully. Anger always has something to tell us. But with idiot compassion, we turn the bodhisattva identity into a kind of impossible ideal, and then hide out in that constructed notion of compassion. We hold on to some Xeroxed image of a saint, an old picture of how a bodhisattva would respond to conflict or confusion, and the Xerox prevents us from responding skillfully to the situation in front of us. Idiot compassion is what happens when we turn the bodhisattva path into a kind of super heroic cocoon. While we are trying to mimic that ideal, we ignore what our emotions are telling us, losing the intelligence that those feelings can offer in knowing how to respond to each unique situation.

Sometimes, the most compassionate thing we can do is say no. Every once in a while, the best way to help another person is to yell at him. This is called an act of wrathful compassion, and it's why many traditional bodhisattvas are depicted carrying iconographic weaponry in Himalayan art, displaying a force that is not caught up within hatred, but that sets firm boundaries which a confused mind cannot cross.

For example, let's say you let someone walk all over you in a contract negotiation because you think you are supposed to be patient and accommodating with that person's desires. "A bodhisattva wouldn't get angry," you say, taking an overly sweet tone during the negotiation. Inside, you feel hurt and disrespected, but you don't say "that's not fair" or push back because you think you are supposed to take a more passive approach, conflating passivity with the bodhisattva's attitude of openness. You project a peaceful image of some ever-smiling Buddha in your mind, becoming someone who pays no attention to how he is valued. When you sign the contract, you deeply resent what you've agreed to. The work that follows is uninspired, and everyone eventually suffers for it. Or maybe a friend asks to borrow money, and you get the sinking feeling as you give it to him that he is going to use it to feed an addiction, furthering his codependence, but you give it to him anyway, enabling his suffering. Codependence and interdependence are two very different things.

If your work involves helping others through teaching, mental health counseling, or any of the myriad activities where we work with others directly, you might experience little moments of idiot compassion all the time, moments where you flee from the present, hiding within your "Superman" ideals of what it means to be seen as a "good" teacher who is always available to every student, a "good" therapist who always provides the most useful feedback, or a "good" parent who never loses her cool and is always on call when her kids need her. These ideals form a cocoon, an unattainable self-image, and from within one's own cocoon, it's not possible to be very helpful.

There are countless tendencies toward idiot compassion that we can begin to notice in ourselves. I think Chogyam Trungpa Rinpoche used the phrase "idiot compassion" humorously, not harshly, not only because he wanted us to be clear about what trips us up along the bodhisattva path, but also so that we might have a sense of humor about the messy task of trying to "help" anyone. Calling something "idiot compassion" is not meant to be a dagger of reproach. For me, keeping this idea in mind allows me to more lightheartedly notice the moments when I think I'm being helpful but I'm really just avoiding what I'm feeling and enabling more confusion. Idiot compassion is actually a good problem for us to have, because at the very least it means we are trying to be compassionate. We are just confused about how to be effective in that pursuit.

It is important to be inspired by the qualities of other compassionate people, but to be a real bodhisattva, we have to let go of fixation on images of what a bodhisattva necessarily does in each situation. We do this by working with our emotions as they come up, and listening to the people in front of us. We can open patiently, while still maintaining boundaries that allow us to conserve our personal resources of time and energy in a sustainable manner, in order to avoid burnout along the path of helping others. The bottom line is that the bodhisattva is still very much on the path of self-awareness and self-care. Otherwise, you just become a martyr-sattva.

FOUR TYPES OF IDIOT COMPASSION

Here are four possible examples of idiot compassion, each of which undermines and distorts the meaning of true compassion.

Being a Doormat

With doormat compassion, we stamp "welcome" on our foreheads, idealizing stories we've heard about how a great being should be able to be patient with anger and aggression from others, and should be able to handle any outrage. We feel, in our fixation, that a bodhisattva should put up with anything. So we decide to silently grin and bear interactions with very difficult people, taking on all the burden of their terror.

There is a famous story in my tradition of an ancient teacher from Bengal, now Bangladesh, named Atisha. Atisha was one of the major pioneers of Mahayana Buddhism, who brought large bodies of teachings on the bodhisattva path to Tibet in the eleventh century. The story says that he had an assistant, known as the Bengali Tea Boy, who was ridiculously annoying. Sometimes we have a hard time working with a person with whom everybody else manages to get along, and we can't believe it. Sometimes we find someone supremely challenging and find out that pretty much everybody else agrees with us. The Bengali Tea Boy was supposedly the latter type. Perhaps he just had a difficult time, as many people do, picking up on subtle social cues, or he just felt shame about his service job and longed for a higher station in life, and so felt that he needed to prove his intelligence all the time, consuming all available space in any conversation. When he served tea, it felt like you were doing him a favor by putting up with him, not the other way around. One of the main marks of a bodhisattva throughout ancient teachings is the ability to remain remarkably calm in difficult situations. So, the story goes that Atisha, wanting to stay on his toes and keep his training in patience strong, invited the Tea Boy to accompany him on the long and grueling trip to Tibet. That seems like an act of patience many of us would be unwilling to bear.

Inspired by this story, we have a little joke in the Shambhala community that the person in your life or work environment who is super annoying is your Bengali Tea Boy, regardless of where the person is from or the person's age or gender. It's meant to be an endearing term of annoyance (if there is such a thing), a role we've all played ourselves from time to time.

While this Tea Boy story is extremely well intentioned and brings needed humor and validation to working with difficult people, two parts of the tale have always bothered me. First, people often forget the story's ending. It's said that when Atisha arrived in Tibet after putting up with the Tea Boy during the whole treacherous trip, he realized that there were plenty of annoying people in this new country as well. In fact, there are plenty of annoying people everywhere—it is the necessary result of multiple beings attempting to share the same space, the friction that results from distinct subjective experiences rubbing up against each other. What Atisha realized was he didn't really need to drag the Tea Boy along for the sole purpose of furthering his own patience practice; he would have plenty of new opportunities to do so. The lesson I take from the story is that we will always have opportunities to work with people we perceive as annoying and difficult, and we don't necessarily need to ride shotgun with every Tea Boy just to feel compassionate. Not every Tea Boy has to be your Tea Boy. Taking on all the difficult relationships you encounter may trigger and deplete you in ways that make it hard for you to show up for your other human relationships. That's not really compassionate, and it's definitely not smart.

The second problem with the idea that you always have to stay in difficult situations with people who trigger you is that it ignores what might be best for the annoying person, the one the bodhisattva is supposed to care about, after all! If our Tea Boy never has any boundaries set, if we never tell him what we are willing to take and what we aren't willing to tolerate, then the Tea Boy never learns how to be aware of his own actions and behaviors. It's quite possible that each Tea Boy remains a Tea Boy because he doesn't ever realize that he's wiping his feet all over the doormat of your humanity.

The doormat version of idiot compassion always involves allowing ourselves to feel walked all over in the name of idealizing what it means to be patient with another person's aggressive behavior. It's an unwillingness to face the uncomfortable truth that it's okay to feel angry and irritated.

Being Popular

No one, not a political leader and not even a great bodhisattva, can be universally liked. But we live in a society of opinion polling and social networking scores, one that encourages us to maximize "likes" and acclaim. The social anxiety of existing in a world where popularity is statistically quantifiable, where we can literally count "likes" and read our approval ratings daily, can lead to a lot of idiot compassion. We have this strange idea that being a decent person means that nobody is ever upset with us. But if you examine every greatly compassionate person throughout human history, they always managed to piss off at least some people, sometimes quite a lot of people. Some of the greatest bodhisattvas in human history drove the powers that be crazy, because that was the only way to enact compassion. For example, if we are going to solve the crisis of global warming, some politicians need to be willing to sacrifice their short-term popularity and financial safety to make tough long-term choices that will make our society more sustainable. They probably will not get credit for doing so.

With the idiot compassion of popularity, we feel the very bodily fear of being disliked, which every human encounters at some point. However, if we are unwilling to stay present with that discomfort, we cave in to the scary thought that our popularity might be replaced by infamy or, even worse, anonymity. We become susceptible to manipulation, because even the threat that somebody might speak ill of us or "un-follow" us causes us to cut deals with people in order to remain on their good side.

For the last few years, I've noticed this peculiar phenomenon on my social media pages. When I share a post or tweet, it is often the vague and generically positive thoughts that get the most "likes" immediately. If I make a statement that sounds more controversial or political, I feel the immediate anxiety that perhaps my intelligence, as well as my standing as a well-intentioned thinker, is about to be attacked. Caving in to this fear, rather than staying present with it, would lead to always trying to calculate the path to maximum popularity. This would be like opening an organic restaurant, but then at the last minute deciding to only serve cotton candy because you know all the kids like it. That restaurant might get popular, but it wouldn't be good for anyone.

When we are able to stay present with the internal discomfort created by the idea that somebody else might be mad at us, we end up becoming a bodhisattva with tremendous integrity. We end up building confidence that we can say what we think and mean what we say, more and more often. This kind of integrity and dignity become contagious, and in the end, even if somebody doesn't agree with us, that person at least respects us for our dedication to living by our principles.

Making Nice

What happens when we are trying to be present for a conflict between others? "Making nice" is the version of idiot compassion that comes about when we cannot stay with the uncomfortable truth of disharmony between people we care about, and instead feel a need to squash or quell conflict. Human relationships have friction and conflict built into them. It is often the case that insight lies within disagreement. When we don't suppress disagreement, we might learn more about where everyone stands and what matters to all the different subjective beings involved. Within the disclosure of multiple perspectives, we may learn something new about the issues involved.

When we rush to try to create harmony, it is often because disharmony makes us deeply uncomfortable, not because we are actually trying to help bring about clarity and insight. This tendency could be even more pressing if we grew up in an arena or household of conflict. We end up saying things to the people who are fighting like, "We need to work this out." Projecting our needs onto somebody else's disagreement is very manipulative and makes it impossible for the parties involved to come to an understanding of what they want and need for themselves. It may also lead us to draw false equivalences between people's behavior, where we just assume that both sides have equal truth because we are unwilling to accept that there might be very valid grievances at play, and that the people involved might never agree to a solution. What we should be saying instead is, "What do you really want here? Do you want to work this out, or do you want to go your separate ways?"

Giving Away Everything

In this version of idiot compassion, we suppress our own needs, feeling like we should just give away everything we have all the time. To be a saint, we should generously offer all our time, all our money, all our energy. The problem here is that generosity is a two-way street. Even if you were to dedicate your life to the benefit of all beings, you should never forget that you are one of those beings! When the lifelong practice of generosity is considered as only an external act, it bends and twists into martyrdom. Many of us hide out in service work, and suppress the uncomfortable feelings that arise when attention turns to taking care of ourselves. If we serve others because we are afraid to be with ourselves, then we need to ask the question: What are we really offering to them except our self-avoidance?

I have often noticed that when I give time or energy to somebody who requests my help, I need to set clear boundaries around what I am able to offer, and under what conditions I'm able to offer it. This is not because I am trying to take some Gordon

Gekko approach to life, but rather, it's a realization that we all need to calculate the resources we can offer today in order to be able to offer ourselves to others again tomorrow. I have also found that clarifying what I can offer when others request my help allows them to be clear about valuing my time and energy. This clarity helps everyone. When I am able to balance generosity with clarity about what I need, my own energy becomes much more sustainable, and the result is that I can actually offer more. If we burn out, we help nobody, and we actually might end up romanticizing destructive tendencies as some kind of spiritual narrative. Thinking that we have to always burn our candle at both ends in order to benefit others is perhaps the greatest idiot compassion of all.

In this way, Sakyong Mipham Rinpoche has been a great example to me. He seems to have an incredible amount of discipline with the usage of his personal energy and the many demands upon his time. Because his commitment to self-care seems so unwavering, he literally seems to grow younger as he ages, and therefore is able to stay present with others over a longer and more fruitful life span. This is very different from somebody like Dr. Martin Luther King, Jr.

One physician estimated that Dr. King, who died at age thirty-nine, had the heart muscle of a sixty-year-old man when he was autopsied, because he refused to take care of himself. While his example is immensely inspiring in so many ways, and while he is one of our American bodhisattva superheroes, one wonders, if he wasn't assassinated, how much longer he could have kept up that pace. One could wonder the same about Chogyam Trungpa Rinpoche, who died at forty-seven. I hope future Dr. Kings and Trungpa Rinpoches live beyond a hundred, and the only path to that outcome is if future bodhisattvas treat generosity as a practice that includes self-care.

THINKING BIGGER THAN "ME"

Rather than thinking of the bodhisattva path as one of forsaking oneself for others, we could think of the phrase "equalizing self and other." From the perceptual standpoint of subject-object, this balance helps us to overcome the objectification of others as a means to further our own pleasure. From this harmony, a direct and situationally appropriate empathy grows. We relate to others based on thoughtful principles applied to specific situations, not on black-and-white rules. Hopefully, we can always find ways to stay open and generous, but without depleting our own life-force energy in the process.

At the same time, the imperative of bodhisattva examples throughout history illustrates that somebody always has to be the first person to think bigger than the cocoon of "me." Where would we be without the beings who have stepped up and been examples of the possibility of opening one's heart and putting others first? These beings always have to be willing to get stepped on or taken advantage of in order to stretch the imagination of those who live in the anxiety that self-absorption produces, those who don't think it's possible to open up at all.

In the "greed is good" world, everybody shrinks away from helping each other. In this frame of mind, all relationships become transactional and commodified. We say things like, "I'm only going to help you if you help me," or "I'm only going to deal with you if and when I know that you won't hurt me." Somebody has to go a little further to stretch her heartmind open and say, "You know what, I might get hurt here. I might get taken advantage of sometimes. I might get my heart broken." But if nobody makes the first move into a kind of compassionate magnanimity, then the anti-bodhisattvas will always win.

If we learn to live in our awareness a bit more, then we also realize that there is no permanent damage that another human being can do to our true home. Of course, we must work carefully with instances of trauma, but when we realize that our awareness is an accommodating space, not a damaged "thing," it becomes safe to extend ourselves a little ways beyond our comfort zone. Ideally, with the obstacle of idiot compassion in mind, we can set clear but porous boundaries for what we are willing to deal with in relationships.

We should also remember that there is no such thing as permanence and apply this to whatever temporary boundaries we set in our relationships. Seeing impermanence can grant us the insight to never shut the door on anyone forever. I remember a conversation I once had with my father. A long relationship had recently ended, and it happened to be with someone whom I had experienced as a major Tea Boy for quite a long time. In an attempt to create good boundaries, I said something along the lines of "good riddance." I don't think my voice was particularly harsh in that moment, but it was clear that I thought the parting of ways was a good thing. Dad cut me off midsentence. "You know, Eth, I really don't think about these things that way anymore. I think that every conflict we have is just a little blip on the radar screen. Everybody we've ever known and loved, we're going to know them again and again and again." While I'm not sure I believe that we will necessarily encounter the same beings again, the reminder is undeniably powerful. The bodhisattva never abandons any relationship permanently. To avoid idiot compassion, we will have to set boundaries and say "not now" to some of our most difficult relationships. That's the only way our practice can evolve. But the bodhisattva never says never. This vast view of time, this willingness to never give up on anyone, is a super heroic trait of forgiveness that any of us can start to embody.

9

EYE TO EYE

The Student–Teacher Relationship

VANESSA HUXTABLE: Rudy, what are you gonna do in life with a fourth-grade education?
RUDY HUXTABLE: Teach third grade!

—*The Cosby Show*

I s it possible to become fully aware and awake without guidance? One of the most important relationships we can have along this path is our relationship with teachers. Given the premise that we cannot traverse this path in isolation, that our universe is relational, we should examine the relationships that help guide us along our journey. These quickly become some of the biggest questions on students' minds: Do I need a teacher, and how do I find one? Where do I get the most useful instruction? How do I know if I need mentorship, advice, and feedback? And what is a guru?

Chogyam Trungpa Rinpoche was asked once if we need teachers in order to complete the path of awakening. His answer was actually very subtle. He said we didn't need them, but that it would be a lot harder without them. That seems like a balanced response.

First of all, without any guidance, finding the right instructions for practice, the right books to study, and the right retreats to go on can make us feel like we're getting lost in an overcrowded jungle of random Google searches. We need some help to even know where to look for help!

The first thing I say to any friend who is really trying to practice and study Buddhism in a committed manner is that it is helpful to have somebody to be accountable to for your practice and path. Accountability is a key word. This is not just someone to feel guilty toward when life gets tough, your practice becomes filled with obstacles, and you can't seem to find the time to work with your mind. The point of accountability is much more positive and supportive than some form of regular confession. Being accountable is about having somebody in your corner who is not just an extra on the set of your life, but someone who cares that you are trying to cultivate your heart and mind, trying to develop compassionate principles in your human relationships. Without someone to be accountable to, it is very easy to forget why we are practicing at all when the going gets tough.

With some kind of guiding presence in our corner, our path becomes anchored by supportive relationships, and it becomes easier to remember to follow through on the intentions we set. With someone to be accountable to, we tend to get sidetracked less often, and when we do get sidetracked, it becomes a moment to learn from rather than a guiltfest that derails us. With the anchor of guidance, we actually learn from our obstacles. Without guidance, obstacles often just stop us in our tracks.

Obviously, having peers and a community, or *sangha*, who are also on the path is quite helpful. Friends support each other's progress, and also bring the needed social component to the journey. We practice together, we remind each other of the development we are trying to accomplish, and then we hopefully have fun together, too. The fun part is crucial. The best dance parties

I've ever been to are the ones thrown by people who just spent a long time meditating together.

It's important to note that we all bring quite a lot of baggage to the discussion of a teacher, and we need to allow space to explore our histories around trust and disappointment in earlier guiding relationships like these. Whenever we talk about looking up to somebody for spiritual mentorship and guidance, especially on a path like Buddhism, which has such a psychological emphasis, we bring with us all the previous expectations, projections, transferences, and disappointments that we've had with parents, elders, mentors, therapists, professors, priests, politicians, and any other form of leadership you could imagine.

It is also interesting to discuss how we craft a relationship to spiritual teachers within our Hollywood culture of celebrity, especially in the era of reality TV, where people are often looked up to for little or no meaningful reason at all. Sometimes, when Sakyong Mipham Rinpoche, my guru, teaches, he sits on a throne above everyone else, as is done in the Tibetan tradition, because gurus are held in immensely high regard. Some people think the brocade-covered throne is a little weird (to be honest, I am one of them—not because I don't think he deserves great respect, but because the throne occasionally distances him from his audience). But if we think having a throne for a teacher who has spent his whole life cultivating compassion and learning the skills of leadership is strange, do we at least also think the spectacle of the red carpet at the Oscars is strange? The question is not whether we offer respect to people we look up to—it's more a question of who we look up to, why, and how we show them respect.

Within this celebrity culture, spiritual teachers are often placed on a very high pedestal, without a clear sense of what exact qualities have earned them that seat, and without clarity about exactly what duties are expected of them as they occupy their position. When we put teachers on a pedestal and we don't know what to expect from them except something vaguely "magical," there's only one place they can go: down. If expectations are vague and enormous, people will always fail to meet those expectations when their humanity is inevitably exposed.

The Buddhist path is about learning to inhabit our own humanity more fully. So, the people we look up to on this path should have some level of mastery of being human. From a Buddhist standpoint, the reason to put people on a pedestal is not to worship them; it's that the teachers demonstrate to us how to be human beings, "extra" ordinary human beings.

I'm assuming you are not looking to worship anyone. If you are, it's probably better to look to rock stars, because you can always hold them at a safe distance and project whatever heroic qualities you like onto them. PR teams are standing by, ready to help us with our projections. Unfortunately, worship has nothing to do with a real relationship, because it distances us from the object of worship rather than connects us to it. Worship has to do with the same kind of grasping objectification we are trying to overcome on this journey.

From the standpoint of basic goodness, though, within every mistake lies a bit of intelligence. Within worship there is a kernel of wisdom; there lie feelings of love, devotion, and commitment. It is much more difficult to travel this path without having people to look up to, people who care about our path, and especially someone to hold us accountable for our aspiration to become more decent and aware humans. Without some kind of relationship to a guiding mentor or mentors, we constantly fall back into our acquired fight-or-flight response, losing confidence quickly and caving in to every doubt that comes along.

Below is a three-part model for types of teacher relationships that originates from the Tibetan Buddhist system. Obviously, this model is greatly simplified, as every student–teacher relationship we have ever had, or might have in the study of Buddhism, has been unique in how it organically develops and what it demands of us as students. But within this traditional trio of student–teacher models, there are some ways to begin to see where we have a good support for our path, and where we might look for a new kind of relationship. It seems that, for most of us, the teacher question is not just a matter of finding one person to guide us or someone to look up to, but is actually more about examining the various ways that this sort of relationship might manifest itself in our life.

THREE TYPES OF GUIDANCE

The Instructor

The instructor is any representative, teacher, or guide from whom you receive information on teachings or practice, which you are then left to incorporate into life primarily on your own. Maybe you attend a meditation course, maybe you download teachings, or maybe your insight is sparked by inspirational quotes from somebody whose words you trust. You can receive instruction either at a distance, such as by reading a book or viewing a lecture online, or in person by attending a class or program.

Reading this book would be an example of following the instructor model, because I'm laying out ideas, yet we can't have a conversation here about anything I'm writing, nor can we discuss how any of it applies to life, directly. Instruction is all about information transmission. Personally, I am so thankful to every instructor who has ever clarified any confusion I had about a process, or better yet, made me fall in love with a subject by transmitting their love for the topic in how they teach. I'm not sure that I have a single curiosity in life that didn't become a deep passion only because I had a great instructor who was able to transmit her own passion for the subject. Unfortunately, sometimes we only recognize the rarity of good instruction later, when we are in the presence of an instructor we don't feel any connection to.

In so many aspects of life, we receive teachings in this one-directional manner, even if they come from something as simple as watching our favorite cooking show to gain ideas and inspiration for recipes. Buddhist instruction can include all aspects of the path of awakening, such as meditation, study, and the application of teachings to our work and our relationships. So, the role of the instructor is quite broad and potentially quite profound.

We should never underestimate the power of preparation and context when receiving instruction. This applies to Buddhism or to any other subject we study. In fact, one of the very first things I would say if asked what studying Buddhism has done for me is that it has made me a more curious and engaged student of everything else I study. The principles and techniques of mindfulness demonstrate that preparation and curiosity are key to learning anything. Buddhist lessons on how to show respect to a teacher have helped me to become a more respectful student of anything that I investigate. When it's time to learn, I take more time and effort to prepare than I used to. Preparation is all about familiarization; then we have to show up fully for a lesson in order to maximize the immersive aspects of mindfulness.

Even if we meet instructors in a one-directional manner, the context for receiving instructions is very important. Because an instructor can't ensure that we put the instructions we receive into practice, it's up to us to show up fully to the learning process.

One of the most interesting aspects of life in the twenty-first century is the effect of technology on our learning process. The modern world allows us to receive instructions with much greater ease than was once possible. One of the problems (and also advantages) that the exponential increase of technology presents is the drastic cheapening of the information we receive. It used to take a long journey, sometimes over dangerous mountains, to receive even basic instructions on how to work with our mind. Now we can receive such instructions—or at least the lifeless Wikipedia replica of those instructions—in a few microseconds online.

In terms of breadth of knowledge, nothing beats twenty-first-century technology. But in terms of depth, we have to consider the effects of receiving information in such a haphazard and superficial manner. My mother is a gourmet cook, for example. If I set aside time and watch and study how she makes her pecan pie, my mind is more respectful and open than if I just watch a YouTube clip—of which there are many—with instructions on how to make pie. If my mother teaches me, it is like preserving a precious gift, watching a chef prepare a dish with love rather than just moving through a mechanical exercise. If I take this view of the context, then I'm more likely to really put in the effort to follow along and receive the instructions. The next time I bake a pie, I'm baking my mother's pie, my lineage's pie. If YouTube teaches me, I probably won't even remember where the information came from in a few weeks. YouTube has no lineage.

In order to fully integrate any instruction into our experience, the teaching has to be important to us. We have to prepare for it and we have to really want it. We have to ask for it and we have to do something to earn it. The traditional analogy for working with an instructor is a student showing up thirsty with an empty cup, waiting for the cup to be filled with nourishing liquid. If we actually make an effort to clean our cup, and present ourselves to an instructor wholeheartedly, then the context for what we receive is much deeper. We also should receive instructions in the context of *sangha*, a community that shares the journey. The support of community makes the instructions we receive much more meaningful, and gives us peer support to contemplate and integrate the teachings into life and practice. Not to get all twentieth century on you, but the best way to do this is always live and in person. You can't get these things from the Internet alone.

If it's not possible to be face-to-face with other people, or even to be with them virtually, then we should at least empty our cup for instructions by creating good time and space to study and learn teachings in our own home. If we are going to listen to a meditation talk, maybe we shouldn't do that while we are also watching a TV show in the background.

While in some ways the instructor model is the most distanced way to learn from somebody, it is no less important than either of the following two teacher relationships. There is nothing like good instructions to clarify our confusion and inspire us to keep going forward along a journey with compassion and mindfulness. However, settling for only a one-way relationship in any learning process leaves us without true guidance and feedback along the path.

The Teacher/Mentor (*Kalyanamitra*)

Many people know the Sanskrit word *guru* as "teacher," but there is another, equally important definition of teacher to be found in the word *kalyanamitra*, which means either "noble mentor" or "spiritual friend."

Different Buddhist lineages explain the meaning of *kalyanamitra* very differently. However, all describe it as a highly meaningful and personal relationship, a two-way street with ample face time and an eye-to-eye offering of guidance and advice along one's path. For simplicity, I'm translating *kalyanamitra* nonliterally as "teacher/mentor," primarily because when most students say they are "looking for a teacher," it is almost always this kind of relationship that they seek.

The teacher/mentor role still requires great instructional knowledge, but the mentor also helps us delve into our individual life situations as we attempt to put the teachings into action in the dynamics of our personal life. This, after all, is the whole trick of the path of awakening, to take good instructions—which are vast, generic, and often vague in meaning—and apply them to one's own life, which is immediate, personal, and specific.

When the Buddha first taught about this type of mentorship, he talked about a space of mutual honesty and shared disclosure. He said the mentor, Mitra, keeps your secrets and also tells you his. He doesn't look down on you or abandon you in times of need. Chogyam Trungpa Rinpoche discussed it as an eye-to-eye exchange, the respectful meeting of two minds.

When we are searching for a mentor such as this, it feels very important to look for someone who knows the path—including various techniques and frameworks for teaching—very well, but who also manifests the qualities of a good listener, because the main job of any mentor is to help you discover your own insights and recognize the wisdom that arises from your own life and practice, rather than imposing her preferences on you. At the same time, a mentor may occasionally give you a gentle (or strong) push toward accountability, pointing out the places she believes you might be stuck or resisting following the intention to live in awareness. In a tradition based on Buddha nature and basic good-ness, the teacher/mentor also offers the student a feeling of "un-conditional positive regard," as the psychologist Carl Rogers said in a different context. Any mentor, and for that matter any instruc-tor or guru, should be transmitting a gentle assurance that the student can use to gain confidence in his awakened nature. A good mentor fundamentally demonstrates that, despite her issues, and despite the student's issues, there is nothing fundamentally "wrong" with anyone, no matter how stuck in karmic patterns we might be.

In my experience on both sides of this type of relationship, the presence of this sort of unconditional acceptance has always been transformative. In the words of Zen Master Shunryu Suzuki, it is this kind of relationship that makes us feel like "we are all perfect, and we could all use a little work." While that sounds contradictory, it's actually the perfect balance for progress to occur. A good mentor, through an attitude of good listening and clear intuition that helps us see where we are stuck, as well as a deep positive regard that reflects insights back to us, can make whatever work we need to do on ourselves seem, well, workable.

These kinds of mentoring relationships, whether they were explicitly Buddhist or not, have meant a great deal to me along my path as a student. Whether helping me with my formal meditation practice, or just listening to me while I was going through a difficult breakup or figuring out my career path in light of my bodhisattva vows, mentors have helped me navigate my own road home during many hard times.

I have approached things from the teacher's perspective as well. I was empowered by Sakyong Mipham Rinpoche as a senior teacher in the Shambhala lineage in 2010, a few days after my thirty-second birthday. When I studied the vow of commitment to being a senior teacher (somehow evading the fine print, I only closely read what the vow said long after I had already taken it in front of Sakyong Mipham Rinpoche), I noticed it said I was a "holder of the Shambhala teachings" and a *kalyanamitra*, a noble mentor toward others. Both of these statements felt like kind of a big deal.

The call to deepen my work in direct relationship to others as a teacher/mentor, and also to help train other teachers, felt both challenging and inspiring. I had been teaching for eight years already, and I had started the Interdependence Project, a secular Buddhist organization, with some friends, so I didn't feel completely unequipped for a leadership role. But I knew I had to really try to develop my ability to listen well. When I worked with students I knew I couldn't ever just tell them what to do even if they wanted me to; many of my students were and are older than me, with greater life experience, even if they have less experience studying and practicing the dharma. We had to navigate the path as a collaboration, but with a sense that my feedback, when given, was meaningful to them. I had to make a conscious effort to study the philosophical, psychological, and ethical teachings of my tradition—and related Western traditions—deeply and consistently. And when questions arose about applying the teachings to career, relationships, family, and whatever aspirations a student might have to help the world, I also had to avoid being overly guarded about sharing my own process in these areas as a practitioner, to the extent that it was relevant to the student's situation.

Sometimes when people ask me what it's like to be a senior teacher in a worldwide Buddhist lineage, I jokingly refer to the scene from *The Cosby Show* mentioned at the beginning of this chapter. Although the joke is a big exaggeration (sorry, Rudy, you do want a teacher with more than a fourth-grade dharmic education), it brings a little bit of lightheartedness to the idea that a teacher must be perfect or enlightened. Rather, the teacher at this stage is most helpful if she can help you stay accountable to your practice, as well as help you to form an experiential bridge between your habitual confusion and your underlying wisdom. This bridging is an unfolding process, and the best teachers always listen deeply in order to understand the process that a student is going through, because teachers know they are in process themselves, applying their practice to life just like you are. After all, all dharmic teachings initially arose from a thoughtful and mindful person looking deeply and compassionately into the lessons of his own experience. It's from this curious and attentive approach to one's own experience that systems and techniques evolve. This is always the method that will work best when we are talking about a journey of learning to inhabit our humanity fully. This constant curiosity about the process of living must be the basis for any helpful form of spiritual mentorship.

The Guru

"Guru" is a word that's best left untranslated, and is almost as ubiquitous in the English language now as the word "karma." And, just like karma, it seems equally misunderstood. In the traditions of Tibet and Shambhala, the guru is an exalted figure, a particular form of teacher who specifically guides and oversees a student's practice and study of Tantric or Vajrayana teachings. The Vajrayana teachings, and the view of "sacred world" that accompanies them, will be discussed in the book's next section.

The important thing about the word "guru" is that it denotes a much more devotional and empowered relationship than those of the first two types of teacher. While the instructor and the teacher/mentor are both worthy of great respect, the guru is the one you make a full commitment to work with for life. The idea is that at a certain point you see the possibility of fully living in your own awareness; at this point, you must commit to your own awakening, and commit to benefiting others as a bodhisattva. On this basis, taking on a guru is a matter of making yourself accountable to someone for life. It's the spiritual-teacher equivalent of getting married, and in many ways when we make the decision to commit to a guru, we make the decision for the same reasons we decide to get married. Not only do we feel great trust under a guru's guidance and example, but we also realize, through a process of maturation, that we need to commit to certain relationships in order to overcome the fight-or-flight response that makes us jet at every sign of discomfort. At a certain point we realize that our fight-or-flight response is—literally—not very evolved. It's when we stay committed to a relationship and a path of deep work with a guiding presence that we actually learn about our own habits fully. That's the idea, anyway.

As both a teacher and a student I have learned the following reluctantly: committed learning is almost always where the deepest learning occurs, and where true personal transformation happens. Obviously, we have to feel that a potential guru is very trustworthy before entering into this type of relationship.

Sometimes people think that they are supposed to have a close personal relationship with their guru. This is almost always not the case. If you examine the history of Tibetan Buddhism, for example, some of the most memorable and carefully recorded guru–disciple relationships occurred with student and guru only meeting a few times over an entire lifetime! There are now a few small Western Buddhist communities where gurus may give students lots of face time and personal guidance as a mentor. But these arrangements are rare, and this role is usually better served by a teacher/mentor.

I'm not going to lie—I often wish I were closer to my guru. And sometimes, when I do get to spend a bunch of time with him, I wish I were farther away! That's how any real relationship works. It's not because I don't love him; it's just that the energy of working with one's own mind, the effort of commitment to fully living within one's awareness, gets deeply intensified around one's guru. Our projections and transferences tend to become more transparent. The literal meaning of the Sanskrit word *guru* has to do with heaviness or intensity. A guru makes our path intense, and we see our habitual reactions in a more immediate and potent way.

It is debatable whether everyone needs a guru to complete the path, and even in my tradition the need for a guru doesn't come up until one is pretty far along on the journey. Yes, working with a guru is sometimes trying, just like any committed partnership. At the same time, my relationship with my guru has taught me many priceless things. Above all else, it has taught me how to stay present with situations longer than I would have if I just obeyed the impulses of my sporadic pleasure-seeking brain. This has in turn helped me learn how to fully commit to being present in my own romantic partnership and close relationships with family and friends. Commitment is the vanguard of cultivating real trust: trust in oneself, trust in our relationships, and trust in our human nature altogether.

NOT PATRIARCHICAL, NOT HORIZONTAL

These teachings are based on the balanced educational premise that everyone needs someone to look up to, yet also that everyone is capable of developing the skills to be of great benefit to others, without exception. This balance creates a fully resolvable tension, a friction between trusting someone else while also trusting your own wisdom. To work with this balance in a healthy manner, both teacher and student need to be deeply respected, as well as held accountable for their roles. While we need to be wary of ethical violations and teachers who are not doing what they say they are doing, we shouldn't throw out the baby with the bathwater and discount the idea of teachers altogether. If we flatten all hierarchies in response to the many abuses of leadership in the past, we quickly start to mistrust the idea of guidance altogether, disbelieving that there's anyone further along in his understanding of awareness and compassion.

Unfortunately, this complete flattening of roles leads us to mistrust the idea of human progress, because if everybody is just spinning their wheels at the same place on the road, it must mean no one really knows where they are going. History has clearly demonstrated the problems with patriarchy and caste systems. Buddha nature—the fact that all beings are fully capable of awakening—is always the great equalizer. If all beings possess Buddha nature, then having different classes of exalted spiritual beings—a spiritual 1%, so to speak—makes no sense. Yet, we have to admit that some people might be further along in their realization of the wisdom we are trying to develop. We think that flattening all power dynamics will make us all more united in our humanity, but that doesn't ever seem to be what happens. The problem with looking up to no one is that it makes us feel even more alone on the journey. If we don't have anyone we trust to guide us, then we are truly stumbling around together in the darkness, only equal to one another in our confusion.

Thus, the Buddhist teachings work best when the guiding relationships we seek—whichever of the three types of relationships we form with a teacher—are somewhere between the two problematic extremes of "Daddy Knows Best" and "Everyone Has Their Own Truth." In my experience on both sides of this relationship, any student–teacher relationship is most successful when you look up to your teachers, but you also look them in the eye. This way, our intelligence is respected, our path feels supported, and we don't feel like we are commuting through this human journey all alone.

PART III

The Sacred Journey

There are many people who are more learned than I and more elevated in their wisdom. However, I have never made a separation between the spiritual and the worldly. If you understand the ultimate aspect of the dharma, this is the ultimate aspect of the world. And if you should cultivate the ultimate aspect of the world, this should be in harmony with the dharma.

—CHOGYAM TRUNGPA RINPOCHE

10

RELIGION, SECULARISM, AND A SACRED PATH

My intensive practice of Tantric Buddhism began in Bushwick, Brooklyn, in 2002. I know, that is a very interesting sentence. Actually, Sakyong Mipham Rinpoche had given us teachings on the preliminary practices of Tantra (also known as Vajrayana—"indestructible vehicle") on retreat in rural Colorado earlier in the year. But I began practicing them while living with close friends at our Bushwick loft in a converted sewing factory. On top of my job, I also had to practice two to three hours a day in order to keep up with the requirements I had been given.

Not particularly a fan of sleep, I was also having the time of my roaring twenties, meeting a huge variety of awesomely creative and politically engaged people, building the kinds of friendships that could fill the pages of many post-collegiate novels. When we moved into the loft, we realized that our landline number spelled out 718-FUN-FORT. It was an interesting moment to begin a mentally intense spiritual practice, which the Vajrayana practices tend to be. It's not like my roommates, my two best friends, were party boys, though. My best friend from high school was studying Zen and running a successful poetry and music series that brought artists from different spiritual traditions together. My best friend from college was beginning a filmmaking career that would lead him to win various documentary awards in a few years. It was a turn-of-the-twenty-first-century bohemia. I had a hard time dragging myself into my bedroom for a few hours every day to focus on the intensely devotional visualization practices that I was expected to complete. I remember vividly one Saturday night, while physically prostrating to an imagined ancient lineage of mostly Tibetan and Indian masters, hearing the sounds of a really good party coming from our living room. Why am I escaping, I remember thinking, escaping into some weird mystical fantasy that I'm just making up, when the real world—the real fun world—is going on without me out there?

IS THIS A RELIGION?

I have often wondered what the role of so-called spiritual practices might be in the real world of the twenty-first century, a world where people are statistically moving away from identification with any one religious tradition at a surprisingly rapid pace. Almost none of the students or friends who I work with on this journey are looking for a new religion. In fact, most of the people I work with are trying to get over the tedious need to identify themselves solidly as this or that. I encounter so many people who don't really want a spiritual identity but still say things along the lines of "If I'm anything, I guess I'm Buddhist."

I grew up with half of my family Southern Christian and the other half New York Jews, but both of my parents felt disconnected from their familial traditions and started studying Tibetan and Shambhala Buddhism in their early twenties. Growing up, I never had much interest in any kind of ritual that I didn't understand as directly related to the life I was living in the world. When, in my own early twenties, I took up studying and practicing the Vajrayana teachings of Buddhism, I was immediately confronted by my resistance to that which seemed archaic and mystical, especially when it separated me from my friends on Saturday nights. Some of this hesitation was about understanding the guru relationship. But much more of it was about the more mystical aspects of visualization and rituals. Life is so short. What could possibly be gained from engaging in rituals that aren't relevant to the here and now?

At the same time, the sacred teachings of Vajrayana (Buddhist Tantra) were enticing to me. The Tantric teachings—with their colors and rituals, visualizations and mantras—brought home so eloquently and vividly all of the most poignant realizations of the earlier Buddhist teachings I had studied on self-awareness and relationships. I was particularly inspired by the Tantric frameworks that delve into the nature of human emotions, even difficult emotions like desire and anger, which I'll discuss in chapter 12. I was floored by the idea that every experience, whether sensory or mental, intellectual or emotional, can be seen as exemplary of the awakened mind in action, if only we can access the right vantage point of awareness from which to view every experience as sacred. It was these teachings that helped me begin to gain real confidence in the sacredness of every emotional and perceptual experience and allowed me to begin to feel truly at home in my own mind.

There is a lively debate as to whether or not the Awake-ist teachings taught by Siddhartha Gautama, and passed down for many generations, qualify as a religion. Though there are many other views on the matter, I think the answer regarding the work of Siddhartha himself* must be no. In studying his earliest interactions with the people he encountered, recorded in the suttas (discourses and teachings in dialogue), it is at the very least clear that Siddhartha was not trying to transmit anything that should be taken on faith. He warned vehemently against blind adherence to his ideas. Meanwhile, the historical Buddha's recorded statements about the possibility of a creator God range from agnostic (refusing to answer the question) to no-holds-barred atheism. At one point, Siddhartha dismisses the idea of an external creator (calling this creator the "housebuilder," which many saw as a reference to the Vedic god Brahma), as if he just beat the "housebuilder" in some wrestling match. One thing is clear: the historical Buddha was consistently offering a series of psychological and ethical tools for working with the very human realities of dissatisfaction and confusion. His emphasis on understanding and alleviating human suffering was the very first thesis of his work, a central thesis from which he never deviated. Time and again, he presented modes of humanistic training designed to alleviate the dissatisfaction caused by grasping, rejecting, and numbing out, which are the nasty symptoms of our commuter's mentality. At the same time, he lived within a cultural narrative that believed in other realms of conscious beings, as well as in rebirth, and so he did not reject these ideas outright. Similarly, I imagine that if Siddhartha attained awakening in a Christian culture, he would not discount the importance of Jesus's example when he taught. And why would he? Jesus was an incredible bodhisattva.

Often, in the earliest dialogues, the Buddha meets people inclined to different spiritual and worship rituals, who ask him

---

*Siddhartha Gautama is also often referred to as Shakyamuni Buddha to note the clan "Shakya" that he was born into.

how he would engage in their rituals. In a favorite sutta, the Sigalovada Sutta, the Buddha comes across a man worshipping the six directions, a devotional practice of the Brahmin class in the region. The man asks the Buddha how he would worship the six directions. Rather than dismiss the man's practice as somehow invalid or guided by theistic faith, the Buddha reframes and humanizes the act of worshipping the six directions, seemingly through spontaneous interpretation, as a practice for relating to and properly respecting our various human relationships. He turns "worshipping the six directions" into a teaching on human interdependence, an examination of how we might properly treat our parents, partners, coworkers, employees, and teachers, and how they might relate to us in return.* This is perhaps my favorite sutta, because Siddhartha does not reject another person's spiritual practice, but reframes and secularizes it.

This approach—finding the human wisdom that already exists in our inherited cultural rituals—is an example for all of us trying to figure out how to be "spiritual" people in the twenty-first century. It's what the Shambhala teachings are all about. Within the realm of opinions on how Buddhism "ought" to be positioned, I contend that Buddhism is most helpful when viewed as a series of practices that can inform, support, and, yes, maybe challenge any other spiritual rituals we choose to engage in. It is a human path to alleviate human confusion. Of course, in many Asian cultures,

---

*The six directions are the four main directions plus above and below. The Buddha places one's parents in the east, teachers in the south, partner and family in the west, friends and colleagues in the north, those who serve us in the lower direction, and holy people in the upper direction. He then discusses how we should treat each of these and how they should treat us in return. Later on in Tantra and the Shambhala teachings, this sort of interdependent mapping of one's life and relationships would be viewed as a "mandala," a sacred circle that artistically represents one's life situation, personality traits, or society through a sacred iconography.

Buddhist rituals did hold a religious place in people's lives, so it is important to respect the various ways that these practices have been adapted into the cultures that have historically held them, not just carelessly co-opt them into our modern paradigm. Still, we have to ask, what is the best way for each of us, as twenty-first-century students in a scientific, globalized society, to treat these teachings?

To me, the view that Buddhist teachings are somehow religious, requiring some form of blind belief, and that you would have to relinquish other spiritual practices in order to pursue them fully, is neither accurate nor helpful. It's not accurate because the Buddha's central thesis was humanistic; he focused clearly on human suffering and the causes of that suffering. At the same time, viewing Buddhism as a religion is not helpful. People from all walks of life become interested in the vast array of Buddhist ethical, philosophical, and psychological teachings, and to declare that they cannot fully participate because they are also exploring another spirituality is severely confining and unnecessary. This is especially true in the Shambhala tradition, where the culture and spirituality of one's upbringing are viewed as our "ancestral" lineages, and we are called upon to make full use of the wisdom of our familial, cultural, and spiritual heritages in order to support our journey in the dharma.

It seems that much of the question of whether Buddhism is a religion really revolves around how vaguely defined the word "religion" itself has come to be. Buddhism certainly rejects the belief in an unseen, separate creator, if that is how we define religion. But Buddhism easily resolves itself with the idea of God as a type of inherent divinity embedded in our worldly experience, not as a distant otherworldly savior. All kinds of positions are possible for Buddhist practitioners, and it's an act of great aggression to tell someone else what he needs to think in this regard, or to impose our own qualifications on the validity of his practice. For example, it's possible to be an atheist who believes in reincarnation, because atheism is only a rejection of a creator God. The Buddhist hypothesis of reincarnation is one of conscious continuity based on psychological cause and effect, and does not require a creator to be logically valid. And Buddhists can certainly connect with "God" as the inherent divinity of all experiences. I am certainly one Buddhist who believes in God this way.

I think religion is best defined as what happens when an ethical or psychological tradition evolves over time and takes on its own cultural and ritualistic infrastructure, which sometimes hardens into dogma. Undoubtedly, this happened many times in the almost 2,600-year development of the Buddhist teachings, just as in any other human system.

In addition to cutting off access to many Christians, Jews, Muslims, and others who could benefit from Buddhist teachings on the nature of the mind, this perceived "religious" limitation of dharma could have an impact on communication with secular fields of knowledge. Applying Buddhist techniques to a wide range of secular pursuits, including Western psychology, social justice, and the arts, might be the most meaningful use of Buddhism in the twenty-first century. If Buddhism were a religion, we would have a hard time relating to the contemplative journeys of atheist and agnostic practitioners, who are the largest groups of people becoming interested in meditation and dharma in the West. The result of the perception that Buddhism is "religious" is that we may do a lot of dicing up of Buddhist ideas in order to find the "secular" parts and make use of them. Mindfulness practice usually survives the chopping block, but the deeper implications of ethics and philosophy (i.e., the bodhisattva's call to consider our interdependence with each other and with the earth) are often discarded, because even though they are extremely helpful practices, we fear these ethics might somehow be viewed as "religious." Mindfulness-based stress reduction and dialectical behavioral therapy are successful and beautiful examples of Buddhist thought applied narrowly to "secular" fields of inquiry. And now we have something called a "mindfulness movement," which is probably just a tiny piece of an "Awake-ist movement" that hasn't felt safe enough to come out of the closet yet.

Beyond just "mindfulness," Buddhist ethics and philosophy are crucial explorations from a scientific and psychological perspective, and Buddhism deserves to be treated in an integrated conversation with Western fields of inquiry as a complete mental system in and of itself. Dzogchen Ponlop Rinpoche calls Buddhism a "science of the mind."* The whole Buddhist system, from start to finish, can be approached as such a science and psychology. The conversation between Buddhist psychology and Western psychology is much more complete and robust than merely the conversation between "mindfulness" and Western psychology. This full conversation can't happen if we try to segregate aspects of the dharma out of an unnecessary fear of "religiosity."

SACREDNESS: OVERCOMING THE SPLIT-PERSONALITY DISORDER OF THE SECULAR/RELIGIOUS DEBATE

Whenever we pose a question, the framing of the question—the possibilities that are allowed by the way a question is structured—is often more revealing than the possible answers to the question. So, when did we start asking the limiting question as to whether

---

*Likewise, when asked about his religion, the fourteenth Dalai Lama answered, "My religion is kindness."

a particular philosophy is either secular or religious? Is that either/or framing really helpful or accurate?

The origins of the spiritual/secular split can be traced to the era after the Age of Enlightenment, when thinkers started to see scientific and rational thought as distinct from faith-based arguments. No doubt, the movement to elevate reason and logic above blind faith was a great step forward in human understanding. However, it leaves us now with an odd framing for all our most important questions, as well as with the constructed belief that experiences and paths need to fit neatly into either the secular-scientific category or the spiritual-religious category.

This is sort of like asking people if they are a Democrat or a Republican. Those words don't really mean anything beyond the framed branding of electoral politics; they are designations of a constructed dichotomy, parties that have actually switched places ideologically in the course of United States history. People who are asked that question should cringe at the limiting frame they are being presented with. For me, the best thing to do would be to step outside the limited frame and say, "I am a progressive who believes interdependence and basic goodness should be the core organizing principles of public policy."

All of this is deeply relevant to understanding where the Shambhala teachings fit in a constructed religious/secular paradigm. To understand the Shambhala approach, it is very important to understand the problems with such an either/or framing. If we look at the quote by Chogyam Trungpa Rinpoche at the beginning of this chapter, we see that he was proclaiming the underlying view of the Shambhala Vajrayana teachings, where spiritual and worldly endeavors are completely integrated in all aspects of life.

When we separate our spiritual self from mundane life in the world, we end up with a kind of spiritual split personality disorder.

This has nothing to do with separation of church and state or freedom of beliefs, which are absolutely crucial to any open society. This has to do with what happens when we each isolate our highest human values from our day-to-day existence. Simply put, this false separation is why we experience life as a grinding commute—because only a tiny fraction of each day seems worthy of being deemed "spiritual." We might meditate or pray or do other rituals, but we view these as an escape from life in the world, not as our path to sanely participating in the world. We go to work and deal with money, but we don't treat our livelihood as a spiritual practice, as our very path to awakening, and this sense of separation between our jobs and our spiritual practice makes us (and those around us) suffer for forty hours a week or more. When we separate our spiritual self from our life in the world, we create a kind of inner schism that leads to a sense of meaninglessness and isolation in our "secular" life.

In order to resolve a dichotomy that was always fabricated, the Shambhala teachings take an integrated approach. Within the Shambhala teachings, the word "sacred" denotes the complete union of secular and spiritual truth. "Sacred" is our word for the panoramic experience of life that occurs after these false dichotomies have collapsed in upon themselves.

The unification of the secular and the spiritual works in both directions. On the one hand, our daily life benefits from spiritual meaning and a sense of majesty. On the other hand, scientific methodologies should be applied to our deepest spiritual questions. Without rational intelligence, any spiritual journey becomes one of blind faith. A spiritual path based on unverifiable ideas is stripped of any real accountability to the world we live in. If our spiritual path is not held accountable to the evidence of direct experience in the world, we have no real measuring stick for how our journey is progressing. At the extreme end of this spectrum, we might pay no attention to climate change because we are convinced the Rapture is coming soon. A more subtle instance of an unscientific spirituality might involve thinking that the number of compassion mantras we recite is more important than how well we treat our romantic partner. In either case, because the measure of spiritual success has nothing to do with real life on earth, we aren't accountable to anything but our own blind faith, which can't be held to any true scrutiny. This is a very dangerous way to approach spirituality. Many atheist thinkers make this point about the danger of an unscientific spirituality quite well.

Sometimes, when we talk about spiritual devotion, which includes devotion to a guru, there is a tendency to turn off our rational brain, to throw out our intelligence, and to hope that somebody else—the guru—will do all the hard work of figuring life out for us. Despite my highly progressive education, I'm repeatedly shocked at just how tempting it still is to let myself believe that somebody else is going to figure everything out about this vast and scary universe for me, and all I have to do is devote myself to his grace and take solace in his shadow. Sadly, this approach only ends in a bypassing of life and an enabling of harmful magical thinking.

SACREDNESS AND VAJRAYANA RITUALS

For some people, spiritual ceremonies are off-putting, but the fact is that we are always already performing rituals. In his book *The Shambhala Principle*, Sakyong Mipham Rinpoche points to the fact that "life is a ceremony." What this means is that every aspect of our agreed-upon cultural activities already demonstrates the qualities of a ritual. When you check out of a store and hand someone your credit card, there is a ritual at play, because there is a mutual participation in an economy, whether we acknowledge it or not. In some cultures, such as Japanese culture, a bow is involved in the exchange of money, a sign of mutual respect and gratitude. In Western society, a handshake developed as the physical demonstration of honest intentions and not carrying concealed weapons. When you stop at a red light, there is a ritual at play; you are bowing to those who are crossing your path. When you place a television as the central element in your living room, it is the same ceremonial act as putting a shrine or altar there. After all, both objects transmit views of how we are supposed to experience ourselves, as either commuters or Buddhas, consumers or citizens. The national anthem at the beginning of a sporting event is a collective meditation on patriotism, whether or not we believe in what we are singing.

As Sakyong Mipham Rinpoche puts it, you can tell what the most important building is within a society by which is the tallest. Within ancient Europe, cathedrals often reached the most soaring heights, as did mosques in the ancient Middle East. Now, in our Western metropolises, we all bow before cathedrals of financial commerce. Our sacred values are implied by our ritualistic choices, whether we agree to them or not. We may not have thrones for gurus or kings, but we do have award shows and tabloids for enthroning and dethroning celebrities. A life lived without ceremony is never possible. Ritual is part of our daily rhythm. Whether or not we treat the rituals of daily life as sacred is completely up to us.

What if you viewed getting a coffee with your best friend as a kind of sacred ceremony? You might bow to your macchiato in gratitude for all of the interdependent beings who brought it to you, and then you and your friend might really listen to each other, holding the stories you tell each other as sacred narratives. I know it sounds cheesy, but that's only because we don't do it enough to normalize the practice as a shared rite. What if you treated money as a kind of sacred energy that you neither feared nor worshipped? You would stop judging it as "dirty," stop chasing after it like a hungry ghost, and start to really think about where your money goes and what values it empowers. What if you treated your clothes as sacred? You would really gain confidence in your own embodiment, and you'd also take care of what you wear. What if pizza was treated as a sacred expression of our cultural heritage? We might learn how to make pizza as a form of participation in a cultural ceremony, totally changing our experience of each slice. What if we treated the work we did and our intention to help others through work as sacred? And most profoundly, what if we treated emotions like desire and sadness as sacred, and developed meditative rituals to honor their place upon the altar of our life? We would no longer treat our own emotions like garbage. With this sort of approach, as well as with practices to encourage this view, all of life becomes meaningful and worth elevating and protecting.

If we held the view that our spiritual and secular lives were never separate endeavors, we would stop commuting toward exalted, peak experiences and start appreciating what is happening right now. Making an omelette might become just as meaningful an act as going to a temple. Going to work on Wednesday morning could reveal the meaning of life to us just as well as an ayahuasca ceremony might. This celebration of the sacredness of the experience we already have, this divinity of the world that already exists, is the core view of the Shambhala Vajrayana teachings. Celebrating the world as it is does not, by the way, mean that we are acquiescing and giving up on progress, no longer interested in helping others, no longer striving to make the world a more compassionate place. Quite the opposite—it is through a sacred appreciation of our world that we can figure out how to connect with it even more fully and find inspiration to conquer the problems we collectively face. The only reason to accept things as they are right now is to find the strength to alleviate more suffering in the future. The only way we are going to gain the inspiration necessary to help the world is if we view it as sacred.

This view of sacredness needs to be understood theoretically before we look at the reason for engaging in Vajrayana practice rituals. The Tantric practices, with their iconographic symbolism, devotional aspects, visualizations, and mantras, are an attempt to create a microcosm of a life lived entirely with ritual dignity and sacred imagination, because when we view our activities as sacred, then we begin to view the space of our own awareness as sacred.

Vajrayana rituals—like bowing, incense, offerings, and mantras—are not just a culturally imported fairy tale. These practices simply mirror the truth that our life is already composed of daily rituals. How sacred ritual manifests is up to each practitioner. But in order to fully awaken, we have to dissolve the false dichotomy between secular and spiritual truths, and start to view ourselves, each other, and the world we share as sacred, 24/7/365.

11

IMAGINING A BASICALLY GOOD HOME

The Practice of Visualization

For all our brain and body know, our world is as we envision it. If we go through our days seeing ourselves as powerless and alone, and the world as a life-or-death struggle for scarce resources, we are effectively setting our brains and bodies on guard and enhancing the threat seemingly posed by each and every event. If, on the other hand, we see ourselves as capable and effective, and the world as a basically safe space for living and learning, we are setting our brains and bodies at ease . . . Crafting a positive vision of life that prepares us to act . . . can help us realize our highest aims for ourselves and our world.

—DR. JOE LOIZZO, *Sustainable Happiness*

One of the most interesting applications of sacredness in the Vajrayana teachings is the focus on imagination, or the practice of visualization. Techniques of visualization, central to the Vajrayana teachings, ask us to train our imaginations to create more positive narratives about who we think we are.

At first glance, imagination might seem to be quite a problem for the path of awakening. Don't our unrealistic fantasies keep us caught in commute? Aren't they the entire source of our problem? When we engage with a foundational mindfulness technique, say, following the breath and trying to be present with sense perceptions as they are, we realize that our attention keeps flying away into fantasies and nightmares. Let's say you are sitting in Austin, Texas, eating a breakfast taco, and your mind keeps getting caught imagining yourself in Paris, savoring a *pain au chocolat*. Mindfulness says "come back," reminding you that you are actually right here in the Lone Star State.

Visualization proceeds from the realization that our minds aren't only innately perceptive, they are also naturally projective. Not only do we receive sensory data, we also generate imagery and emotional experience based on what we imagine.

It is our ability to imagine that helps us to create powerfully positive intentions for how we live our life. Sitting in Austin, dreaming of Paris, you might begin to use your mind's projective capacity to conceptualize a journey you want to make someday soon. Every journey starts by imagining that such a trip could happen. Every meaningful creative process begins with some kind of fantasy. We start with imagination, which leads to real action. The practice of visualization asks the question: What if your imagination could be consistently trained as a contemplative practice, enlisted in the service of helping yourself and others?

It's as if we have a movie projector in our minds that conditions our experience of the present moment. At first, this projective tendency might seem like a big problem, an obstacle to overcome. We might think the idea of mindfulness is to stop the movie in our minds altogether, to cease the pretense of how we would like things to be, getting back to how they really are. Let's turn the lights back on in the theater of the mind and get down to what's real. As a foundational principle, all Buddhist practices are based on clear perception, using the naked and direct honesty of mindfulness practice as a basis to create a bare attention and direct experience of the present reality.

At the same time, if Vajrayana is about ritualizing every aspect of our consciousness in the service of awakening, then paying attention to the way things really are includes making use of the mind's imaginative capacity. The point of self-awareness is not to turn off our projector, per se, but to study the projector, to realize that the projector is always on, and to notice that our experiences are projections that arise in the theater of the heart-mind. The point is not to stop projecting, but to see the projections for what they are. If we do that, we can begin to alter the projection, shifting our self-image, recrafting our ideas about other people, and revisualizing the world we all share.

Visualization is not just some spiritual event—it's a basic cognitive process. If you are preparing for an important meeting or event, for instance, you often fantasize about everything that could possibly go wrong beforehand. This is basically just an anxious mind generating a negative, insecure, and incapable image of itself. With visualization, the very space of our imagination, often dominated by fantasies of the future and nightmares of the past, could be converted into a kind of mindfully creative space, a kind of movie studio that actually benefits sentient beings.

It's also important to note that visualization is not just a feature of Vajrayana meditations. In fact, imagination is used in the relational meditations of Buddhism, such as lovingkindness and compassion practices, where we generate the images of ourselves and other people in our life in an attempt to cultivate more nurturing attitudes toward all sentient beings. Creating mental projections is part of what the mind does, and so it is a feature of every meditative tradition.

Within the Vajrayana view of sacredness, it may be helpful to look at three different approaches to visualization practice.

THE PSYCHOLOGICAL APPROACH

As Dr. Joe Loizzo points out in his book *Sustainable Happiness*, our experience flickers back and forth between present-time sensory information on the one hand, and memory and plans on the other. Our cognitive framework functions in a manner that ping-pongs back and forth between sensory perception and imagination, as our brain works to fill in major gaps in our flickering sensory intake by visualizing what's happening. So, the practice of visualization harnesses what we are already doing.

Within this theater of the heartmind, we have to ask about the nature of the narrative that we have constructed and taken to be real. As we discussed in chapter 4, we have to recognize that the self-image we are projecting is often quite a negative one.

Let's imagine this strange scenario: A group of Buddhas, completely enlightened beings, go to the movies together. When they arrive at the theater, they find out that the movie playing is the story of their own lives, except told from the perspective of materialism and confusion. The versions of the Buddhas depicted on the screen aren't enlightened at all—they are scared, selfish, scattered, and totally disconnected from the present moment (imagine a bunch of neurotic, chain-smoking Buddhas). The characters are given a cynical motivation for reading their lines, and a kind of anxious apathy permeates their interactions. Imagine that the Buddhas in the audience become slowly more and more obsessed with the story, the way we all become obsessed with our favorite dramas and horror stories. In their obsession, the Buddhas buy more popcorn and settle in to watch the movie again, and again, and again, eventually coming to believe that the selfish and frightened characters on the screen depict who they really are. Imagine that this group of enlightened beings, through the conditioning of their projective karma, eventually forget altogether that they are even in a movie theater, and begin to believe that this horror show is their real-life biography, depicted in a high-definition, 3-D, documentary format.

This is a highly simplified allegory of how our confusion actually comes into being from the standpoint of the Vajrayana. The Tantric view is that there is already a complete Buddha dormant within each of us, but we've individually and collectively become addicted to horror movies that we mistake for documentaries. From this perspective, our whole society is caught up in a kind of shared horror story, imagining ourselves as zombie consumers rather than empowered citizens: afraid, insecure, incapable beings who have no choice but to wander through life grasping after fleeting pleasures, needlessly competing with each other instead of collaborating, isolating ourselves from the plight of those whose stories we don't understand. Because our whole society is both constructing and watching this shared screenplay simultaneously, the physical world begins to take on the qualities of this horror movie, and it becomes more and more difficult to distinguish the theater of our experience from the screen of our own projections.*

In this age of virtual reality and imaginative storytelling, how would a being who has forgotten his own enlightened nature reconnect with his confidence? The answer is to learn how to project a different kind of story, to learn a more awakened kind of filmmaking. This is the formal practice of visualization.

Before engaging in this practice, of course, we would have to become aware of the fact that we are sitting in a mental theater, both projecting and reacting to the movie of our life. This realiza-

---

*From the standpoint of traditional Buddhism, this slow projection of one's reality onto the outer world is also how we end up with different psychological realms of beings, such as the hell realms, hungry ghost realms, and jealous god realms, etc., which are depicted in ancient maps of the psychological realms of samsara.

tion that our true home, the heartmind, has both the perceptive and projective qualities of a theater is embodied in our commitment to self-awareness as the basis of our journey. The next step is to develop great empathy for and camaraderie with the other beings caught up in watching the same horror movie, or whatever horror movie they happen to be watching in their theater next door. As the Vajrayana-practicing poet Allen Ginsberg said in his epic poem "Kaddish": "nothing to weep for but the Beings in the Dream, trapped in its disappearance, sighing, screaming with it, buying and selling pieces of phantom." This weeping for "the Beings in the Dream, trapped in its disappearance" can represent the bodhisattva's commitment to staying present in and compassionate about human relationships, engaged with the rawness of their intensity and their impermanence. It also represents the accountability inherent in the truth that, while life may operate like a movie (or, as more traditionally taught, like a dream sequence), the movie has real consequences for the beings who are caught up in believing in the story's objective reality. Generating the bodhisattva's intention to care for others—the prerequisite built into all Vajrayana visualizations—is what distinguishes these types of imaginative practices from something like "The Secret," for example. If visualization is engaged in for merely pleasure-seeking reasons, it fails to distinguish itself from any other kind of virtual fantasy, and just becomes a mental video game. The bodhisattva only visualizes himself in a BMW if that car turns out to be of great benefit to many beings.

On the basis of these two crucial commitments—to honest self-inquiry and to benefiting others—Tantric practitioners realize that they can use visualization to reconstruct a more optimistic and confident narrative about themselves and the world they inhabit. We can learn to write a more compassionate script and recast the movie of our life.

In the psychological approach, visualization is treated as a kind of abrupt transformation of one's inner narrative. In order to do this, we often call upon the imagery of meditational Buddhas and bodhisattvas (also called *yidams* in Tibetan), to remap our minds around the presence of enlightened qualities. Instead of watching the movie where we are inadequate and never get what we want, we use our meditation to build an inner movie set where we become great heroes of wisdom or compassion, satisfied that we have what we need, confident that we can help others.

Joseph Campbell pointed to the fact that every society in human history has had archetypal narratives of a hero's journey that fit a remarkably common pattern of storytelling. In our Western culture, I am constantly fascinated by the extent to which the comic book superheroes of the twentieth century have become the Hollywood heroes of the twenty-first century. No matter how old we all get, we all need to visualize heroes, and we will pay good money to escape into fantasies where life is not so difficult and heroes support us every step of the way. In classical Tantric Buddhist practice, you invoke your own superheroes, named Manjushri and Tara, who possess the very ordinary superpowers of wisdom and healing compassion, respectively. In Shambhala, even the various phases of the journey are embodied by archetypal beings known as the four dignities.

Mastery of self-awareness is embodied by a powerful yet gentle tiger who remains content and mindful with every step it takes. Mastery of relational awareness is embodied by an energized and joyful snow lion who never stops interacting with others playfully. Mastery of emptiness is embodied by a mythical half man–half bird creature called a *garuda*, who soars across the sky and never needs to land. Mastery of the Vajrayana teachings and mastery of the environment itself is embodied by the dragon, another mythical creature, who exerts a powerful influence without even announcing itself. Within the Tantric practices of Shambhala, these mythical creatures are called upon to embody the most powerful aspects of our mind's capabilities.

As my friend and colleague, the Buddhist teacher and psychologist Dr. Miles Neale likes to comment, the psychological approach to imagining oneself either in the presence of bodhisattvas (called front-visualization) or embodying the qualities of an archetype yourself (called self-visualization) encourages us to believe that we can shift a deeply acquired negative self-image into a more capable and confident sense of who we are. With the psychological approach to visualization, we are utilizing a classic hero's narrative of compassion, wisdom, and confidence to slowly transform our story of insecurity, inadequacy, and selfishness.

THE DEVOTIONAL APPROACH

There are some visualization practices that one can do without a commitment to a guru, but when one fully enters into visualization practices, one does so having committed to a guru relationship, and with at least a preliminary devotional connection to the lineage of awakened masters that the guru represents. From this standpoint, the awakened Buddhas and bodhisattvas that we visualize in these imaginative practices are not merely self-generated photocopies. Rather, imagining awakened beings and archetypal symbolism represents an investment in a lineage of human mastery and human empowerment. Whenever I think of this devotional aspect of visualization practice, I remember the ghostly Jedis in the forest at the conclusion of *Return of the Jedi*. If we devote ourselves to the path of awakening, then our visualization can connect us more and more with a humble yet confident devotion to our lineages.

In the devotional approach, the idea is that by connecting with these archetypal beings and fields of logo-based symbolism (bodhisattvas, mantras, and sacred environments), we are actually connecting with the awakened mind of our gurus and their predecessors along this journey, the previous "Jedis" who have empowered these symbols and rituals with potency and meaning. By tapping into the field of visualized symbolism, we are—through our connection to the gurus—tapping into the lineage of the awakened mind directly.

The idea is that while the archetypes might not make immediate sense or always seem totally relevant, they have been enriched and empowered by the practice and struggles of masters who came before us. Through devotion and by committing yourself to working with your guru, you build trust in the idea that you are not alone; you have history's support for feeling capable and confident in your own mind. From this standpoint, visualization is a practice of plugging into a power source that has existed for a long time, of trusting that we don't have to work with our awareness all on our own.

THE MYSTICAL APPROACH

The mystical approach to visualization is the one place along our path where our current scientific understanding may not suffice, where the practice can't be described so simply as a personal psychological transformation. This mystical approach carries the outrageous idea that the visualized bodhisattvas might represent real energies, real types of conscious beings who exist beyond the spectrum of sensory reality and whose energy can be called upon by those who intend to benefit others. This mystical approach to a bodhisattva like Manjushri or Tara requires us to be open to the space beyond our sense perceptions. Even in this mystical approach, it is crucial to note that a visualized bodhisattva is never an external savior; it is simply an energy source, a type of consciousness that can be invoked. It is not necessary to believe that the bodhisattvas are real beings, but it might be useful to be open to the idea that there is more to reality than just what we perceive with our limited scientific technology.

Of course, it is completely fine to engage in visualization with a psychological purpose in mind. But we should be aware that the classical interpretation of visualization's effectiveness is actually on all three of these levels at once: psychological transformation, devotional empowerment, and mystical blessings. If we truly create an integrated paradigm where spiritual and scientific truths are not viewed as isolated from each other, then spiritual practice would include the possibility of both psychological and mystical outcomes. At the very least, being open to our own awareness would mean that we were not cutting off the possibilities of how vast the universe truly might be. If we are going to avoid falling into the trap of blind faith, looking for some superman to save us, then we have to at least work strongly with the psychological approach. If we want to gain confidence that we are not alone in our journey, that we do stand on the shoulders of previous Jedis, then we should be open to devotion as part of the visualization process. Whether or not we think the archetypes that we imagine correspond to real entities is up to us. Some of the greatest shamans and saints in history believed that these beings existed in some way. I try to always stay grounded in the psychological and devotional approaches to the rituals of Tantra, while staying open to mystical possibilities.

NOT MAKING ANYTHING UP

No matter what tradition of Tantra we practice, by the time we begin to work with visualization, it can be assumed that we have a deep rapport with the teachings on emptiness discussed in chapter 7. This means we have at least some ability to notice our fixation on any narrative—especially our own spiritual narratives—as a potentially problematic obsession. While we engage in imagination and visualization, we should notice how our story about reality can block us from being available to the present moment as it is right now, a space that no story can adequately describe.

If visualization practice is primarily about transforming our inner narrative, then it is equally important to realize that no narrative is solid, even an enlightened and empowered one. All Buddhist visualizations end by dissolving the imaginative phase and returning to resting in naked awareness, plugging fully back into one's immediate perceptual and emotional reality. Without dissolving the visualization, we might just end up fixating and fantasizing on a new hero's narrative, a new type of comic book or Disney movie. But having a new story to fixate upon is not the point. The point of visualization is to return to the present moment more confidently, more empowered and available to others.

Thus, all visualizations eventually lead toward a phase of practice known as either the "perfection phase" or the "dissolving phase," in which we rest within our awareness, vividly and openly, not making anything up, not manipulating experience at all. In order to bolster this space of vivid awareness, where we directly investigate the nature of thoughts, emotions, and perceptions, two popular systems of meditation emerged in Tibet, most commonly known as Mahamudra and Dzogchen. These directive systems of mindfulness and awareness are meditations on the nature of consciousness itself, tools for looking directly into what the mind is, how it perceives, and how it projects.

This reality check—that all visualizations must be dissolved—which is the beginning and end of all good practice, should be a constant reminder for all spiritual practitioners, lest we turn into a new kind of fundamentalist. We should be wary of using these very ancient filmmaking tools to escape into a New Age fantasy. Insofar as the practice of visualization gives us confidence and empathy for our real life, it is useful. As soon as it becomes a kind of make-believe to take us away from dealing with life, it becomes a kind of spiritual bypassing, a harmful exercise in entertainment, a kind of Buddhist movie that furthers our escapist tendencies.

During those lonely Saturday nights in Bushwick when I would choose to practice visualization, I had to keep strongly in mind that the point of these long sessions was to train to return to my real life, confidently and compassionately. If we keep our commitment to self-awareness in our hearts, as well as maintain our commitment to being heroically available for others, then we can begin to transform our inner story lines. This will give us the inspiration to invest more time in practice, maybe even on Saturday nights, when there's always a great party going on somewhere.

I 2

SACRED EMOTIONS,
SACRED ENVIRONMENT

So far, the ideas in this book have followed a certain logic regarding the evolution of the subject-object relationship. At first, we discussed our commuter's mentality of materialism (samsara), where we chase after impossible safety within the fleeting objects of experience, whether those objects are physical, intellectual, or emotional. Then, in the journey of self-awareness (Hinayana), we learn to take responsibility for our own mind, and begin to live within awareness. Stepping onto the path, we get to know our own subjective experience, learning about the heartmind through meditation, study, and ethics. In the journey of relationships (Mahayana), we realize the extent to which we—in our mindless commute—have objectified other human beings, and we practice connecting with them as subjects in their own right, recognizing that their journey is not isolated from our own. Now, in the Vajrayana, we see the sacredness of all experiences. In the Tantric teachings, both our awareness and the object that our awareness experiences are held to be sacred, already possessing the qualities of wisdom and compassion. How does this sacred view change our experience of coming home to our own awareness, and how does it change our relationship to the world around us?

In the last chapter on visualization, we discussed how visualization could slowly help us replace an inner narrative of inadequacy with one of confidence and compassion by guiding our imagination toward the heroic qualities we already possess, hidden and embedded in our consciousness. While visualization practices are meant to be engaged in over long periods of time, there are also methods for recovering confidence more quickly, tuning back into *bodhicitta* in a more immediate way. The Shambhala Vajrayana teachings use a series of practices called windhorse meditations to complement the confidence-building work of visualization. As we train in the practice of windhorse, we increase our ability to recall our confidence more quickly. Windhorse connects us with sacredness in a very immediate way, and can help us to reconnect to our awareness within the heat of difficult moments when we need it the most.

Why is this strange hybrid notion of windhorse used to symbolize the arousal of sacred confidence? In his teachings on windhorse, Jeremy Hayward, an Acharya of Shambhala, describes the widespread usage across many ancient cultures of the term "wind" to denote the most basic and powerful energy of our humanity, from chi and prana in the Eastern health systems to "Holy Wind" in the Native American language of the Navajo. "Wind" represents the emotional forces that blow powerful energy through our bodies and minds, energy that we often feel overwhelmed by.

Again, from a materialistic standpoint, the purpose of spiritual practice is to rid ourselves of negative emotional states like anger, desire, fear, and pride. Losing the view that our minds are sacred, we just want our difficult feelings to go away. Trying to stay present during an emotionally charged moment can feel like sitting within a hurricane. But within Tantra, a realization about the nature of emotions as energy comes about. Mainly, we realize that emotions actually *are* energy, and that energy is neither good nor bad in and of itself—it can warm or destroy, power or pollute, facilitate or interrupt—but that it depends entirely on how we use it.

The "wind" in windhorse has to do with seeing emotions as a kind of sacred energy source for the heartmind. With any kind of energy, there are two basic possibilities. Either the energy can be utilized destructively, as a harmful pollutant, like coal or fossil fuels, or it can be used to create fusion, solar energy, and "wind" that can power the turbines of our highest aspirations. In the Vajrayana teachings, the fact that energy can always be used either constructively or destructively is referred to as "coemergence." Whenever an emotion arises in the space of our awareness, it creates a powerful wind that can be either harnessed as wisdom or fixated upon and treated neurotically and destructively. When the emotion is fixated upon, when it freezes as a habitual pattern, its neurotic and destructive tendencies are called *klesha* in Sanskrit. When the emotion is not fixated upon, but is instead accommodated and harnessed, it becomes windhorse.

The "horse" in windhorse refers to the ability of a skillful person to harness and ride the energy that arises in one's mind. You could think of the practice of "raising windhorse" as the act of harnessing emotional energy.

Raising windhorse involves a series of meditative techniques for abruptly creating a karmic gap where there is enough space to name and feel the energy of presently arising emotions. In practice, the mind abruptly returns to its own awareness, with all the confidence it can muster, and then begins to connect intimately with whatever type of energy is present in the current situation. When this connection is made genuinely and mindfully, according to the teachings, an emotion—desire, for example—ceases to be destructive, and becomes sacred instead. At that point, the energy of desire can be harnessed, and we can actually use that energy, rather than shy away from it, in order to benefit the present situation. That's the idea, anyway.

ENLIGHTENED EMOTIONS

Sacred Desire

You are probably accustomed to the downside of desire. Classic Buddhist teachings have no shortage of description of the aspect of desire that is *klesha*, destructive and harmful patterns. For many of us, the addictive tendencies related to passion—the grasping and groping and seemingly unending grind of *wanting*, the feeling that there is a gaping hole within us—is the reason we began practicing meditation in the first place. Many of my friends first came to this path because they were struggling with a particular addiction. Many others came because they were struggling with heartbreak, the pain and longing of losing someone they desired so completely. Anyone who becomes familiar with the pain of desire would love to find some way to stop the painful torment of having to reach and grope for pleasure and beauty and meaning all the time. At the very least, desire makes us distractible and unsettled. In human relationships, if desire is not used constructively, it can lead to deceit and manipulation, to a life where we claim mighty intentions and altruistic values but end up getting jerked around like puppets tied to the whims of our passions.

None of these problems, however, is intrinsic to the experience of desire. When we harness the energy of desire and ride it without clinging, we see the truth of interdependence, of how deeply connected we are to every other being. Within the Vajrayana teachings, the wisdom of desire is referred to as Padma (lotus) energy. If we can move past the obsessive stuckness of desire, we begin to appreciate beauty and discern what we want to connect with. Our longing is what guides us to craft positive intentions and what eventually leads to the bodhisattva's journey. We appreciate ourselves and fall in love with others. We fully taste a piece of chocolate and appreciate its subtleties. The energy of desire is not intense because it is problematic; it's intense because it is powerful. If we have the methods to create enough of a gap to experience desire, we can handle its power and make thoughtful choices on how to wield it. Wouldn't that be ideal—to long for something and actually have a choice about how we pursue it?

In these sacred moments, we realize that desire is none other than love itself. Desire is an electric field of love: love for dessert, love for music, love for romance, and love for all beings. If we can learn to create space for desire, to see it arising in the home of our awareness, then we can choose to ride it and, in so doing, become passionate about the things we do. Through practice, the energy is harnessed and we become like human magnets, using our charm to wake people up rather than to manipulate them. After all, a passionless bodhisattva is not going to inspire anyone. If you want to communicate with others, you always have to learn how to flirt well. This is what the wisdom of desire knows. At the end of the day, the sacred aspect of desire is synonymous with love— love for one's own mind, love for others, and yes, even love for chocolate, in moderation.

Sacred Anger

We live in a truly violent world, and we have all suffered through war because of the actions of people who cannot control their anger. In addition to questioning hatred and violence in the outer world, the Shambhala and traditional Buddhist teachings urge us to become familiar with just how brutal our internal landscape really is, how much we judge and beat ourselves up with thoughts of how we are failing at life. Possibly the most destructive energy a person can feel is resentment, which is what happens when anger hardens into an entrenched narrative. Resentment is like a clog in an artery in the heartmind. Even worse, anger can turn inward and freeze into depression. Hopelessness is the most frozen form of self-aggression.

At the same time, there is a constant battle among contemplative practitioners and activists on the appropriate use of anger. This seems to be an argument that activists often win, perhaps because many activists are intuitively in touch with the wisdom of anger. Community organizers and philosophers like Saul Alinsky point out that touching anger is one key to inspiring a group of people to get off their (meditation?) seats and do something about the state of the world. Within the Tantric teachings, the wisdom of anger is called Vajra (thunderbolt) energy.

The wisdom of anger is actually a pure form of deep sadness, a clarity of consciousness that witnesses avoidable suffering and stays present to instances of injustice. The wisdom of anger also allows us to see all the petty logical inconsistencies we spew to justify our confused actions. Wise anger knows when it is in the presence of hypocrisy, when somebody is sloppily claiming that the way things are is the way things have to be. Anger can have a strong bullshit detector for silly arguments, a radar attuned to pointing out when views are conflicting and lead to suffering, or when someone is claiming that $2 + 2 = 5$. With awareness, anger can be a key motivating force to action, as it can shake us from our stupor and force us to bear witness to the fact that something is wrong. If anger is used appropriately, it can bring clarity to what is missing in the situation, as well as skillful action, rather than righteous aggression, to pacify real grievances and heal wounds. Therefore, within awareness, it is always crucial to leave space for anger. It should never be discounted as an unwise emotion, no matter how destructive it might feel at times.

Sacred Pride

Studying these teachings forces us to confront the relationship between confidence and arrogance. Stereotypically, spiritual people are meant to be humble, heads bowed low, waving off praise. They would have a hard time even writing a résumé, because they would always be downplaying their abilities. I know many Buddhist practitioners who experience guilt and shame when they have to enter any of the arenas of life—such as job interviews or school applications—that require them to engage in anything that even resembles self-promotion. There seems to be a dominant spiritual narrative that we are supposed to underplay our strengths at all costs, engaging in false modesty in order to win "humble points," and saying we are bad at things that we are actually good at. And we are supposed to regard this dismissal of our worth as a form of humility.

In many classic texts, arrogance—taking excessive pride in your own skills, and inflating the attention you want paid to you—is a major downfall. When pride is thought of as gluttony— taking up too much space or needing to see your name up in lights all the time—then it is a major problem, a *klesha* related to greed and an inflated sense of self-importance, that Stay Puft Marshmallow Man of "ego."

But, at the same time, we are encouraged to develop great confidence in our ability to see clearly and react well to circumstances, a kind of innate capacity to respond to situations intelligently. The wisdom quality of pride is called Ratna energy, a kind of enriching jewel capable of constantly generating abundant gifts for everyone. From the standpoint of Vajrayana, it is only when we take pride in what we have to offer that we can become truly generous; if we don't value ourselves, then we have nothing to offer to others. Within the space of awareness, pride means gaining confidence in our own resources, feeling self-sufficient and low-maintenance instead of malnourished and praise-starved. Within its manifestation as wisdom, pride alchemizes into a feeling of innate wealth and worthiness. The wisdom of pride generates a relaxed confidence that you will always find the resources you need to thrive, which lets you become increasingly magnanimous toward others.

Sacred Jealousy

Let's face it—a large portion of our most anxiety-producing thoughts are spent comparing ourselves to others. On a recent flight, I got bumped up to first class for no extra points or cost. I decided to take the upgrade because, come on, who wouldn't take a free upgrade? I remember sitting there, after a long weekend of teaching, clinking ice cubes in my complimentary beverage, feeling quite important about my early boarding status, watching people stream past me into a more claustrophobic coach cabin. I wondered: How much of the perceived value of this experience is the joy of the experience itself, and how much is the feeling of knowing that I have it better than those poor suckers behind me? Are they looking at me as they shuffle past, wondering if I'm a VIP as they struggle to get settled in their less special reality? The service in first class might be slightly nicer, the seats slightly bigger, but the reason it costs many times more and is so sought after is the comparative status it offers you. It's not that you have something pleasant—it's that you have it better than someone else; the very title tells you that there's implicitly a "second" class behind you, even if that's not what we call it anymore. "First" means that you are ahead of the rest, which means, in the language of the commuter's mentality, that you are safe. Safe for a moment, at least, until the paranoia of status starts anew.

In our world, virtually everything can be made statistical, and once quantified, it can become a polluting fuel for the comparative mind: the *U.S. News and World Report* numerical ranking of the university you attend (aim for single digits), the number of followers you have (aim high), the size of the clothing you wear (aim tiny). When our goals become comparative, we end up with the constant paranoia of an existence of always being weighed on hidden scales, living with the stress of keeping our elbows out in anticipation of others trying to get ahead of us. All of this is a distortion of the wisdom of achievement, which lies hidden within the emotional energy of jealousy and envy.

In Tantra, the family of emotional energy related to jealousy and accomplishment is called Karma, or action, energy.* We set goals that create a sense of health and enjoyment for ourselves and that benefit others, without falling into the trap of needless comparison. Like everybody else, a Buddhist needs to set intentions and aspire toward marks of progress. If we don't reach for outcomes, then nothing gets done. When we relate to this type of emotion—the longing to succeed and achieve something—within the space of open awareness, it ceases to be problematic jealousy. After all, every moment of painful comparison we experience is merely revealing to us something about what we would like to accomplish for ourselves. For example, if you go to a friend's art

---

*Within earlier teachings, karma refers to the "action" and reaction of our habitual patterns and conditioning. In Tantra, karma refers to the emotional energy of jealousy, achievement, activity, and production. Both meanings arise from different applications of the word "karma," which literally just means "action."

opening, and feel jealous at the accolades your friend's work receives, it might mean that you long to reconnect to your own creativity.

When viewed as sacred, jealousy guides us toward projects we would like to undertake, meaningful intentions we would like to reclaim. This accomplishing energy of production and action, which lies dormant within all our jealousies, helps us to see activities through to the end. It overcomes the disheartenment that sets in when the road toward achievement turns out to be longer than we thought it would be. The awakened form of jealousy, called "all-accomplishing" wisdom, helps us to identify obstacles to our goals and face them in a no-nonsense, "get it done" manner, without procrastinating and without worrying what everyone else is doing that might be "better" than our project. The energy lying within jealousy, when harnessed by the practice of windhorse, helps us to be effective and swift in achieving things that bring about well-being and, most important, that allow us to help others.

Sacred Fear

Yes, even fear—along with all of the anxiety, resistance, paralysis, and the destructive habits that come with it—has wisdom. From the standpoint of the Shambhala Vajrayana teachings, fear may have the most profound wisdom of all emotions.

Of course, we all know something about the neurotic aspect of fear. An unaware relationship to fear causes us to overreact, or else to freeze in paralysis, avoiding showing up to real life because fear overwhelms us into panic. When examining my own anxieties, I take great solace in the findings of contemporary neuroscience and evolutionary biology as they relate to Buddhist thought. We have to remember that our experience of the mind is deeply entwined with the structure of our nervous system. When I study the current understanding of the limbic system and the amygdala, it makes sense that we humans experience fear so often. Our human nervous systems still contain many of the same functions as those of the earlier species we evolved from, species whose very survival was threatened constantly, and who passed on their reptilian and animal brains to us. It makes sense that being afraid that you might not make your rent payment this month can provoke almost the same nervous response as thinking that a predator is about to eat you. Inhabiting a human nervous system is kind of like living in a house where the doorbell and the burglar alarm make exactly the same sound. Because we are still mammals, we can have great compassion toward our fears, as well as toward the fears of others, no matter how irrational they sometimes seem.

Examining fear in relation to our survival instinct and nervous systems, I return again and again to one of the most famous analogies in all of Buddhist history. In this ancient parable about fear, a man walks into his hut and sees a dark form slithering along the ground and thinks that it's a snake (in ancient India, a bite from a poisonous snake was probably one of the worst ways to die). A torch light reveals that it's really just a rope on the ground that someone left lying around. Witnessing the neurotic aspect of fear always has to do with seeing how fear leads to false assumptions about the present moment, and how those falsehoods trigger our survival instinct when our survival is not really in question. We are afraid that a friend is mad at us when she actually really like us, or we don't dance because we think we will look awful, when everyone else is just waiting for us to get down. Because we so often mistake ropes for poisonous snakes, we cower and hide and excuse ourselves from participation. We miss our life.

When the Shambhala teachings discuss the meaning of "fearlessness," they don't look at it as some idealized state where the emotion no longer occurs. Again, as we know from the discussion on karma and habit, idealizing a state without feelings is actually our whole problem, the source of our desensitized tendencies.

This numbness makes us terrified of being with the emotions and thoughts that move through our minds moment by moment. By contrast, the brave warrior's way of dealing with fear is to see it as a profound emotion, and move toward it as a sacred experience that links us with every other human who has felt terrified at one time or another. This moving toward fear, rather than trying to reject it, is, ironically, what we call fearlessness.

As Pema Chödrön has said, "Fear is a natural reaction to moving closer to the truth." Connecting with fear, we get up close and personal with the vulnerability and fragility of being a human being. When we take a sacred approach to fear, we begin to resensitize and overcome our numbness. Fear becomes a motivation to open up, to be a brave and flawed person among other flawed people. Working with fear forms the basis for accommodating every other emotion. This energetic quality of accommodating and accepting fear can be called Buddha energy, which is the most basic emotional energy in the Tantric system of emotions, related to the most foundational level of spacious, accommodating awareness, which allows an experience to be exactly what it is, without evasion or judgment. It is exactly this kind of accommodating awareness that will help us to become more familiar with fear.

A person facing her fear models a kind of authentic realness. The energetic quality of fear is no different from the energy of being alive—fear runs through our veins and our nervous system as our most basic power source. You might have a fear of heights, because you understand your body is fragile and gravity is no joke. You might get nervous when you step up to ask someone out, because when you actually look in her eyes, her existence ceases to be theoretical. I might be afraid of protesting an unjust war or economic distortion, because I don't want an arrest on my record, because that would stab at my sense of solid self, my reputation as a "good Buddhist guy."

Life is unstable; life is electric. Fear, when we can face it, grounds us in our body and annihilates the pretense that we are supposed to be anywhere else. Fear destroys the naïve spiritual premise that we might "transcend" our human experience, and encourages us to be right here. When we accommodate fear, we just show up, perhaps shaking a little, but good enough to be worthy of what's in front of us. From the viewpoint of sacredness, fear is saying to us, "This is really happening. You are really alive right now. These jitters you feel are the basic life force of your heart and mind, your windhorse. Please stop wishing for another now!"

This approach to fear as the most fundamental emotion connecting us to our humanity still does not mean we have to seek it out. We don't have to become some kind of daredevil or kamikaze meditator, dive-bombing into our worst anxieties in order to aggressively achieve liberation. That cavalier attitude would be another way of bypassing the present moment, an intense form of spiritual and emotional materialism. We don't need an extreme spiritual practice—we just need to work bravely with whatever fear we naturally experience.

Speaking personally, I experience fear so many times each day that I can't even keep track. Fear is always with us, and we can take a friendly approach to viewing it as a valid and meaningful experience, a recurring energy that shows us our own beating heart, and shows us that we are alive and awake. The full experience of fear is a prelude to every moment of growth along our journey. Fear is the most sacred emotion of all. Fearlessness is what happens when we approach a moment of fear as sacred, and treat its arrival as if the doorbell is ringing, rather than the burglar alarm sounding.

These five families of emotional energy—Buddha (fear), Vajra (anger), Ratna (pride), Padma (desire), and Karma (jealousy)— form a basic Tantric map showing us how we can begin to navigate our various emotional experiences as sacred and awake.*

THE ENVIRONMENT IS ALIVE: *DRALA*

What does the world of objects, the environment, begin to look like when we start to experience our mind as sacred? It's actually a pretty simple equation: as we come to respect our own mind, we come to see the sacredness of the atmosphere with which our mind interacts. Within the Shambhala teachings, the sacred energy of a particular environment is called *drala*, a Tibetan word that literally means "beyond or above enemy." The problem for the commuter in each of us is that, as we grasp after the objects of experience, the environment risks being reduced to a bunch of dead and lifeless inputs for our momentary pleasures. We don't see the environment as a living and animated space itself, because, with-

*This is my interpretation. In traditional Tantric teachings, the "Buddha" family of emotional energy is not linked with a specific emotional response. Rather, it is the basic family from which the other emotional energies described above come. On the neurotic side, Buddha energy is linked with our most primal tendency to desensitize, or numb out against present experience. On its wisdom side, Buddha energy describes our most fundamental level of awareness, an open space that is able to accommodate all emotions and perceptions. However, when we experience the vulnerability of the present moment fully, our most primal response is fear. According to the Shambhala teachings, fear is always the most fundamental reaction to fully witnessing the groundless nature of our life. From this standpoint, the deepest emotion we must befriend is fear, and thus it is linked with the most foundational level of awareness and emotional energy here.

out self-awareness, we don't experience ourselves as fully alive. The commuter's world—the consumer's world—becomes wrapped in dead plastic. If the world is inanimate and unsacred, then all that's left to do is consume and dispose of it.

But if the mind is held as sacred, then the environment that the mind engages with becomes sacred as well. The Shambhala teachings point us toward a total transformation of the subject-object experience, in which the rousing of windhorse allows us to view our subjectivity as a sacred space, and the study of *drala* enables us to see the environment of objects as alive and sacred, too. Instead of trying to consume resources, we begin to view ourselves as the stewards of a living environment. We connect with the living quality of the food we eat, whether it is vegetarian or animal protein, we see cultural vibrancy in the clothes we wear and pick them carefully, we see the energy created by the buildings we design, and we see sacredness in the natural environment and construct our society to be in harmony with that sacredness. On the deepest level, interdependence is about seeing that subject and object are never separate, but always exist relationally, while the Tantric teachings utilize ritual and ceremony to see subject and object as sacred. The only way the human race will be inspired to create a sustainable relationship with the earth is if we hold both humans and the ecosystem as sacred entities worthy of coexisting.

Most of the cultures of the ancient world had stories to bring the natural world to life, so that people would come of age feeling like the natural world was a living being to be respected. Many creation myths and tribal narratives have this sense of humanizing nature. Within the shamanistic lineage of Shambhala's ancient Tibetan heritage, the alive energy of the natural world was given a similar narrative of sentiency, and *drala* was not only viewed as the sacred energy pervading the environment, but also as invisible spirits, beings who protected the environment and could be called upon by those whose minds were not caught up in grasping. Either way, whether we think of *drala* as the sacred energy of our environment, or as the spirits who inhabit that environment, the result is the same: as we come to see the sacredness of our own mind, we appreciate the sacredness of our world.

With a commitment to self-awareness, a commitment to relationships, and a commitment to sacredness through the dissolution of unnecessary boundaries between spiritual and secular understanding, we can begin to talk about society's journey home, the road we are on collectively, as a group of human beings.

PART IV

Society's Journey

It is no measure of health to be well-adjusted to a profoundly sick society.

—KRISHNAMURTI

Like me, you could . . . be unfortunate enough to stumble upon a silent war. The trouble is that once you see it, you can't unsee it. And once you've seen it, keeping quiet, saying nothing, becomes as political an act as speaking out. Either way, you're accountable.

—ARUNDHATI ROY, *Power Politics*

13

THE WISDOM OF NO ESCAPE
FROM THE WORLD

Early Buddhist texts, as translated, have a tendency to place a surprisingly negative spin on the notion of existing in the "world." Worldly life is often depicted as a dirty realm inhabited by those still caught up in their samsaric commute, those blinded by activities of commerce and romance, those who have yet to get serious about the spiritual journey. Before we start thinking that Buddhism is some world-denouncing pursuit, we have to understand the cultural context of such ancient statements.

When Siddhartha lived, all of society was divided into small tribal city-states. Up until very recently in human history, this was mostly still the case. In ancient India, if a person became serious about his spiritual path, he left the city behind and "went forth" into the wilderness just beyond the city, to engage in contemplative and yogic practices.

To understand the context of the Awake-ist teachings in the

twenty-first century, we have to recognize a very recent historical development: escape from society is now almost impossible.

Growing up, my mother's apartment was on the Upper West Side of Manhattan, and our block was named Edgar Allan Poe Street, because Poe wrote several of his major works living in a farmhouse near that site in the 1840s and '50s. For anyone familiar with Manhattan, this should give you some pause. This was a bit more than a century and a half ago, and there was a farmhouse, and a large surrounding farm, right on Broadway, in what is now a densely populated island metropolis. If Poe wanted to get away from the "world" for a writer's retreat (or a meditation retreat), all he had to do was stroll a few miles north up Broadway! The city, and for all intents and purposes the "world," simply ceased to exist two miles downtown. This is very similar to what the Buddha did a few millennia earlier, when he left his father's estate in the small tribal region of Shakya to pursue his personal awakening in the forest, which was most likely right outside the city. Thus, when an ancient text describes "worldly concerns," it is very important to understand that this is actually a geographic designation, not an existential one. The "world" really just encompassed the frenetic endeavors of life in the city, that place of hustle and bustle, lust and heartache, career and ambition, art and entertainment, government and politics. Deeply pursuing spiritual practice meant leaving the city behind.

Nowadays, by contrast, the entire East Coast of the United States, from the southern suburbs of Washington, D.C., all the way to north of Boston, has the continuous population density of a city, forming one massive "megalopolis." There is no escape from the world anymore. In truth, because all phenomena are interdependent, the idea of escaping the world, or of somehow being "in it, but not of it," was always just an existential fantasy, a delusion of transcendentalism. But now even the fantasy of leaving the world behind seems gone. Even my favorite meditation retreat center, in the remote Northeast Kingdom of Vermont, several hours away from the nearest city of Montreal, has had wireless Internet for many years.

The Road Home has been written on the fundamental premise that there is no escape from your own mind, because it's where you live, whether you like it or not. So, if there's no escape from your own mind, and there is also no escape from "the world" anymore, what does this mean for the journey of awakening?

It means we must see the interdependence between the journey of the individual and the journey of the society in which that individual lives. This crucial relationship between personal and communal realities is also outlined in early Buddhist teachings, with their emphasis on embracing *sangha*, a community of practicing peers. It isn't the case that the earliest Buddhist teachings were completely isolationist; they just de-prioritized "worldly concerns" for certain historical reasons that are no longer valid, if they ever really were to begin with. Personal transformation and societal transformation have always been completely interwoven— it is merely a recent evolution in human history that has allowed us to be irrevocably confronted with this timeless fact. The bad news is there is no escape from engaging in society. The good news is that there is no need to. Because we can't escape the world, we must embrace the world as part of our practice.

RECONCILING PERSONAL RESPONSIBILITY WITH INTERDEPENDENCE

The historical Buddha mentioned two difficult-to-reconcile facts about the way reality is structured. First, echoing the sentiments of personal accountability that we discussed in chapter 2, he said that sentient beings are the inheritors of *their own* karma. This was a call to accountability and self-empowerment, not an attempt to blame people for their difficult circumstances or experiences. It means that, at the end of the day, only an individual can work with his own mind, his own habits, his own conditioning. This first relevant premise seems quite conservative, or libertarian, on its face. It seems to be a very "pull yourself up by your bootstraps" way of looking at life. Taking personal responsibility to heart is also how we overcome the idea that some relationship—spiritual, romantic, or otherwise—is going to swoop in and save us from the tough job of working with our own life situation. The basic premise of Buddhism is that there is no savior to worship: nobody is going to save you from your own mind. Nobody can get into the heart of your experience and fix anything for you. If you want to make your own internal experience more hospitable, only you can do that work. Others can always support and guide you and spark insights, but ultimately you are your own boss and the agent of understanding your mind and opening your heart. Nothing has been more profound for me than taking this teaching on accountability to heart, especially when I fall on hard emotional times and must remind myself that my heartmind is my true home.

Now, the Buddha—as well as countless wise ladies and gentlemen throughout history—also said that all phenomena are completely interdependent. Nothing ever happens in a vacuum. Whatever you built, you didn't build it all alone. In societal terms, this truth puts a huge dent in much of the logic of self-creation that currently enables a massively unequal accumulation of resources among a very few members of our society. In spiritual terms, whatever awakening you achieve, it is conditioned by the influence of others. Even the Buddha had teachers. He awakened because of a supportive environment where all the necessary conditions were present for his journey. He didn't even teach himself how to meditate!*

Cocreation is just the very way our universe is structured, the way everything happens. If you are reading this book on paper or on a device, the very surface you are reading from connects you with countless other beings, from the paper mill to the Apple or Kindle factory, as well as to everyone those people ever connected with. Without those people, some of whom toil in horrible conditions, this book could not happen.† Whether we see it or not, we support, influence, and condition each other's experience all the time. If you are reading this in a café, and the barista was kind to you and you said something sweet in return, that exchange may influence the quality of thoughts and feelings you both have for hours into the future, as you interact with many other people. The pond never stops rippling. The immense suffering that exists in our shared society implicates all of us, and is akin to the "silent war" that Arundhati Roy declares cannot be unseen once it is witnessed.

How do we reconcile the two teachings above—personal responsibility for karma, and interdependence—which seem to directly contradict each other? Here's what I believe. The second premise, interdependence, provides the proper and appropriate context for understanding the first premise, personal responsibility for one's karma. In other words, it is when we begin to witness interdependence that we see the true importance of personal

---

*It's said that Siddhartha studied with two different masters of concentration before going off on his own. He saw strengths and limitations in their practice methods—namely, the confining attempt to permanently objectify states of concentration. He later utilized and evolved their meditative methods into his own system of meditation.

†I explored the philosophy of interdependence in detail in my first book, *One City: A Declaration of Interdependence*.

responsibility. Once we see that nothing happens in a vacuum, that's the exact moment that we are properly inspired to become accountable for our own mind.

If we separate personal responsibility from the context of interdependence, we end up psychologically and spiritually disabled, holding to a vision of life that is isolated, fearful, and compassion-deficient. We end up with Thomas Hobbes's awful interpretation of this sacred world as "a war of all against all." We end up with Gordon Gekko's emotionally crippling falsehood that "greed is good." For our political leaders, or anyone else, to preach personal responsibility without preaching interdependence is to engage in an unintended cruelty, because it leads us to isolate our view of personal transformation outside of its true context, which is always the community and society in which we exist.

The version of personal responsibility that comes from seeing interdependence holds each of us no less accountable for learning to work with our own mind. But when we see interdependence, we experience ourselves as connected, brave, and deeply empathetic. This transformed view makes all the difference in the world.

On the deepest level, even the thoughts that arise in our head during meditation are cocreated with the society in which we live. Sakyong Mipham Rinpoche makes this point beautifully in *The Shambhala Principle*. When we think any thought, it is a reflection of our cultural heritage, our education, and our socialization. Even when we sit down to meditate alone, we hear the voices of our parents (whether kind or harsh) and we think within the ideological frameworks of our education (whether encouraging or oppressive). When song lyrics come to us in meditation, we are hearing the music of our culture (whether it manifests as brilliant art or apathetic consumerism).

While our relationship with our experience is deeply intimate and personal, each time we sit down to meditate, we are plugging into our social conditioning. Within the home of our awareness, the thoughts we think and the emotions we feel link us to all other beings who have ever influenced us, especially those people who most directly taught us how to relate to our thoughts and emotions. Every thought and feeling we have is influenced by family, teachers, and the community in which we live. The bad news is that this means none of us has ever had a completely original thought—all of our thoughts are momentary expressions of an inherited social context. This doesn't mean we are uncreative, though, because we each get to synthesize the ideas we inherit into new and brilliant expressions.

If we only looked at personal accountability for karma, we would end up with claims about reality that make no sense. It would be preposterous to argue that all those self-loathing thoughts that tell you that you are "not good enough"—those thoughts that constantly beat you up—are somehow independent of all the advertisements you saw today that sold you an aggressively idealized and airbrushed version of how to be you. It would be both cruel and inaccurate to claim that the sense of self experienced by an impoverished or historically oppressed person in our society exists separately from the social messages, both subtle and obvious, which that person receives daily. As Sakyong Mipham Rinpoche puts it, "Many of the thoughts we take to be our own are really coming from social ceremonies that have been grafted onto our mind." Why does he use the word "ceremony" here? Because he is drawing a link between the rituals an individual practices in her spiritual life and the rituals that we engage in when we participate in society. As we've said, according to the Shambhala teachings on sacredness, every communal act is a social ceremony, whether it's a trip to the grocery store or navigating the system of streets, highways, and traffic lights that allows us to arrive safely at work.

This incredible fact—that even our most personal and private thoughts are interdependently constructed with our society—is the ultimate downfall of all our libertarian tendencies, whether those tendencies take the Eastern form of the yogi or the Western form of the cowboy. The view of interdependence necessarily moves us beyond the naïve notion that our spiritual journey can be isolated from our societal context.

THE THREE LEVELS OF PRACTICE

In 2006, I was introduced to Eric Schneiderman who, at that time, was an attorney and New York State senator. He is currently the attorney general for the State of New York. I was in the process of setting up the Interdependence Project with some friends, a nonprofit organization committed to integrating secular Buddhist practice with activism, the arts, and ideas from Western psychology.

While not a Buddhist (his spiritual practice is Judaism), Eric had a broad background in both Eastern and Western philosophy and an interest in Buddhist thought that began when he was a student of the young professor Robert Thurman. After receiving Eric's advice on social activism, I joined together with the meditation teacher Sharon Salzberg and other thinkers from the worlds of dharma, yoga, activism, arts, and politics to develop a philosophical framework for what a journey of awakening might look like when (1) personal accountability, (2) interpersonal awareness, and (3) political and cultural engagement are all held in a holistic balance.

We adopted the name "transformational activism" to denote a practice of integrating these three levels of engagement into one sacred practice. Many of my contributions to this growing movement have come directly from my study and practice of the Shambhala teachings under the guidance of Sakyong Mipham Rinpoche and others. The scope of the Shambhala teachings includes a radical view of enlightened society that compels us to place any traditional teachings of Awake-ism in their broadest possible social context, in order to cultivate both societal institutions and a cultural environment that supports awakening for all individuals who share in our society. Out of our collaboration, we developed a simple framework for considering awakening on these three levels, three aspects of engagement that always occur simultaneously.

Level 1: Personal Practice—Living in Awareness

The introduction and first section of this book were devoted to the path of self-awareness. While so many people come to the Buddhist path because they want to help others and change the world, there is no way around making personal transformation through the practice of meditation and ethics the foundation of one's path. Without a committed practice of self-awareness, we end up trying to affect our relationships and our society while still in the same state of mind that creates our habitual patterns. For example, maybe we go to an antiwar rally with no idea how our own aggression operates in the realm of thought and emotion, and with no tools for dealing skillfully with the angry thoughts and feelings that come up toward those with whom we disagree. As Einstein said, "We cannot solve our problems with the same thinking we used when we created them."

By always having an active practice of self-awareness, whether on the meditation cushion or the yoga mat or elsewhere, we draw a harmonious balance between personal accountability for the workings of our minds and our interdependence with other members of society. Therefore, the foundational component of any activism, and of any bodhisattva activity, is progressive action on a deeply personal level. We might not normally think of mind-body health and awareness practices as "progressive action," but in fact, they are. If we change the way we relate to our own mind, we necessarily begin to shift the way we relate to others. If we learn to resensitize and slowly overcome our aggression and our greed, we affect every human relationship and the society in which we exist.

Level 2: Interpersonal Practice—Awakening in Relationships
Sakyong Mipham Rinpoche has pointed out that the basic building blocks of any society are the relationship between two individuals. This view has its roots in Buddhist psychology, where it is demonstrated that the mind can only hold one object in attention during each moment. When we are mindful, we experience our social presence as a series of momentary connections with one other being. These moments of interpersonal connection are like the Lego building blocks of our social awareness. The second section of this book addressed the bodhisattva path in a contemporary context, the journey of working in relationships. With each relationship—with our partners, our family, our friends, our dates, our coworkers, our neighbors, our creative partners, and strangers—we experience ourselves in community. We must each engage in these personal relationships with mindfulness and empathy, both in order to work with our own mind more skillfully and to navigate our society more effectively.

Without this sometimes missing link of interpersonal practice, "society" becomes a vague abstraction. We cannot think about an abstract concept like "all people" or "all beings" until we start to form direct and mindful relationships with each being we encounter. Without a constant mode of relational awareness, as well as practices to awaken our relational being, society will remain a series of shapes and colors, like a Rothko painting. Interpersonal awareness is the key link between the personal and the collective.

Level 3: Collective Practice—Toward Enlightened Society

On the third level of our practice, the societal level, the truth of interdependence comes into its full measure. Likewise, it is on the societal level that our understanding of sacredness, as we discussed in chapter 10, becomes crucial. Again, sacredness refers to the holistic view that our spiritual self and our worldly existence can never be isolated from each other. Thus, whatever divinity is available to human beings, whatever our highest values might be, the only place we can witness that divinity directly is within our life in society.

An activist holds the implicit view that our institutions, as well as the political decisions made by a community or society, are the key factor in how individuals experience themselves within that society. Here, politics no longer refers to simplistic and outdated divisions like Democrat or Republican, or even conservative and progressive. Instead, politics refers to the need to engage with society fully in order to help each other awaken. Traditional Buddhist spiritual teachings, among other practice traditions, often only go so far as the second level—the interpersonal level of service—in their ethical mandates, commenting on the need to engage compassionately in relationships of service along the bodhisattva path. But with the awareness of this third level, we start to ask deeper questions about human suffering and confusion. For example, we might have a spiritual mandate to serve others, and we might volunteer at a soup kitchen or a prison. This would be practice on the second level. But collective practice refers to questioning and transforming the very structures that necessitate so many soup kitchens and prisons in the wealthiest society that has ever existed on earth. Without asking the questions "Why are there soup kitchens to begin with? Why does the United States incarcerate five to eight times the number of people than does any other wealthy nation?" we won't really get to the systemic root of collective suffering. Unless we get at the institutional structures that mold our personal and interpersonal experience, our understanding will be incomplete. If our practice is going to truly help the world, it must evolve beyond personal awareness and service work into a true sense of participation in society, of questioning the decisions that we have made together about how our society should be arranged. This is the deepest lesson of interdependence. Society always implicates us as its participants and primary agents of transformation (or as agents of the status quo), no matter how much we would like to shirk our duty and claim the spiritually impossible status of being "in the world, but not of it."

In the Shambhala teachings, the third level of collective practice is divided into an engagement with both the social and the cultural realms. Here, "social" refers to the set of institutions and systems (including huge institutions, such as the economic and political systems that we live within, all the way down to a school board, for instance) that condition the minds of every individual. The "cultural" refers to the shared environment in which we experience ourselves as creative beings, capable of expressing ourselves to each other. The cultural sphere is where awakened creativity and artistic endeavor become crucial, which we'll get to in chapter 15.

As we have seen, the Buddhist teachings on emptiness and nonfixation demonstrate that nothing about our world is fixed—rather, it is mainly the frozen narratives of human minds that hold our social reality in place. Therefore, no single thing about the way our society runs is set in stone, however much it feels like the gears are always turning at someone else's command. The institutional decisions that a society makes have no solid ground, no fixed nature. Even the lines that divide countries are superimposed onto physical terrain. It is a mark of great spiritual laziness to take the world we inherit as a given. It is constantly in flux, and it is our own projective mind that creates it. A true visionary sees society itself as a shared projection, a kind of hologram we are all cocreating with no permanent basis, one that can always be reimagined based on the shifting views of human nature that we hold.

Reimagining society is therefore an extension of the logic of sacred imagination that we discussed in chapter 11. We are choosing together—day by day—to participate in a shared projection, a collective movie with millions of directors. Of course, within the massive inequalities of our society, it often feels like a few directors have much greater power over our shared movie, but, in the reality of Buddha nature, each individual has the same potential to awaken to the script.

CONTEMPLATING THE THREE LEVELS TOGETHER

When viewed together as a sacred path, these three levels of practice—the personal, the interpersonal, and the collective—offer a clear template for a journey of awakening. When all three levels are held in awareness, we have the chance to examine which aspects of our life we might be focusing on, and which levels of practice we might be avoiding. Each of us—whether we have any familiarity with Buddhist teachings or not—tends to be really good at cultivating compassion and mindfulness on at least one of these three levels of practice. More rare is the true practitioner, who finds a complete and harmonious balance between all three, day in and day out.

A classic stereotype of someone who practices only the personal level of awakening is a cave-dwelling yogi, the one who has abandoned "the world" in order to liberate himself from confusion. It is crucial to note that, in the paradigm of the Shambhala teachings, this solitary yogi is not the idealized image of a practitioner. Of course, each of us can benefit from deep periods of retreat and practice where we learn the subtleties of how the mind really works, and how thought and emotion lead to action. Periods of retreat are a big part of the Shambhala path. However, the Shambhala ideal of an awakened being, of a Buddha, is called the Rigden, a Tibetan title denoting an enlightened leader of society who attains full enlightenment through engagement in every aspect of society. At the center of all Shambhala shrines is an archetypal representation of this Rigden figure, replacing the historical Siddhartha Gautama, whose path to enlightenment involved (at least temporarily) leaving society behind.

Meanwhile, some of us are very inspired to take care of others interpersonally, within small communities and the organizations with which we work. Some of us, like a loving mother, devote ourselves wholeheartedly to service within a small group of relationships. But, like that overwhelmed mother, we often do not have the time to work on our own personal growth, nor do we raise our gaze to examine and stay present with the dilemmas facing our larger communities and society. The overwhelmed mother would be an example of somebody focusing intently on the second level of practice—the interpersonal level.

On the third level, many activists know what it is like to work themselves to the bone in the name of justice and compassion, to try to change policies and systems within a community or society. Likewise, many artists and writers know what it's like to stay up all night dreaming of expressions that might change the way others view themselves and the narratives that shape their experience of reality. For many people in both of these groups, burnout and disappointment arise because they often lack the tools to work with their own heartminds as they set about changing culture and society. In the name of a larger mission, they may also often fail to stay fully present in their personal relationships. The burned-out activist would be a fitting stereotype to describe somebody who is focusing only on the third level of practice—the collective level.

Within this three-part framework of personal, interpersonal, and collective, we have the beautiful opportunity every day to contemplate the balance among these three levels of awakening. I try to do one practice that engages in these three levels daily. On the first level, I practice meditation and yoga each morning, in order to establish an ongoing ground of befriending myself and coming home to my own awareness. On the second level, I try to generate compassionate and good listening and right speech for my partner, my family, my friends, my students, and my coworkers, noticing when I want to avoid a certain relationship. This interpersonal level is sometimes as simple as remembering that a phone call often works better than an e-mail, or just remembering the practice of bringing home flowers. On the third level, I try to stay aware of political, social, and cultural realities and apply the principles of mindfulness, compassion, and interdependent sacredness to my engagement with whatever issues I take on. I try to remember activities of transformation that not only help individuals, but also transform the shared views and policies by which we collectively live.

It is with the balance of these three levels that we become full practitioners of a social vision, in which the journey of awakening becomes fully integrated with all aspects of life. When this happens, we experience the sacred collapse of constructed divisions between our worldly existence and our spiritual awakening. It is by balancing our commitment to practice on all three levels daily that a scared world can become a sacred world.

When we began our collaboration, Eric Schneiderman said, "I hope your communities come to see their meditation and yoga practices as profound *political acts* and to see their political work and social engagement as profound *spiritual practices*." Imagine a world where all of us held that view.

14

SCARED WORLD
VS. SACRED WORLD
3 S's and 3 C's

Let's return for a moment to the teachings on personal karma, and the three poisonous tendencies—grasping, rejecting, and desensitizing. Again, when these three problematic reactions are described as nouns, they are described either as passion, aggression, and ignorance, or greed, hatred, and delusion.* Within iconographic Tibetan depictions of an individual's commute through samsara, these three poisonous strategies are symbolized by a rooster (representing passionate grasping), a snake (representing aggressive rejecting), and a pig (representing ignorant desensitizing).

Professor and Zen teacher David Loy writes compellingly about the ways that these three poisons have been institutionalized

---

*Within Indo-Tibetan Buddhism, the trio is usually translated as passion, aggression, and ignorance, whereas within Zen and Theravada you more often see greed, hatred, and delusion.

in our social systems. He analyzes subjects such as corporate personhood and the military-industrial complex as a way to begin to explore what a dharmic social theory might look like. The most compelling aspect of using these three poisonous reactions as a way to begin to explore the link between the personal, interpersonal, and collective levels of practice is its theoretical simplicity. Any theory of society that is not rooted in the insights of personal practice will be ill-fitting, and from a contemplative standpoint, it will also be unscientific. Such a framework allows us to apply the insights of our personal practice to our collective experience.

In creating a dharmic social theory, the most scientific approach is to utilize the insights of personal practice to build our understanding of what is happening on a systemic level. In other words, if the cultivation of a certain state of mind, like empathy, is demonstrated to be beneficial on the personal level, it would also be beneficial to create social institutions that foster those same qualities. On the other hand, if a state of mind was demonstrated to be repeatedly destructive to the psychology of an individual, it would also follow that creating social structures that encourage that state of mind would be destructive for society as a whole.

EXPERIENCING THE POISONS ON A COLLECTIVE LEVEL: THE THREE S'S

What happens when the three root poisons gain power not just over individuals but in society at large—when they become embedded in the interdependent systems and institutions in which individuals operate together?

When our habitual strategy of desensitizing becomes socialized as an avoidant norm, we turn into a society of people incapable of resting in the present moment, repeatedly avoiding the real conditions of human life on earth. This numbness manifests as a society of distracted multitaskers and frenetic commuters. One of the main markers of a desensitized society is a group of overly busy people, constantly distracted by technology and entertainment, unable to look reality in the face, unable to ask deep questions about what really matters. In this society, we settle for infotainment rather than information and consume entertainment rather than appreciating art, preferring to numb ourselves instead of looking deeper. We seek Hollywood melodramas to watch at a distance, rather than finding ways to engage in our live communities fully. This habitual poison of ignorance manifests as a society of people who avoid—avoid themselves and avoid eye contact with each other. In such a society, human connection is devalued and the world becomes something we watch on screens.

Another manifestation of a desensitized society is a for-profit media, in which the interdependent narratives of events are always framed, spun, and decontextualized in the search for quick, marketable content. In such a media environment, we often pay more attention to the dramas of celebrities than to wars and oppression, because to pay attention and open our hearts would be to resensitize, which is always a painful process. Sometimes it is just easier to focus on a TV show than to hear news of a new war over scarce resources that are seemingly becoming scarcer all the time.

The individuals of such a society experience themselves as constantly *scared*, the first of the three S's. When we live in a constant state of avoidance, the simple truths of life become deeply threatening. We become scared of feeling emotion, scared of boredom and space, scared of knowledge, and deeply and tragically scared of our imminent death. Death should be a close friend, because death happens to every human being, yet many times if we just speak its name, we are accused of being morbid, one of the surest signs of a society that attempts to avoid reality.

In a related way, in an ignorant society, youth is airbrushed and commodified, and the elderly, rather than being celebrated and honored for their wisdom, are shuffled off behind closed doors.

Even if we don't consciously experience fear as the landmark of our desensitized society, we might just experience a state of apathy, turning the single word "whatever" into our preferred mantra for cultural participation. "I don't really pay much attention to what's going on in the world. I know I probably should, but . . . whatever."

This "whatever" mentality is nothing more than fear frozen into disengagement. "Whatever" really means that we tried to be sensitive in the past, tried to get involved, but then we got hurt and disappointed, and so we gave up. When "whatever" becomes our mantra, the prospect of lifting our eyes from our various distractions, of feeling our world and all of its suffering beings, becomes deeply threatening. Apathy is the rusted armor worn by a scared human being.

Within a state of ignorance, we become avoidant of our fellow human beings if they fall into any available category of "otherness," categories that are easily constructed and manipulated in order to accentuate fear. Who, after all, in this interdependent world of commuters, is *not* an immigrant? And what leader hasn't made a mistake? As in the classic Buddhist story of the snake that is really a harmless rope, ignorance causes us to live in a panic constructed by darkness, in both subtle and obvious ways. Because we have created institutions of numbness, we all experience ourselves as scared to turn on the light. This social conditioning is one of the reasons it is so difficult to begin to allow ourselves to feel the space of our own awareness within meditation practice. When we spend lifetimes numbing out against now, even the gentle stillness of the present moment becomes a threat. Even slowing down long enough to look at your own heartmind becomes an act of revolution against the sheer pace of our social karma.

When the poison of grasping and fixation becomes embedded in our economic exchanges, we experience ourselves as *selfish*, the second of the three S's. When desire becomes an obsession, it manifests as greed, narrowing the scope of our awareness as we cower in object-management mode, trying to make ourselves permanently safe. When this mentality becomes institutionalized, we begin to think that consumerism, the outermost layer of materialism, is the only safe path available to us. Hiding out in the survival-frenzied portion of our brains, we mistake instant gratification for lasting happiness. The problem with fixated desire is that in our narrowness we lose any sense of larger context, the awareness of interdependence that is necessary for any healthy societal participation.

As they helped shape the views of human happiness that mold the value systems of the modern world, many profoundly influential political economists—from Adam Smith to Milton Friedman—mistook narrow self-interest for some form of deep contentment. They then produced a theory of value and exchange based on institutionalizing greed as serving the greater interests of society, mostly because of an odd definition of the word "profit," which fails to take any social context into account. Critiquing this logic is in no way a critique of capitalism, as many different forms of free market systems are possible, and markets can operate within the frame of many different ethical priorities. However, the lazy assumption that greed—which is demonstrably harmful to the individual who gets caught up in it—is somehow beneficial when replicated across our social institutions does not stand the test of any contemplative analysis of how lasting happiness is actually achieved.

Again, a basic premise that becomes an axiom when looking at the relationship between the insights of one's personal practice and the insights of our societal systems is that, if a state of mind is destructive for the individual, it cannot somehow become helpful when reproduced socially. Research is beginning to demonstrate that the most extreme accumulations of wealth damage an individual's ability to empathize with others. The ability to feel and care for another human's experience is one of the main precursors for personal contentment and fulfillment. If greed causes an individual to become less happy by damaging the pathways of empathy—which the Buddha himself clearly said was the outcome of becoming stuck in greed—then greed cannot ever lead to societal happiness. Only systems of empathy can do that.

When the poison of aggression and rejection becomes a social norm, we experience ourselves as *separate*, the third of the three S's. Always seeing other people as potential threats results in our having to be constantly on guard and ready to preemptively strike back against "enemies." We live in a state of protective isolation, with a nervous system on code red all the time. Shambhala teachings emphasize our self-aggression, which refers to deep-seated habits of rejecting oneself as unworthy. This leads to alienation, a feeling of not belonging in one's life, a dark sense of isolation. When the aggression of separateness manifests toward others, we create barbed wire between ourselves and their experiences. We compete with coworkers, rather than collaborate. We send out the drones of war, rather than communicating and negotiating. Out of this feeling of separateness, we engage in true acts of violence against ourselves and each other, hoping to eliminate the "cancerous" elements. We create declarations of independence, rather than declarations of interdependence.

THREE C'S: OVERCOMING SOCIETY'S ADDICTION TO THE THREE POISONS

We have to ask ourselves repeatedly along this path if any other way of relating to our mind is possible. Simultaneously, we can also ask if another way of relating to society is possible.

Fortunately, we all have at least glimpsed another way of existing in society, which is based on the premise of learning to live in awareness, allowing ourselves to begin to feel the present moment, the most basic way that mindfulness counteracts our wandering commute. While it provides no defense against vulnerability, self-awareness slowly creates a sense of worthiness and belonging. As we have seen, when we are actually able to come home to our own awareness, we become *courageous* instead of only scared, because we begin to see, looking directly at experience, that there's no emotion we can't (eventually) handle. We can slowly begin to accommodate whatever feeling visits us. With courage, we are no longer experiencing a life lived in the dark, worrying about each day's unfolding as a series of theoretical snakes that might bite us at any moment, because we are repeatedly shining a light on our experiences. It's this courage that allows us to reclaim our sentient sensitivity, remembering how to feel and to appreciate that we *can* feel. With this courageous attitude, we become curious about our existence, a curiosity that helps us to overcome ignorance. As we become more curious, we see that reality is structured interdependently, and we actually want to understand the experience of other people.

This curious attitude leads us to become *compassionate* instead of selfish, as we begin to widen the scope of what matters to us, recovering our inherent ability to empathize. When we empathize, we start to explore definitions of personal happiness that now include the happiness of other beings, and we experience an inclusive sense of contentment that comes from knowing that other people are enjoying their lives as well, which makes us feel truly safe. With compassion, we overcome our self-absorption, the fastest road to nihilism.

Compassion leads us to feel *connected*, rather than separate. As we empathize and feel into the space of others' subjective experience, we lose our tendency to believe that reality is a constant battle against the "other." As we connect with interdependence more and more, we realize that there is no "other," at least not on the level of ultimate reality. Self and others form an inclusive totality with each other, like protons and electrons, and our care extends to members of society who we used to greet with aggression and disdain. Meanwhile, our intelligence leads us to create skillful boundaries, so that confused individuals cannot exert undue power over any system of relationships. We might love all sentient beings, but we don't vote for confused beings to lead us anywhere.

Which of these is actually the nature of human society, the three S's or the three C's? Is human society fundamentally broken? Does the future of the human race lie with the pessimistic appraisal of the three S's or the optimistic and inspirational vision of the three C's? And if human nature is really explained by the three S's, then what kind of future could we possibly have?

I remember being in New York City right after September 11, 2001, and feeling the greatest palpable tension between these two views that I have ever experienced. I returned to New York five days before September 11, after spending most of my first post-collegiate year living at Karme Choling, a Shambhala meditation center in rural Vermont. I remember the shock of the tragedy just as I was trying to transition back into city living and figure out how to pay my rent, but more than that I remember how compassionate, courageous, and connected all New Yorkers seemed to be in the days that followed. We were experiencing a massive gap in our social karma, a collective feeling of vulnerability, which provided the space necessary for us to connect with the three C's. And then the Bush administration and a for-profit cable news media swooped in with a revenge narrative crafted in the spitting image of the three S's. It was during the next few weeks that I decided to do a meditation teacher training. While I could not put words to it until a few years later, it was clear that the decision was based on feeling the tragic pull between these two visions of human nature, and feeling like the three S's were a dark manifestation of shared karmic patterns that I needed to commit myself to uprooting.

Rebecca Solnit writes about opposing visions of human nature that occur in the aftermath of disasters in her book *A Paradise Born in Hell*. She argues that disasters can often bring out the very best, not the worst, in humans. One organizer interviewed by Solnit states: "We in New York did not see the world or anyone as our enemy, and that same sense of solidarity and mutual aid within the city also extended to our wanting with all our might to prevent war and further killing in the world." Unfortunately, the Bush administration was too caught up in the three S's to look at what was actually happening in New York City in the aftermath of the attacks.

Many famous thinkers throughout history have felt their own conditioning toward greed and aggression and had no idea how to work with these as karmic forces, and therefore came to the conclusion that these forces must be "human nature." But master meditators have looked at the same qualities again and again in meditation, and determined confidently that the three poisons are very deeply ingrained habits, not our intrinsic nature. Until we begin to look deeply at our own mind through meditation, we might not believe that there's any other way to live in this world.

Conflating human habit with human nature is, sadly, a self-fulfilling prophecy. Samsara survives on the circular momentum of these closed, self-fulfilling loops. If we say that human nature is "a war of all against all" then we will create a system in that negative image, then look back later and claim we were right all along. "You see!" we will say, "I am feeling greedy right now, and so are the people I surround myself with! That proves that humans are inherently greedy!" Of course, this is the exact same type of hermetically sealed logic that holds that one unseasonably cold day in one city somehow disproves the larger truth of global warming.

So, when Thomas Hobbes said that human society was by nature "a war of all against all," it's not clear what within his own subjective experience of life he was drawing on to make this claim. When ancient economists said that the purpose of human life was to "maximize personal utility," it's not clear which human hearts they were actually studying psychologically. Most of the humans I know aren't really looking to maximize anything; they are looking to feel a sense of belonging and contentment and have somehow been taught that maximizing something or other is the way to feel most alive. Even using the cold phrase "utility" to describe human joy makes me think that the people creating these terms might not have known what the quality they were attempting to describe (contentment, fulfillment, satisfaction) actually feels like.

One of the most frustrating aspects of the Buddhist path, one that can lead us to great disappointment and even depression at times, is that meditators frequently fall into the trap of disheartenment, thinking that our stuck habits are in fact our nature. Guess what? We don't overcome our self-aggression the very first time we meditate. For many years, we may just notice the intensity of aggression's harsh *voice*. We may get disheartened and think that this self-aggression is our true nature. When we make this mistake, we lose confidence in Buddha nature, our potential to be the person we want to become. We each have many moments where we believe Hobbes was right (in early Buddhist narratives, the part of Hobbes was played by a being called Mara, and his enticing voice of doubt and negativity visited the Buddha frequently). In these moments, we think the best we can do is create utility-maximizing strategies for living out our life as scared, selfish, and separate. When our societal institutions reinforce this cynicism, and our daily participation in society mirrors these dark beliefs back to us, it becomes even easier to fall into this trap. After all, our nervous system is set up for a kind of interdependent mirroring with others, so if all social messages point to our basic *badness* and original sin, it's going to be very hard to feel that basic goodness is anything other than the naïve mythology of a few happy-go-lucky foreigners from a preindustrial culture. The three C's become like that mystical dragon that we're not sure really exists, a vision that all of us want to believe in but can't really bring ourselves to live by, like the lyrics of a John Lennon song.

When we work with our own personal practice, we slowly gain confidence that many of our personal strategic defenses were just mistaken karmic responses, acquired habits of defensive evasion that can be slowly shifted. We gradually gain confidence that there is, in fact, another way to live. We gain this confidence not just because the three C's feel much better, but also because we realize through practice that even the three S's are just a form of societal cocoon, a sort of frozen social intelligence. Both the three C's and the three S's come from basic goodness, as everything does. But just as we must learn to shed the layers of our personal cocoon in order to truly appreciate our own mind, we can only fully witness the basic goodness of our society by gradually leaving behind the three S's.

In parallel to our personal story, it is only through engaging with a deep contemplative journey that we can clarify what we believe about human society at its very core. This transformation does not happen quickly. If I had to make a numeric approximation, I would say that before I began meditating, I acted from belief in the three C's about one percent of the time. Now, it's closer to ten percent. While I still have a long way to go, just the transformation that has occurred so far has made me appreciate my own life immensely, and has made me more available and connected to other people than my teenage cynicism would ever have allowed me to dream I would be. Just the progress that I have made so far has convinced me that I want to live in a world of collaboration, not one of fear and isolation. Subsequently, I have become more and more optimistic that we can cultivate the existing wisdom of our economic, environmental, and political institutions into structures that mirror back to each of us our interdependence and our basic goodness. I am optimistic about engaging in the collective level of community and society as a part of my practice, not to overthrow some evil elite, some wrongly empowered "other," but because I have gained confidence that a society based on the three C's will be a much happier one. I have this confidence because my practice has demonstrated that a human life based on the three C's is a happier life.

There are so many systems of collective engagement that we could analyze to explore whether or not our social structures and hierarchies encourage the three S's or the three C's. Of course, much of the time what we experience is complexity and ambivalence, an experience that takes the form of a blending of optimism and pessimism about human nature and the nature of human society. You could apply the logic of the three S's and the three C's to any area of inquiry—your field of work, your family dynamics, your meditation *sangha*, your artistic community.

We can let our own interests guide us in applying this social framework to a wide array of social systems. It is no accident that as a Buddhist I am interested in economic systems of human value, and how resources are shared. My own practice—as well as working with students—has made it immensely clear that maybe the greatest psychological obstacle we all face is a sense of personal worth. Our views of value shape our sense of the worthiness, or unworthiness, of our life. The issue of how we perceive our own value on the personal level, how we value each other on the interpersonal level, and value the planet on a collective level, seems to be at the very root of our society's sense of self, our deepest sense of belonging in this world. As we live in a world where a tiny group of billionaires hoards more resources than the poorer half of humanity, and as our collective resource consumption pushes us all to the brink of environmental collapse, the issue of wealth seems to have the most direct implications for how we value human society on this increasingly endangered planet. The point of a compassionate analysis is never to vilify enemies, but rather to look at how systems of thought influence the individual, and how an individual can affect relationships and collective experience as a practice of awakening. Because nothing is fixed, any time we relate to ourselves or others with confidence in the three C's, we slowly shift the entire organizing principle of our society, just a little bit.

15

THE CULTURE OF AWAKENING
Art and Transformation

The purpose of a work of art is bodhisattva action. This means that your production, manifestation, demonstration, and performance should be geared toward waking people up from their neurosis. Being an "artist" is not an occupation, it is your life, your whole being.

—CHOGYAM TRUNGPA RINPOCHE

There is a classic encounter captured on video where Allen Ginsberg asked Chogyam Trungpa Rinpoche, in front of a large audience, about the enlightened possibilities of jazz music, the blues, and rock 'n' roll. Trungpa answered, with a playful humor, that jazz and the blues both had enlightened possibilities, but rock 'n' roll had lesser possibilities, claiming rock was too "Coca-Cola-oriented." Ginsberg pressed Trungpa Rinpoche, his guru and friend, on the point, but came to no conclusion. There are some times that I have to respectfully disagree with the founder of my lineage. I'm just happy that it was too early to discuss hip-hop or electronic music, because I fear Trungpa Rinpoche might not get those, either. I think rock 'n' roll, like any other form of music or art, has the ability to aid our awakening, rather than just being the distracting sound track of our groggy commute through materialism. Whether or not you agree about rock 'n' roll's enlightened potential, the fact that Trungpa Rinpoche attracted such amazing artists as students says a lot. In many ways, it was his artistic emphasis that attracted both of my parents to study with him.

There is no doubt that Trungpa Rinpoche was at heart an artist of renaissance versatility. He was deeply interested in and well-trained in poetry, photography, theater, flower arranging, calligraphy, painting, and many other forms of creative expression. My mother, who spent much of her life as a painter before becoming a Buddhist psychotherapist, comments that even when he was teaching traditional dharma and philosophy, it was as if Trungpa Rinpoche were painting with his words. This gives many of his transcribed oral teachings a mystique and a creative magic that can be both deeply inspiring and difficult to penetrate.

This tradition of dharma art as part of practice has been fully passed down as a central element of the Shambhala teachings and culture. Sometimes when I see Sakyong Mipham Rinpoche, he will ask me to compose a poem right on the spot. Poetry is a huge part of our lineage, and I had the great fortune of receiving my first real lesson in poetry as a young child from Allen Ginsberg, when a few of us "dharma brats" were invited to his East Village apartment to write poems with him, which felt in retrospect like a real transmission of the Shambhala lineage. Now, when the Sakyong asks me for a spontaneous poem, I consider it a way to reconnect with my lineage. While whatever I come up with for him is usually very far from my best work, the process keeps me on my toes, and keeps me aware of the fact that creativity is forever part of my path of awakening.

Why do the Shambhala teachings devote so much energy to creative pursuits and dharmic art forms? As one senior student and artist, Jack Niland, put it in the documentary *Crazy Wisdom*, Trungpa Rinpoche saw that "in order to create an enlightened society, you have to change the culture, and in order to change the culture, you have to change the art." While it could be argued that our economic and ecological systems condition our sense of self more deeply than our cultural sensibilities, the way a society experiences itself is always based on its artistic and cultural practices.

So many artists I know feel an ongoing tension between their passion for creative expression and their longing to be a bodhisattva, wanting their voice to benefit others, rather than just carelessly throwing more fuel upon the great bonfire of consumerism. What does it mean to make your creative process sacred and awake? It means that you are looking at your own artistic practice as inseparable from your spiritual path, and you are exploring the effects of art on the personal, the interpersonal, and the collective levels all at once.

On the personal level, engaging in a creative process can aid your meditation practice, and allow you to see your mind's habits and wisdom directly as you move through a mode of expression. For me, while I have dabbled in other forms of expression, writing has always been the way I understand myself and my world. I've identified as a writer since before I identified as a Buddhist.

On the interpersonal level, we might sit and contemplate the intention for our creativity with an eye toward how it connects us with others. Because creative people often spend so much time alone, contemplating the interpersonal level of our intention is a good way to maintain perspective. Of course, one way to ruin any work of art is for the artist to be too forced or rigid with a sense of purpose. However, without sacrificing the freedom of our work, we can always contemplate the intention behind the ongoing process of our art-making itself. If the intention of art is just a sarcastic "whatever," or if the effect of one's creative output is to foster more distracted consumerism, then that intention should be questioned deeply. Besides, "whatever" art has already been done, ad nauseam.

Without our intention being too forced, creative practitioners can think about our process as an aspiration to benefit others through whatever we produce. Often, at the close of a writing session, I actually recite a short dedication of merit, an aspiration that whatever has been produced might be helpful to both myself and others. Practitioners often close a meditation session with such a dedication, offering the merits of our practice to our own future benefit and the extended benefit of others. This is a great way to set an intention for any practice and clarify our reasons for being on the path. A creative session can be structured very similarly to a meditation session (candles and incense optional).

On the collective level, we can think about how the output of our creative process changes the way that communities perceive themselves. For a painter, for instance, on this level of social engagement, it's not just about having an innovative technique; it's about the way people experience themselves at his opening. For a poet, it's not just about vocabulary and meter; it's about the community that gathers at the reading. For the chef, it's not just about the cuisine, but who gets invited to the meal and how the ceremony of sharing nourishment is conducted. For the filmmaker, it's not just about the special effects and editing; it's about what the audience does after they leave the theater. For the entrepreneur, it's not just about testing the product, it's about how engaging with that product allows people to experience their own minds.

STUDYING CULTURAL NARRATIVES

If we are going to make the collective level of experience part of our practice, we also have to become students of how we tell communal stories, and how those embedded stories frame our views of human nature and the nature of society. We have to study how dominant cultural narratives have empowered the three S's, the three poisons. If we train ourselves to become aware of the views underlying more superficial expressions, we can see the total malleability of the stories we tell ourselves and each other about who we are. Without sacrificing aesthetic or emotional power, we can cultivate narratives that empower the three C's, rather than worshipping the three S's.

Understanding narrative is crucial to seeing the shared views of human nature that underlie our social systems. When conflict arises, the narratives that have shaped our views guide our response to the moment at hand. The engrained plot of our favorite childhood novel tells us whether another person is to be competed with or collaborated with. The actions of our favorite movie character mold our belief in interdependence or isolation. The first romantic comedy we ever saw shapes our sense of partnership, whether it leads us toward thinking love is about needy salvation or about connected empathy. It is no accident that many of our most famous conservative libertarian thinkers trace their beliefs back to reading one seminal novel by Ayn Rand.

In contemplating the effect of narrative, I often think of different usages of the word "aspirational." Within something like a Hollywood screenplay, the word refers to a story structure where the audience is encouraged to lust after the socioeconomic status of the main characters and the environment in which they live. It is truly amazing how subtle and pervasive messages of grasping after greater social status are in our shared stories. But, in a Buddhist context, the word "aspirational" almost always refers to our bodhisattva intention, the wish that our actions and practices in the world would help free ourselves and many others from confusion and suffering. That's quite a stark contrast in usage and intention.

We can also explore how our response to conflict is karmically conditioned by cultural narratives of revenge. In October 2001, CNN covered the United States' retaliatory bombing of Afghanistan with the tagline "America Strikes Back." This was an obvious link to a narrative that everyone could connect with, perhaps the most popular narrative of Generation X—the second *Star Wars* movie, *The Empire Strikes Back.* CNN was apparently unaware of the irony of this tagline, unintentionally having the United States stand in for Darth Vader's evil empire. It bears at least contemplating: If we hadn't all been raised eating popcorn while watching revenge narratives, what would happen to our support for any war? The military-industrial complex is interdependent with the stories we tell about how conflict is handled, even if we think they're "just movies."

Within every story that we tell each other, within every ad we create, within every cultural text we produce, we are either disempowering people and reinforcing their experience of the three S's of scared, selfish, and separate, or else empowering them to experience themselves as the three C's of courageous, compassionate, and connected. Of course, as the three S's and the three C's are interdependent with each other, our cultural stories are usually much more complex than a simple either/or, helpful/harmful dichotomy, which is why remembering the underlying basic goodness is so crucial.

Meditation practitioners have huge tools in our arsenal, if only we would use them, to study how story lines empower culture and how culture empowers the systems that shape individuals. When we meditate, we begin to experience, through the repetition of witnessing thoughts, how empty yet powerful our own story lines are. From this personal exploration, we start to recognize that all cultural narratives are by nature fluid, empty of any solid sense of how stories "must" be told. The point of dharma practice is not to try to live without any narrative. The point is to see how all narratives

have a holographic nature. Because we spend so much time cultivating awareness of the nonsolidity of our views, we also see how
our actions are molded by the stories we tell each other. Practitioners of mindfulness are in an important position to help transform our shared narratives about human nature.

By studying arts and culture, and viewing our awakening as a
cultural matter, we begin to shift the environment in which we
personally, interpersonally, and collectively experience our lives.
By becoming students of art and culture, with curiosity about how
culture affects our relationship to our mind, we naturally also become students of enlightened society.

16

CONCLUSION
Coming Home

I was present once while Dzogchen Ponlop Rinpoche offered refuge vows to a small group of his dharma students. In many lineages, this refuge vow is the formal ceremony of commitment for becoming Buddhist, a proclamation that you are on the path of awakening for life. At this ceremony, you stop saying, "If I'm anything, I am a Buddhist," and you start saying, "Umm . . . I guess I'm a Buddhist now." Again, when you take such a step, you have to determine for yourself what it means, in terms of what other spiritual traditions you might study or how you will integrate the Buddhist practices and teachings into your own life in a meaningful way. No matter your individual circumstance, becoming a Buddhist is a commitment to living within awareness and working with these teachings, befriending yourself, and proclaiming your mind as your true home.

When he spoke about the meaning of the vow, Ponlop Rinpoche reminded us that, traditionally, students would have a tiny bit of their hair cut during the ceremony by the teacher presiding over the vows. His explanation for this ritual struck me as somewhat ironic. He said that hair is a way to distinguish ourselves, to feel special in our style, and that when we take on the path of awakening, we should feel like we are no big deal. He said "there should be no sign" that we are Buddhist.

THERE SHOULD BE NO SIGN

I have often thought of what it really means to be a student (and also a teacher) of Buddhism in the modern world. As Buddhism becomes more and more popular, as the so-called mindfulness movement evolves into a more robust social movement that includes the humanistic study of ethics, psychology, philosophy, art, and politics, those who practice dharma become more heavily scrutinized for how we live our lives. Sometimes this scrutiny is very fair (who doesn't want people to practice what they preach?) and sometimes it holds us to impossible standards of robotic perfection, where even the smallest mistake causes someone to sarcastically comment, "*That's* not very Buddhist of you." The other night I was watching an episode of the popular animated show *Family Guy*, where one character jokes to another that Buddhism is a religion of "annoying white people." That made me smile, and I quietly thanked *Family Guy* for the shout-out. At the same time, it made me cautious about the cultural role that Buddhism is adopting in our world.

The cultural theorist Slavoj Žižek has an interesting critique of Western Buddhism. He argues that because Buddhism teaches us how to be accepting of what is arising in the present moment, it is actually the perfect spirituality to be co-opted into the consumer capitalist framework as a way to make ourselves feel spiritually protected while the world goes down around us in the flames of greed and aggression. Žižek's view seems to be that acceptance (i.e., learning how to rest in the gap between our karmic conditioning and our reactive impulse) equals some kind of passive acquiescence to the status quo. Of course, anyone who practices meditation knows that acceptance is not about acquiescence. Acquiescence is about numbing out, but acceptance is a profoundly difficult practice of resting with the intensity of the gap. We cannot make different choices for our future, either personally or collectively, until we intuitively understand the psychological forces that have shaped the present. If we try to alter the future without fully understanding the present, we simply re-create the habitual problems of the past. This enslaving circular motion of habit is what it means to be lost in commute, caught up in samsara. This is why we practice "acceptance."

It's not really clear that Žižek cares much about the fate of Western Buddhism or even knows much about meditation, because his general analytic style is to use many different cultural phenomena as foils for his playful provocations about modern society. It's quite possible that his analysis of Western Buddhism is just on par with Seth MacFarlane's *Family Guy* mention, a provocateur's method to gain a few easy laughs and stir people up. I understand this playful impulse completely, because I make fun of my own tradition all the time, too. Believe me—the only way to dedicate your whole life to something is to never take it, or yourself, too seriously.

But Žižek's critique of the potential dangers of Western Buddhism becoming co-opted into a materialistic and privileged mind-set should be very well heeded.* To avoid the danger of

---

*A May 28, 2014, article in Bloomberg's *Businessweek* carried the deeply ominous headline "To Make a Killing on Wall Street, Start Meditating."

Western Buddhism becoming a new form of spiritual material- ism, we need to always place the practice of self-awareness within the context of being a decent and engaged citizen of our commu- nity. If we always open our eyes to the truth of interdependence, our personal practice will remain grounded in a larger human vision of a compassionate society, a vision to conquer greed and aggression as structural institutions of communal life. If we closely examine our own experience, we will cease using lazy arguments about the selfishness of human nature to accept confusion and human degradation as foregone conclusions. When Buddhists become known for being at the forefront of action regarding the larger social justice issues facing their communities and societies, only then will we have a meaningful response to accusations of self-obsession or spiritual narcissism.

Meanwhile, when I contemplate Ponlop Rinpoche's teaching that "there should be no sign" that one is a Buddhist, I think he meant that we can try to live our life as a model example, with- out any cultural trappings. To do so, we need to stay relevant and fully involved in the communities in which we live, fully steeped in our own cultures, willing to embody our own time and place on this earth. For me, the teaching that "there should be no sign" that I am Buddhist means that normalcy and decency, grounded living, are the highest priorities. Spiritual accoutrements are op- tional, and are most likely just a distraction.

My life is pretty straightforward. I live with my partner in Brooklyn. I wake up in the morning and meditate, and try to get in a yoga practice every day. If I don't feel like practicing, I listen to a little music first to get inspired, maybe Prince or Nina Si- mone, or other musical masters of *bodhicitta* and windhorse. After daily practice, I try to figure out how I can be present with my own mind throughout the day, present with my relationships, with the organizations I work for, with my students, with my community, and especially with my society. I try to eat well, with a sense of grateful connection for all the causes and conditions that brought food to me. I make a lot of mistakes every day, and I try to learn from the obstacles I witness in myself, free from shame or guilt about the fact that I am, indeed, a human. When I teach dharma, I make occasional reference to the cartoons of the 1980s and the hip-hop music of the 1990s. I make no apologies for discussing the Care Bears when I'm giving a lecture on lovingkindness or De La Soul when speaking about the "ego." After class, I argue with friends about art, politics, and film, and proclaim my belief that Radiohead is the best band of the last twenty years, still the closest thing that my generation has to the Beatles, a fact I find both awesome and sad. I like my coffee strong and my occasional whiskey on the rocks, and I know that if I am not very mindful with either of these beverages, trouble is bound to ensue. Sometimes I get cranky, usually late at night when tired. Sometimes when I get super cranky, I want to give up—give up on myself, on others, on the world. Then I remember that I just need some sleep, and I wake up the next morning and do it all over again.

There should be no sign.

I hope we can get over the idea that this tradition is exotic in any way. Awake-ism is not an Indian tradition, it is not a Southeast Asian tradition, it is not a Tibetan tradition, and it is *definitely not* an American tradition. It is one hundred percent human, a human lineage of transmissions and practices about coming home to ourselves and taking care of each other. For me, Buddhism's relevance is entirely reducible to how well it prepares us for living in our world. Whenever we deviate from the reality of our humanity, becoming overly theoretical on the one hand or engaging in magical thinking about transcendence on the other, everything that Buddhism offers ceases to help us. While it certainly behooves us to deeply study the cultural and historical context of any lineage that we receive—in order to increase respect for the ancestries from which this human wisdom originates, as well as to understand that all good tools arise in a given cultural context—historical study is not really the point. If these teachings are meaningful, they will touch people only because the people who currently practice and hold these teachings are sane, balanced, caring humans who help transform our societies into more sustainable, more inclusive, and less violent places.

WHAT YOU NEED FOR THE ROAD

The first thing we need is to enter the journey of self-awareness by committing to a regular meditation practice. This is the way that we learn to come home to our own awareness. I would recommend a short daily practice of ten to fifteen minutes, building up to the possibility of attending longer retreats, which create an experience that just isn't possible with a short daily practice. If your practice is stuck, get to a retreat as soon as you can.

In order to succeed with practice, we need great patience, instead of a get-rich-quick mentality where we are constantly waiting to be zapped with ray guns of insight. Again, there are some popular spiritual thinkers who promise sudden shifts in consciousness, but in my experience the path is always slow and gradual. Making a commitment to practice and then seeing the commitment through over the course of your life is the only reliable way to see long-term transformation. All of the shifts on this journey are slow, sometimes glacial, as if we are tilting a planet ever so slightly on its axis. In the long term, if we tilted the Earth even one degree, it would change the climate tremendously, but from outer space it might look like very little has happened. This is a good analogy for the effects of long-term practice. If you've recently fallen off the wagon with meditation, it might be because of the disheartening thought that you should've already transformed yourself and should feel completely at home by now. With true gentleness, we are willing to let this journey be as long as it needs to be.

I would also begin at some point to look for guidance and mentorship in the form of teachers. While this might be a process of trial and error, having guidance along the path—someone in your corner who cares about your awakening and encourages you to keep setting an intention to use your practice to benefit others—is such a meaningful support.

Finally, I would look for peers and a community of like-minded practitioners who are trying to cultivate the same values that you are, a group of people who view their practice as a means to greater societal and cultural engagement. While *sangha* can be annoying at times, it is the only thing that can truly exemplify the larger collective aspirations that we hold.

If we change our attitude a little bit every day, and try to become consistent students of the personal, the interpersonal, and the collective levels of our experience all at once, we can eventually cultivate immense gratitude for our life and for our opportunity to exist in an interdependent society. Beyond any other effects, these practices and teachings have made me incredibly thankful that I get to be a being, and have helped me arise just a little bit out of the trap of my own self-obsessions into a deeper level of care and intimacy with other beings. I plan to be on this road for the rest of my life, because, ironically, it does take (at least) a lifetime's journey to come home to yourself and to be present with others. A journey with intention and compassionate connection is an entirely different road to travel from the déjà vu circles of a zombie commuter. If we take on the journey of self-awareness, while keeping interdependence in our hearts, we can put an end to our grasping commute, and start to live in a society of human goodness, ready and able to help each other begin to feel at home.

SUGGESTED READING

Each section is arranged by the order in which it is suggested to read the books in that section.

MEDITATION PRACTICE

Salzberg, Sharon. *Real Happiness: The Power of Meditation*. New York: Workman, 2010.

Mipham, Sakyong. *Turning the Mind into an Ally*. New York: Riverhead, 2003.

Ferguson, Gaylon. *Natural Wakefulness: Discovering the Wisdom We Were Born With*. Boston: Shambhala, 2009.

Nichtern, Ethan, and Sharon Salzberg. *Buddhist Meditation: An Introduction Across Traditions*. New York: IDP Recordings, 2015, audio download.

SHAMBHALA TEACHINGS

Trungpa, Chogyam. *Shambhala: The Sacred Path of the Warrior.* Boston: Shambhala, 1984.

Mipham, Sakyong. *The Shambhala Principle: Discovering Humanity's Hidden Treasure.* New York: Harmony, 2013.

Hayward, Jeremy, and Karen Hayward. *Sacred World: The Shambhala Way to Gentleness, Bravery, and Power.* Boston: Shambhala, 1998.

OVERVIEW OF THE BUDDHIST PATH

Trungpa, Chogyam. *Cutting Through Spiritual Materialism.* Boston: Shambhala, 1973.

Nhat Hanh, Thich. *The Heart of the Buddha's Teachings.* New York: Broadway, 1999.

Ray, Reginald. *Indestructible Truth: The Living Spirituality of Tibetan Buddhism.* Boston: Shambhala, 2000.

Bodhi, Bhikkhu. *In the Buddha's Words: An Anthology of Discourses from the Pali Canon.* Somerville, Mass.: Wisdom, 2005.

Kapleau, Roshi Philip. *The Three Pillars of Zen.* New York: Anchor, 1989.

BUDDHISM AND WESTERN PSYCHOLOGY

Welwood, John. *Toward a Psychology of Awakening: Buddhism, Psychotherapy, and the Path of Personal and Spiritual Transformation.* Boston: Shambhala, 2000.

Brach, Tara. *Radical Acceptance: Embracing Your Life with the Heart of a Buddha.* New York: Bantam, 2003.

Hanson, Rick. *Buddha's Brain: The Practical Neuroscience of Happiness, Love, and Wisdom.* Oakland: New Harbinger, 2009.

Epstein, Mark. *Thoughts Without a Thinker: Psychotherapy from a Buddhist Perspective.* New York: Basic, 1995.

Chapman, Susan Gillis. *The Five Keys to Mindful Communication: Using*

Deep Listening and Mindful Speech to Strengthen Relationships, Heal Conflicts, and Accomplish Your Goals. Boston: Shambhala, 2012.

COMPASSION MEDITATION PRACTICE

Chödrön, Pema. *The Places That Scare You: A Guide to Fearlessness in Difficult Times.* Boston: Shambhala, 2001.

Salzberg, Sharon. *Lovingkindness: The Revolutionary Art of Happiness.* Boston: Shambhala, 1995.

CONTEMPORARY AND SOCIALLY ENGAGED BUDDHISM

Nichtern, Ethan. *One City: A Declaration of Interdependence.* Somerville, Mass.: Wisdom, 2007.

Rinzler, Lodro. *The Buddha Walks into a Bar . . .: A Guide to Life for a New Generation.* Boston: Shambhala, 2012.

Ponlop, Dzogchen. *Rebel Buddha: A Guide to a Revolution of Mind.* Boston: Shambhala, 2010.

Trungpa, Chogyam. *True Perception: The Path of Dharma Art.* Boston: Shambhala, 2008.

Williams, Angel Kyodo. *Being Black: Zen and the Art of Living with Fearlessness and Grace.* New York: Viking, 2000.

Loy, David R. *The Great Awakening: A Buddhist Social Theory.* Somerville, Mass.: Wisdom, 2003.

TANTRIC BUDDHISM

Trungpa, Chogyam. *Journey Without Goal: The Tantric Wisdom of the Buddha.* Boston: Shambhala, 1981.

Rockwell, Irini. *The Five Wisdom Energies: A Buddhist Way of Understanding Personalities, Emotions, and Relationships.* Boston: Shambhala, 2002.

Simmer-Brown, Judith. *Dakini's Warm Breath: The Feminine Principle in Tibetan Buddhism.* Boston: Shambhala, 2001.

Allione, Tsultrim. *Feeding Your Demons: Ancient Wisdom for Resolving Inner Conflict.* New York: Little, Brown and Co., 2008.

Brown, Daniel P. *Pointing Out the Great Way: The Stages of Meditation in the Mahamudra Tradition.* Somerville, Mass.: Wisdom, 2006.

ACKNOWLEDGMENTS

None of us has ever had a completely original thought. Especially me.

I would first like to thank my parents, Janice Ragland and David Nichtern, for being basically awesome, for introducing me to these sacred teachings as a template for how to be myself in this world, and for giving me the feeling of home. I would also like to thank my extended family, because this path is about seeing all sentient beings as family, and that has to start with one's *actual* family.

I would like to thank my guru, Sakyong Mipham. You are the most quietly brave and impeccably disciplined person I have ever met. Please live a long life. Also, many "jedis" have passed away, and their memories linger. Chief among them is Chogyam Trungpa Rinpoche, whose example of fearlessness always makes me smile and cry at the same time.

I have many other teachers and mentors, and they all have titles, so I hope they forgive titular omission for brevity's sake. For inspiring this book, I'd like to especially thank: Sharon Salzberg, Miles Neale, Suzann Duquette, Gaylon Ferguson, Dzogchen Ponlop, Eric Spiegel,

Arawana Hayashi, Carol O'Donnell, Pat Enkyo O'Hara, and Eric Schneiderman.

I would like to thank the community and students of both Shambhala and the Interdependence Project. Our relationships have crafted my approach to the dharma. Our interactions sharpen and soften me continuously, a priceless combination.

I would love to thank the literary team that made this book possible. Thanks to my excellent Brunonian editor, Gabriella Doob, for "getting" my voice and for paying such insightful attention to this text. To Jeff Seroy and the whole wonderful team at Farrar, Straus and Giroux, thanks for everything you did to make this book as polished and accessible as it could possibly be, and to help connect writer with reader, a sacred interdependence. And thanks to my not-so-secret agent and dear friend, Lisa Weinert, who has been kind to my writing ever since we met in Mr. Hubner's ninth-grade English class.

I would like to acknowledge a few dear comrades and homies on the path of dharma and the path of life during the long arc in which this book was conceived. The only reason this list isn't much longer is my desire not to massacre trees. Thank you, Kim Brown, Ericka Phillips, Greg Zwahlen, Lodro Rinzler, Chris "Kodomo" Child and Hilary Schaffner, Juan Carlos Castro, Robert and Amy Chender, Andrew Buckland and Maria Azcue, Heather Coleman and Alex Lambert, Seth Freedman, Kate Johnson, Christine Aziz, Caitlin Strom, Patrick Groneman, Lawrence Grecco, Jerry Kolber, Caroline Contillo, Adam Lobel, Josh Silberstein, Dave McKeel, Meredith Arena, Crystal Gandrud, Ellen Scordato, Jon Miller and Claudia Cividino, David Perrin, Whitney Joiner, Matthew Steinfeld, Evan Rock, Abigail Rasminsky, Ian Koebner, and Jeff Zimbalist.

Finally, and crucially, I'd like to thank my amazing partner, Marissa Dutton. I wandered around looking for you for a very long time. Then I came home to you while writing this book, and now you're stuck with me. Everyone I know thanks you. ☺

A NOTE ABOUT THE AUTHOR

Ethan Nichtern is a senior teacher in the Shambhala Buddhist tradition and the author of *One City: A Declaration of Interdependence.* He is also the founder of the Interdependence Project, a nonprofit organization dedicated to secular Buddhist study as it applies to transformational activism, mindful arts and media projects, and western psychology. Nichtern has taught meditation and Buddhist studies classes and retreats across the United States since 2002. He is based in New York City.